LIBRARY IN A BOOK

DRUGS AND SPORTS

Fred C. Pampel

Facts On File

An imprint of Infobase Publishing

Drugs and Sports

Facts On File, Inc.
An imprint of Infobase Publishing
132 West 31st Street
New York NY 10001

ISBN 10: 0-8160-6575-6
ISBN 13: 978-0-8160-6575-2

Library of Congress Cataloging-in-Publication Data

Pampel, Fred C.
    Drugs and sports / Fred C. Pampel.
        p. cm.—(Library in a book)
    Includes bibliographical references and index.
    ISBN: 0-8160-6575-6 (alk. paper)
    1. Doping in sports. I. Title.
        RC1230.P36 2007
        362.29—dc22   2006020536

Text design by Ron Monteleone
Graphs by Sholto Ainslie

Printed in the United States of America

MP Hermitage 10 9 8 7 6 5 4 3 2 1

This book is printed on acid-free paper.

CONTENTS

PART III
APPENDICES

PART I

OVERVIEW OF THE TOPIC

CHAPTER 1

INTRODUCTION TO DRUGS AND SPORTS

On March 17, 2005, several well-dressed, muscular, and physically fit men appeared before the House Committee on Government Reform to testify about accusations that they had engaged in illegal and unethical behavior. The hearings drew more TV crews and photographers than any other in history—even those in 1998 on the impeachment of President Bill Clinton. When the questioning began, one witness jabbed his fingers at the representatives to emphasize that he never did what he had been accused of. Another refused to answer questions about his actions because, he said, it would harm others, violate his right to privacy, and unnecessarily bring up the past. Still another went on to say that the accusations were false. Representatives and the media greeted the denials with skepticism, implying that illegal behavior was widespread.

The seriousness of a congressional hearing and the heated and defensive denials of witnesses suggested something sinister and immoral—perhaps organized crime, stock fraud, or corporate dishonesty. In fact, the witnesses, Rafael Palmeiro, Mark McGwire, and Sammy Sosa, were famous current or former baseball stars and record holders who had been brought before Congress to answer questions about something else often considered sinister and immoral—the use of performance-enhancing drugs called anabolic steroids.

The hearings illustrate an ugly fact and ethical challenge for sports today. Although athletes are expected to provide moral guidance to youth, many of them from a wide variety of sports have relied on anabolic steroids—drugs used to build muscle, endurance, and speed—to enhance their performances. Only recently, however, has the extent of the scandal come to the attention of the public and underscored the links between drugs and sports.

Drugs and Sports

Besides steroids, other illegal substances used by athletes to improve their performance have proliferated. A wide variety of stimulants, growth hormones, narcotics, painkillers, and substances to increase oxygen-carrying capacity in the blood have been outlawed by athletic authorities, but their use by athletes persists. For example, in 2005, a French newspaper has claimed it has evidence that Lance Armstrong used a banned substance in winning the Tour de France several years ago—a claim Armstrong vigorously denies.

More recently, allegations about Armstrong's use of drugs have been overshadowed by a new scandal: The 2006 Tour de France winner, American Floyd Landis, tested positive for steroids during the race. Landis denied using banned drugs and appealed the doping charges against him but has been dropped from his team and faces a ban from racing.

The problem of drug use in sports goes beyond a few well-known, highly talented, and very wealthy athletes—it also affects youth throughout the country. Mirroring the trend in professional sports, steroid use has spread to boys who want to improve their muscular appearance and athletic performance in high school sports. More surprising, steroid use has been rising among teen girls who use the drug to help lose weight and maintain a toned look. According to one study, "More than a half million 8th- and 10th-grade students are now using these dangerous drugs, and increasing numbers of high school seniors say they don't believe the drugs are risky."[1]

Why the concern? Some might respond that use of steroids and other substances differ little in principle from the use of vitamins, nutritional supplements, laser eye surgery, and other medical procedures to improve physical performance. The difference is that steroids and other drugs have side effects that ultimately hurt rather than improve the health of users. Drugs in sports additionally raise thorny ethical issues about fairness in competition. If some athletes willingly risk their long-term health to improve current performance, it gives them an unfair and unnatural advantage over others and forces competitors to risk their health by trying to keep up with those who use drugs. In the words of journalist Peter Lawson, "Unless something is done soon, international sport will be a competition between circus freaks manipulated by international chemists."[2]

One should not overstate the problem. Most athletes compete fairly and without using banned substances, and broad statements about the use of drugs can wrongly tarnish their reputations. Even so, that fact makes the cheating by those who use drugs all the more unfair. And it does not deny the attraction of athletes to the advantages offered by drugs and of youth to shortcuts for athletic success. Drug use in sports is a problem that will not go away soon.

4

DOPING BECOMES A PROBLEM

Whenever and wherever societies have prized sports competition, athletes have searched for ways to gain advantages. Most efforts have gone into finding ways to train and eat better, but the search has sometimes gone even further. Ancient Greek athletes ate the testicles (or testes) of lambs, thinking that the male organ would provide special strength and muscle size. Observing the effects of castration on animals, herders and farmers had known for centuries that removing the testes weakened male strength, aggressiveness, and sexual desire. It stood to reason that doing the opposite—consuming testes—would improve athletic skill and sexuality.

Ancient athletes and warriors also searched for stimulants from plants that would improve endurance and courage. Greek soldiers ate hallucinogenic mushrooms, and Roman gladiators used stimulants. Strength and endurance proved most crucial for battles, hunts, and rituals, but the benefits of plants with energizing properties could aid in sporting events as well.

Modern drug use in sports reflects much the same desire as in the past but differs in effectiveness. Improving on folk knowledge about performance-enhancing drugs, scientific discoveries in the 19th and 20th centuries revolutionized the nature of sports competition. Rather than relying on cooked testicles or rarely found mushrooms and plants, athletes can choose among dozens of substances synthesized in labs, manufactured for maximum effect, and available for daily use.

The use of drugs to enhance athletic performance became common enough in the last century to get its own name—*doping*. In sports, doping refers to the use of chemicals and substances to boost performance. The International Olympic Committee (IOC), the governing body of the Olympic Games, refers to doping in somewhat more detail as the use of any substance that is foreign to the body, taken in abnormal amounts, or taken by an abnormal route into the body with the sole purpose of unfairly enhancing performance in competition. This definition does not always clearly distinguish between illegitimate drugs and accepted medicines or nutritional supplements, so more recent definitions refer less informatively to doping as the use of prohibited substances. The key, however, remains the use of drugs to gain unfair advantage in competition.

The term has an unusual derivation. *Dop* comes from the Kaffir dialect of South Africa. It referred to the use of stimulating liquor by tribe members during religious ceremonies. Dutch settlers to South Africa adopted the term, and by 1865 it had spread to Amsterdam, where swimmers in a canal race were accused of taking *dop*. By 1889, it appeared in an English dictionary referring to a narcotic mixture of opium used for racehorses.

With the letter *e* added since then, *dope* has taken on many meanings, including recreation drugs, while *doping* most often refers to the human use of drugs in sporting activities.[3]

SPEEDBALLS TO AMPHETAMINES

Early forms of doping involved the use of stimulating chemical substances and drugs. During the late 1800s, six-day, continuous bicycle races became increasingly popular in Europe, and competitors began to take "speedballs" to stimulate activity and prevent fatigue. Speedballs mixed heroin and cocaine into a frightening concoction, while alcohol, caffeine, nitroglycerine, ethyl ether, strychnine, and opium were used as well. Taking poisonous or damaging substances such as strychnine, nitroglycerine, and ethyl ether sounds bizarre, but in carefully measured amounts, they gave athletes a boost. Strychnine, for example, is a stimulant in small doses and a deadly poison in large doses.

The first documented use of stimulants in the Olympic Games came in 1904—only eight years after the modern Olympics had started. Thomas Hicks, the U.S. winner of the marathon, collapsed at the finish of the race. His handlers admitted giving him strychnine and brandy during the race to keep him going. Hicks survived but expressed no guilt over his tactics, saying that "I would rather have won this race than be president of the United States."[4] Olympic participants, all amateurs rather than professionals at the time, received no payments, prizes, or endorsement fees for their victories. The goal of winning still motivated Hicks and others to use drugs, even at the risk to their health.

The potency of stimulants improved dramatically with discoveries in the 20th century. Amphetamines, drugs that stimulate the brain and central nervous system in ways that increase energy and alertness, had first been chemically synthesized in 1887. Yet, new and more potent forms developed in the 1920s and 1930s led to wider use. First adopted in the 1930s by students and truck drivers needing to stay awake for long periods of time, amphetamines later helped counter combat fatigue among soldiers during World War II. From there, the stimulant spread to athletes, who liked the boost of energy it gave.

Early evidence of amphetamine use in sports came in the 1952 Winter Olympics in Oslo, Norway. Several speed skaters became ill and needed medical care to recover from the excess amphetamines they took. Bicycle racers seemed particularly likely to use the drug. In one 1955 race, five of 25 urine samples taken from riders tested positive for such stimulants.[5] A few years later, "pep pills" were found in the locker room of U.S. women swimmers during trials for the Olympics. Used now for speed events as well as endurance events, stimulants attracted athletes in a variety of sports.

The seriousness of the problem became obvious with several amphetamine-related deaths during competition.[6] In the 1960 Summer Olympics in Rome, Knut Jensen, a Danish cyclist, collapsed, fractured his skull, and died during the road race. Tests revealed the presence of amphetamines in the blood. In 1967, a British cyclist in the Tour de France, Tommy Simpson, died during the race from complications related to amphetamine use. Contributing to publicity about the dangers of stimulants, a French soccer player and French cyclist both died in the next year from amphetamine complications.

Although common in many other sports, the use of stimulants most affected long-distance cycling. By 1965, nearly one-quarter of amateur cyclists and more than one-third of professional cyclists were using amphetamines.[7] One five-time winner of the Tour de France, Jacques Anquetil, summarized the attraction in 1967: "For 50 years bike racers have been taking stimulants. Obviously, we can do without them in a race, but then we will pedal 15 miles an hour [instead of 25]. Since we are constantly asked to go faster and to make even greater efforts, we are obliged to take stimulants."[8]

Still other drugs with legitimate medical purposes came to be misused by athletes. Various forms of painkillers, for example, allowed athletes to compete even when injured. Injections of Novocain into sore shoulders, pulled muscles, or twisted ankles eliminated pain that would otherwise keep athletes from performing at their best. Various forms of sedatives, barbiturates, tranquilizers, and muscle relaxants could also aid performances. These "downers" did not increase strength or speed—in fact, they did the opposite by slowing reflexes. However, they helped athletes in certain sports such as golf, archery, or rifle shooting deal with nerves and pressure.

Despite the benefits they brought, all these forms of doping had a drawback. Speedballs, amphetamines, painkillers, barbiturates, and other drugs brought only short-term gains. They might improve performance on the day of the competition but did not bring lasting training benefits. And tests done on the performance day would reveal the intake of these illegal substances. A different sort of performance-enhancing drug came to be adopted more slowly than stimulants. It would ultimately prove to be more popular and more threatening to the integrity of sport. Anabolic steroids, a form of human testosterone, would bring long-term benefits that endured for months after their usage ended.

TESTOSTERONE FROM THE LAB

Building on the dreams of ancient athletes who ate animal testicles to increase their strength, scientists in the 19th century began to discover ways to supplement the body's production of the male hormone testosterone. The goal of the scientists had little to do with sports—they wanted to develop ways to improve health and extend lives. But the creation of testosterone in the lab and the discovery of ways to deliver it to the body would profoundly affect sports.

Early Experiments

One early discovery demonstrated the nature of male hormone delivery. In 1849, a German professor named A. A. Berthold castrated roosters, which typically reduces the size and color of the red combs on their heads. However, Berthold then surgically implanted the testes into the abdomen of the roosters. When the combs stayed large and bright, he correctly reasoned that substances from the testes were released into the blood to develop and maintain male sex characteristics.

Although castration and surgical implantation of the testes had little practical value for humans, perhaps the substances in the testes could be directly injected into the bloodstream. A claim to do just that followed several decades later. In 1889, a 72-year-old French scientist named Charles Edouard Brown-Sequard injected himself with semen, blood from the testicular veins, and juice extracted from the testicles of a dog or guinea pig. After removing the animal testicles, "He then smashed these testicles and brewed them in a salt solution, giving rise to a sort of 'testicle stew.'"[9] He then claimed that self-injecting the stew improved his physical and mental energy, offered free samples of his testicular liquid to others, and promised it would rejuvenate those brave enough to try. Scientists today discount the claims—Brown-Sequard coincidentally died soon after his experiment—but the work eventually led others to examine the effects of hormones more scientifically.

Two Austrian scientists, Oskar Zoth and Fritz Pregl, later made the connection between testicular extract and athletics in an original, but ultimately flawed experiment. They injected themselves with the extract of bull testicles and then observed the consequences of the injections by measuring changes in the strength of their fingers during a series of exercises.[10] In a paper published in 1896, they concluded that the extract increased muscular strength and suggested that athletes adopt it as a training tool. Such conclusions had a flaw, however. By experimenting on themselves, Zoth and Pregl might have unconsciously acted in ways to favor their belief that the extract could improve their strength. Such bias apparently led them to conclude incorrectly that the extract (rather than their hopeful expectations) caused the increase in strength. Modern scientists, who use neutral subjects for experiments, have not found much benefit of simple extracts from animal testes.

However crude and flawed the tests, the claim about benefits of the male hormone had a kernel of truth. As scientists in the 20th century soon discovered, the testes produce a hormone called testosterone, which causes the development of male sex characteristics such as sperm production, growth of facial and body hair, and development of muscles, bone mass, and sex drive. Although present in small amounts in women, testosterone comes primarily from the testes and reaches much higher levels among males. The presence of both large amounts of testosterone and muscle mass in males made early efforts to use testicular extracts for muscle building seem logical.

The first step toward a scientific breakthrough came from isolating the male sex hormone from animal testes—and indeed proving to skeptics that such a hormone actually existed.[11] In 1926, two American scientists at the University of Chicago, Fred C. Koch and Lemuel C. McGee, isolated a small amount of a male hormone from 40 pounds of bull testicles. When injected in small amounts, the substance returned the sex characteristics (such as the red comb) to castrated roosters. In later research, Koch and colleagues gathered the male hormone extract in larger amounts from 10,000 pounds of bull testicles and observed its effects on a castrated human. The inefficient extract of the hormone from bull testicles, however, made use of testosterone in large amounts impossible.

Other critical scientific breakthroughs came in 1935. Dutch professor Ernst Laquer determined the chemical structure of the male hormone isolated from bull testicles and gave it the name testosterone. Next, two scientists independently synthesized human testosterone. A Yugoslav chemist, Leopold Ruzicka, and a German chemist, Adolf Butenandt, received the 1939 Nobel Prize in chemistry for this accomplishment. Now, testosterone could be created in the lab and used to treat men with inadequate testosterone and, ultimately, to improve athletic performance.

The First Anabolic Steroids

Although able to synthesize testosterone in the lab, scientists had more trouble administering it to patients. Unless modified, pure testosterone proved ineffective when given as pills or injections. The chemicals broke down in the body and were excreted before they could get to the muscles, bones, and organs. By 1935, some simple chemical changes overcame this problem, and products became available to treat patients with low levels of the male hormone. Although many advances have occurred since then, current steroid products stem from these early discoveries.

Drugs and Sports

Testosterone with chemical modifications became known as anabolic steroids—the name used today for the muscle-building drug. Anabolic steroids are simply a human-made form of the male sex hormone. Anabolic refers to the process of building complex tissues from simpler molecules, especially the building of muscle. Steroids can replicate the anabolic functions of testosterone to increase the body's muscle mass, bone density, burning of fat, and efficiency in transporting oxygen in blood.

However, synthetic testosterone caused other changes besides building muscle. It also had androgenic properties, a term that refers to the development of male sex characteristics. These characteristics include enlargement of the prostate gland, growth of dense body hair, deepening of the voice, increased acne from oil produced by glands, greater sexual interest, and intensified male personality characteristics such as aggression and competitiveness. The term *anabolic-androgenic steroid* more precisely describes the nature of synthetic testosterone, but both *anabolic steroid* or *steroid* are terms commonly used to mean the same thing.

To avoid confusion, note that other forms of steroids also have medical uses that differ altogether from those for anabolic steroids. Corticosteroids refer to a related set of hormones that suppress the immune system and symptoms of inflammation. Unlike anabolic steroids, these types of steroids have a variety of legitimate medical uses such as for easing the symptoms of rheumatoid arthritis that do not contribute to growth of muscle mass. Steroids written about here refer to the anabolic-androgenic type.

For many decades, scientists and pharmaceutical companies tried to separate the anabolic and androgenic effects of steroids. Most users wanted the anabolic benefits of increased muscle mass without the androgenic side effects. Men and women with otherwise normal sex characteristics preferred to avoid the acne, mood swings, or extra hair that comes with steroid use. Despite much experimentation, however, efforts to separate the two effects have not fully succeeded.

Anabolic steroids found use for legitimate medical purposes. Steroids helped treat unusually low levels of testosterone and low sexual desire among men, and problems of menopause and osteoporosis among women. Without knowledge of proper doses and timing of intake, initial treatment involved little more than experiments, but several studies reported success. Along with the early medical use of anabolic steroids, it did not take long to realize that those with no medical conditions could use them to improve their performance. Rather than restoring testosterone to normal levels, steroids in these cases could increase normal levels to unusually high levels. As many suspected early on, the extra testosterone would likely have ergogenic properties, or properties that increase muscular capacity for work and enhance performance.

German Nazis may have been the first to take advantage of steroids for enhancing performance. Some claim that German athletes prepared for the 1936 Olympics in Berlin by taking testosterone, and that German soldiers in World War II took early forms of steroids to increase aggressiveness. Scholars generally discount these claims,[12] which may have emerged because the scientists who synthesized testosterone were German. However, one intriguing historical fact suggests a link between steroids and Nazism: Adolf Hitler was injected, according to a diary of his doctor, with a testosterone derivative to treat a variety of illnesses.[13]

By the 1940s, publicity about the possible use of steroids for athletic performances began to emerge. In a 1945 book, *The Male Hormone*, writer Paul de Kruif summarized studies of the consequences of the new synthetic testosterone. "It changed them, and fundamentally . . . after many months on testosterone, their chest and shoulder muscles grew much heavier and stronger . . . in some mysterious manner, testosterone caused the human body to synthesize protein, it caused the human body to build the very stuff of its own life."[14] In years to come, athletes would discover the truth of these claims for themselves.

Breakfast of Champions

It is difficult to date the first use of steroids to improve human athletic performance because initial adoption occurred informally and in secret. Some stories suggest that bodybuilders in California during the 1940s and 1950s experimented with steroids.[15] With the goal of building and shaping large muscles, bodybuilders would gain obvious advantages from steroids. Yet no proof exists that they adopted the drug before other athletes.

The earliest documented use of steroids occurred in the 1950s among Olympic weightlifters in the Soviet Union. Combining training with steroids, the Soviet team enjoyed remarkable success in world competitions, a success that did not go unnoticed elsewhere. In the 1952 Olympics in Helsinki, Finland, for example, Soviet weightlifters won seven medals, and suspicions grew that their accomplishments somehow came from hormones. At the 1954 World Weight-Lifting Championships, the team physician for the U.S. lifters, Dr. John Zigler, had his suspicions confirmed about use of steroids by the Soviet team. Over a drink, a Soviet team physician admitted as much. Then at the 1956 World Games in Moscow, Russia, Zigler witnessed Soviet athletes taking steroids.

Wanting to replicate the success of the Soviet team, Zigler introduced the practice to American weightlifters. However, the health drawbacks of steroids worried Zigler. As one side effect, early steroid products enlarged the prostate gland, which blocked urination. Zigler had observed some of the Soviet athletes using catheters, small tubes inserted through the penis into the bladder, to urinate. He did not want his athletes suffering the same problems.

Only in 1960, after several years of experimentation with steroids, did some of the weightlifters Zigler helped become champions. Zigler started to give a new anabolic steroid product call Dianabol (manufactured by Ciba Pharmaceutical Company) to three U.S. weightlifters, Tony Garcy, Bill March, and Lou Riecke. "All three were good lifters, but not the best in the country. Very quickly, all three made astonishing progress, gaining muscle mass as well as strength. All three became national champions and March and Riecke both set world records. . . . Soon the secret was out, and anabolic steroids began to spread from sport to sport in the United States and beyond."[16]

With this success, steroids spread quickly. In their history of doping, two scholars say, "Anabolic steroid use was apparently not a major problem at the 1960 Olympic Games. . . . By 1964, however, the secret behind the startling progress of a number of strength athletes began to leak out, and as a result steroids were soon being used extensively by athletes in all the strength sports."[17] Besides weightlifters, those competing in throwing events (e.g., shot put, hammer throw) found steroids helpful. By 1968, track and field athletes concerned with speed and endurance rather than pure strength had also followed the example of athletes in other events. Anabolic steroids improved the performance of sprinters, hurdlers, and middle-distance runners. By the estimate of one participant, one-third of U.S. athletes had used anabolic steroids in preparing for the 1968 Olympics.[18] An informal poll of track and field contestants at the 1972 Munich Olympics found that 68 percent used some form of anabolic steroid in their training.[19]

Making fun of both the slogan of Wheaties cereal ads and doping among top athletes, users started calling steroids the "Breakfast of Champions."[20] Few athletes would admit to the use, however. In 1971, Ken Patera, a U.S. weightlifting champion, became one of the first to publicly disclose his steroid use. After losing to his Russian competitor, Vasily Alexeev, in the previous year, he hoped the 1972 Olympic Games to come would be different. He said, "Last year, the only difference between me and him was that I couldn't afford his pharmacy bill. Now I can. When I hit Munich next year, I'll weigh about 340, maybe 350. Then we'll see which are better—his steroids or mine."[21]

Soon the use of steroids spread beyond Olympic events to professional sports. By 1969, one investigative journalist claimed that almost every team in the National Football League (NFL) and American Football League (AFL) had players who took steroids.[22] The same likely occurred among college football teams. Ken Ferguson, a successful college player at Utah State University said in 1968 that 90 percent of college linemen and likely all college football players who became professional players used steroids. Even some high school football players began to try them.

Some women began to use the product as well. One notable athlete, Tamara Press of the Soviet Union, won gold medals in the shot put and discus in the early 1960s. Known as the Flower of Leningrad, Press had a remarkably muscular and powerful physique for a woman. She and several other women suspiciously retired from competition in 1967, the year before the start of chromosome testing to make sure women competitors were genetically female. Although some thought that Press might have male chromosomes, she and others more likely used steroids.[23]

THE AUTHORITIES RESPOND

At least initially, sports physicians viewed steroids as similar in nature to vitamin supplements. They willingly prescribed them to athletes, and lacking knowledge of proper doses, failed to stop athletes from overusing the products. Reasoning that if a small amount helped them, then a large amount would help them even more, athletes often took amounts two to five times greater than recommended for medical use. Since steroids had not yet become illegal or prohibited by sporting organizations, little was done to stop the misuse. Dr. John Zigler, who first introduced steroids to American athletes, saw the misuse of the product and came to regret having introduced it.

Things were clearly getting out of hand. A 1969 exposé alerted fans and the country more generally of the extent of the problem. In a three-part article on "Drugs in Sport" in the popular magazine *Sports Illustrated*, Bil Gilbert described the widening use of drugs, the beneficial, yet artificial effects they have on performance, and the threat of turning sporting events into a competition among chemists for the best new drug.[24] Like many others, Gilbert criticized sporting organizations for not taking action against use of drugs in competition.

Initial Olympic Drug Testing

Olympic authorities began to express concerns about the growing popularity of stimulants among athletes and took tentative steps toward testing in the 1960s. Until then, no rules or tests existed for the use of performance-enhancing drugs in sports. In 1960, delegates at the meeting of the International Olympic Committee (IOC) complained about use of "pep pills" and asked for more scientific research on its dangers. The IOC, a nonprofit organization that supervises the Summer and Winter Olympic Games, took action the next year. It set up a medical committee to investigate doping among athletes and make recommendations on what steps to take.

At its 1964 meeting in Tokyo, the IOC took a firmer position. It condemned doping, required that athletes sign a pledge of no drug use, and asked national organizing committees to make their athletes available for drug tests. Those committees found to promote drug use were threatened with punishment. Despite strong public statements, however, the IOC had no way to enforce its rules. Prevention of drug use initially had to rely on cooperation and good will rather than testing and punishment.

The next steps involved mandatory testing. The IOC first set up a medical commission for drug testing in 1967 and began taking urine samples the next summer at the 1968 Olympics in Mexico City. The banned substances that the tests sought to find included alcohol, stimulants, cocaine, hashish, vasodilators (that cause the blood vessels to expand), and opiates such as morphine, heroin, or opium. Rather than test all competitors, personnel selected a sport at random each morning and tested 10 randomly selected participants in that sport (or two members from a team sport). If urine tests done before the event revealed evidence of drugs, the athletes could not compete.

Early Problems

Despite good intentions, the tests were largely ineffective and failed to eliminate doping. Reflecting a problem that would occur from then on, many of the participants found ways to avoid being caught by the test. One weightlifter talking about amphetamines said,"Everyone used a new one from West Germany. They couldn't pick it up in the test they were using. When they get a test for that one we'll find something else."[25] Only one drug disqualification occurred: Swedish entrant in the modern pentathlon, Hans-Gunnar Liljenwall, tested positive for excessive alcohol and became the first Olympian disqualified for drug use.

Further contributing to the ineffectiveness of the Olympic procedures, most of the tests available in 1968 could not reliably detect drug use. Using urine samples from the athletes, the tests had to search not for the substances themselves, but for traces of metabolites. In metabolizing or breaking down banned substances, the body creates metabolites or byproducts that pass into the urine. Tests aimed to find these by-products, a task that chemists had only begun to master. Both false positives and false negatives occurred commonly. A false positive wrongly concludes that an athlete used a substance and unfairly leads to disqualification of innocent athletes. A false negative misses drug use and allows cheaters to compete.

Why did the IOC not use blood tests instead of urine tests? That might have allowed a direct search for drugs in the blood rather than a search for metabolites in urine. Olympic officials then—and until only recently—worried about the risk of injury, transmission of disease, or trauma to athletes from the use of needles. While urine is excreted routinely and needs only to be collected in a jar, taking blood involves a greater threat to privacy and health. Sports federations did not want to take the risks associated with blood tests.

The flaws made it possible for athletes to use drugs and not get caught. Some athletes devised clever but dishonest ways to fool the tests. Men would sometimes use a catheter to insert someone else's urine through the penis and into their bladder and later present a sample of clean urine to testers. Women would sometimes insert condoms filled with someone else's urine into their vaginas and release the clean urine into the sample jars. Less extreme methods of drinking excessive water or using diuretics—drugs used to release water from the body—would dilute urine and make it harder to find trace materials.

Those athletes whose urine tested positive still had ways to beat the system. They could say that eating poppy seed rolls caused them to test positive for heroin, or that over-the-counter ibuprofen or cold medicines were misinterpreted as a stimulant or barbiturate. Still others could say that their sample had been mishandled, mislabeled, or contaminated. Indeed, few quality controls for the early tests had been put in place, and the best procedures were not used consistently. For example, in the 1970 Weightlifting World Championships held in Columbus, Ohio, tests of the medal winners revealed that several had used stimulants. Yet, the International Weightlifting Federation decided to reject the tests and reinstate the medals for the winners because not all lifters at the championships had been tested.

Another example illustrates the controversy that resulted from punishment for doping. A gold medal–winning American swimmer at the 1972 Munich Olympics, 16-year-old Rick DeMont, tested positive for ephedrine. Although legitimately used to treat asthma, ephedrine has stimulating properties that led the IOC to ban its use and to revoke DeMont's gold medal. DeMont appealed the decision, arguing that he used the medicine for his asthma. After the IOC rejected the appeal, groups in the United States, including the American Academy of Allergists, protested the ruling. They called for changes in the rules that allowed athletes with asthma to use ephedrine.

Dr. Robert Voy, a physician who later took over drug testing for the U.S. Olympic Committee (USOC), summarized the attitudes of athletes during early testing: "The athletes knew better than anyone that the drug testing posed little threat to them. They scoffed at testing notices and went right on with their routine drug use with little fear of detection."[26] He noted that the medical authorities also recognized the limits of their tests. They saw that known users of drugs often came up negative in the tests and realized that stripping someone of a gold medal for a positive test would cause enormous problems. According to Voy, "This gave rise to a less libelous approach to testing called sink testing, used to prevent false positive reporting and legal challenges. This now nonexistent method meant all samples were collected but either were not tested or were simply poured down the drain."[27]

Even if existing tests had been more effective, a critical flaw remained: No testing was done for steroids. The high profile of stimulants led Olympic authorities to give little attention to steroids in their early tests. Steroids in fact were not even included among the banned substances listed in 1967 by the IOC. Users largely kept the practice secret, and little was done to stop it. More important, no test for use of steroids existed at the time. Many members of the IOC called for better tests, more clearly stated policies, and more severe punishments. By the time these would be put in place, however, drug and steroid use had spread even more widely than it had during the 1950s and 1960s.

A MODERN EPIDEMIC

The emerging use of drugs and steroids during the first 70 years of the 20th century warned of greater problems to come. Over the next two decades, from roughly 1970 to 1990, drug use in sports, particularly anabolic steroids, would spread to such an extent that some would call it an epidemic. In his 1991 book, *Macho Medicine: A History of the Anabolic Steroid Epidemic,* Dr. William N. Taylor argued that the number of steroid users exceeded 3 million, and spending on steroids sold in the black market exceeded $4 million.[28] Other performance-enhancing drugs likewise grew during these decades. While improved testing would eliminate reliance on many stimulants and barbiturates commonly used in the past, new forms of doping would continue to give some athletes an edge in competition. Despite attempts by officials to keep the problem under control, athletes often stayed one step ahead of the testers.

The years around 1990, however, marked a change in attitudes and, perhaps, a change in usage of drugs in sports. A few years earlier, the discovery that Ben Johnson, the 1988 Olympic gold medal winner of the 100-meter race, had tested positive for steroids received much publicity, and his disqualification helped direct attention to the problem. Other publicity, particularly articles about the use and dangers of steroids by professional football players in *Sports Illustrated*, also highlighted concerns. Even the popular television show *60 Minutes* devoted a story in 1989 to the spread of steroids and the risk they present to sports.

Senators and representatives began to take action about the same time. Passage of the Anabolic Steroid Control Act of 1990 made steroids a controlled substance. The law prohibited steroids from sale or possession without a prescription and prohibited physicians from writing steroid prescriptions for ergogenic or cosmetic reasons. It also increased penalties for illegally selling steroids, required better records by manufacturers, gave the Drug Enforcement Administration the power to investigate the illegal manufacturing, distribution, or possession of steroids, and added steroids to government-supported, drug-abuse prevention programs.

Negative publicity, more sophisticated testing, and new laws nonetheless have not ended the problem. By all accounts, use of steroids (under a variety of slang names such as the gear, juice, and roids) and other drugs (amphetamines, clenbuterol, human growth hormone, and blood doping products) that improve sports performance has continued since 1990. Indeed, new scandals involving steroids in baseball and illegal blood substances in cycling have emerged in the last several years.

OLYMPIC SCANDALS

By the end of the 1960s, word about the benefits of steroids had spread to most Olympic sports. Usage figures are difficult to come by because athletes rarely admitted to taking drugs, and tests failed to find all the users. Given the small number of athletes who tested positive during the Olympic Games, some officials naively thought that they had the problem under control. Yet many others believed steroid use had come to dominate the games. For example, one informal survey of track and field athletes from seven nations found that 61 percent had used steroids in the six months before the 1972 Summer Olympics in Munich.[29]

Likely reflecting only a small part of the problem, documented instances of use of steroids and other drugs by Olympic athletes include the following:

- In 1976 at the Olympic Track and Field Trials in Eugene, Oregon, 23 U.S. athletes failed drug tests.

- In 1976 at the Montreal Summer Olympics, eight athletes out of 275 tested showed positive results for steroids.
- In 1979, the International Association of Athletics Federation, the world-governing body for track and field, banned seven women athletes from Eastern European countries for positive drug tests.
- In 1980 at the Moscow Summer Olympics, a new and informal test for steroid use revealed that 20 percent of those tested failed.
- In 1983 at the Pan American Games in Venezuela, 15 athletes from 10 nations tested positive for steroids.
- In 1984 at the Los Angeles Olympics, Thomas Johansson of Sweden, who won the silver medal in Greco-Roman wrestling, became the first medal winner to test positive for steroids, and Martti Vainio of Finland lost the silver medal he won in the 10,000 meters race because of a positive steroid test.[30]

These isolated cases failed to capture the public's attention. In 1988, however, an Olympic scandal gave worldwide publicity to steroid use in sports.

Ben Johnson and the 1988 Olympics

Although not the only user of steroids in the Olympics, Ben Johnson of Canada became the Games' most famous cheater. Born in Jamaica in 1961, he moved to Canada in 1976 at age 14 and began training in track. Over the next 12 years, he emerged as the world's fastest man, winning a bronze medal in the 100-meter race at the 1984 Los Angeles Olympics, a silver medal at the 1985 World Cup Championship in Australia, and a gold medal at the 1986 Commonwealth Games in Scotland.[31] In 1987, he set a new world record in the 100 meters, and his performance so impressed other sprinters that rumors of steroid use began to circulate.

At the 1988 Summer Olympics in Seoul, Korea, Johnson met his chief rival, American Carl Lewis, in the finals for the 100 meters. Lewis had won four gold medals, including one for the 100 meters at the 1984 Olympics, and fans expected a close race. To the surprise of most, however, Johnson easily defeated Lewis, shattering the world record with a time of 9.79 seconds and coming in well ahead of Lewis's second-place time of 9.92. The resounding victory left Lewis dejected but boosted the morale of Canadian athletes and fans. Johnson said he felt pleased by his performance, victory, and gold medal, and believed he could do even better.

From that point on, things went badly for Johnson. The day after his victory, analysis of the first of the two urine samples he had given immediately after the race disclosed evidence of stanozolol, a steroid. The next day, Johnson, his trainer, and representatives of the Canadian Olympic team came to observe the test of the second sample, which turned out as well to contain the steroid. Worse, the analysis indicated long-term use rather than a single application. All involved, including Johnson, denied that he had taken any drugs and specifically denied taking this steroid. Still, Johnson and his trainers had no explanation of how it had gotten into his urine. An IOC committee met to consider the evidence and decided to disqualify Johnson and revoke his gold medal. Canadian Olympic officials appealed the decision, arguing that the positive test must have resulted from deliberate sabotage, but the committee denied the appeal.

Once announced, the disqualification received massive publicity. Other winners of medals in less popular sports had tested positive for steroid use, but this scandal, involving the high-profile 100-meter race to determine the world's fastest runner, had much more impact. Canadian newspapers devoted pages to the story of the nation's disgraced hero, and television stations likewise aired extensive updates, interviews, and commentaries. The U.S. media, now interested in the gold medal newly awarded to its star, Carl Lewis, also gave the story much attention. The scandal became worldwide news, making concerns about the Olympics, cheating, and drugs a topic of conversation among the public.

Information on Johnson's drug use followed the games. A Canadian commission appointed under the direction of Charles L. Durbin, a Canadian judge, to investigate use of banned drugs for performance enhancement produced more facts.[32] Johnson eventually admitted using steroids supplied by his trainer, Charlie Francis, on a regular basis since 1981. During those years, he successfully hid his steroid use from drug tests. Through confusion or carelessness, however, he had come to inject a steroid that would not disappear by the time of the 1988 Olympic events. His physician, Dr. Jamie Astaphan, may have provided the steroid, but without telling Johnson and others exactly what it contained.

Johnson was banned from competition for two years, lost his Olympic medal, and had his 1987 world record deleted from the books. While subject to random testing over the next two years, he still trained in the hope of making a comeback. However, he never regained the speed he showed while on steroids. Although making the 1992 Canadian Olympic team, Johnson finished last in the qualifying heat and did not race in the Olympic final. In a 1993 race in Montreal, worse was to come—he again failed a drug test for steroids and was banned from competition for life.

Some have complained that Johnson served as a scapegoat. Many other Olympic athletes, although never caught, also used drugs. A *New York Times* article on the 1988 Olympics stated, "At least half of the 9000 athletes who competed at the Olympics in Seoul used performance-enhancing drugs in training, according to estimates by medical and legal experts as well as traffickers in these drugs."[33] Yet others who failed tests were not disqualified or publicly humiliated in the same way as Johnson.

Critics of Johnson's disqualification point to U.S. runner Florence Griffith Joyner. She won three gold medals at the 1988 Olympics, reaching a record time in the women's 100-meter race that many had thought impossible. Her time in the Olympic trials of 10.49 seconds shattered the existing record of 10.76—an astonishing improvement. In the Olympic finals, she won a gold medal with a time of 10.54. Many believed that she must have used steroids to run that fast. She consistently denied the accusation and never tested positive, but the rumors continued. Her unexpected death from an epileptic seizure in 1998 at the young age of 38 restarted the rumors about past steroid abuse and how it harmed her health. While her defenders say that no evidence has ever indicated drug use, skeptics suggest that she differed from Johnson only in the ability to avoid detection.

The East German Doping Machine

Although largely hidden at the time of Johnson's disqualification, a greater scandal involving drugs and the Olympics was in the making. This scandal involved government leaders in some nations who encouraged or even required their athletes to take performance-enhancing drugs. Such encouragement presented a new threat to the Olympics. With the help of trainers and physicians, individual athletes and team members had taken drugs, but they had done so in secret. Most hid their drug use from high-level national sports authorities in the worry that, if discovered, they would be banned from competition before even making it to the Olympics. In the 1970s, however, sports leaders in some nations did the opposite.

Rumors of government-supported drug use began with the Soviet Union and other former communist nations of Eastern Europe. Because steroid use first emerged among weightlifters in the Soviet Union, the government appeared not only to tolerate its use but also to actively aid its athletes in getting access to the drug and avoiding detection. Other communist nations in Eastern Europe, where the lack of democracy, a free press, and access of outsiders made it easier for the government to hide its activities, also came under suspicion.

As it turned out, however, one nation took drug use among its athletes to extremes. East Germany, a communist nation split off from West Germany after the end of World War II until reunification in 1990, took considerable pride in its athletic achievements. It used victories over West Germany in sports competition to claim the superiority of its economic and political system over democratic and capitalist systems. Ultimately, East Germany pushed its athletic goals to excess by forcing its young athletes to take steroids. Although suspicions of misuse of steroids had been raised for decades, proof of these suspicions came in the 1990s after the reunification of East and West Germany. Papers of the former communist government demonstrated shocking and unethical use of drugs for sports performance. This evidence led one writer to describe the sports effort as the East German doping machine.[34]

The success of East German athletes in the Olympics was indeed stunning. In the 1968 Summer Olympics in Mexico City, before the widespread adoption of steroids, East Germany won 25 medals compared to 26 by West Germany.[35] Only four years later in Munich, the East German count rose to 66 compared to 40 for West Germany; eight years later in Montreal, the East German medal count reached 90 compared to 39 for West Germany. Success came in the Winter Olympics as well: East German medals jumped from four in 1968 to 23 in 1980, again bettering their West German counterparts by a large margin. Since winners came from all sports, it appeared that athletes gained from something more than good coaches and training.

The improvement in the performance of women swimmers was most startling—and raised the most suspicion of illegal drug use. Amazingly, the women's swim team won 11 of 13 gold medals in the 1976 Olympics, and their competitors could see why. The women swimmers appeared mannish—they had broad shoulders, large muscles, excess hair on the body, and an aggressive and intimidating attitude. Competitors believed that the women must be taking steroids. When one American, wondering about that possibility, asked an East German official why the country's women swimmers had such deep voices, the official dismissed the concern by saying, "They came to swim, not to sing."[36]

In fact, the beliefs about steroid use proved true. According to records of Stasi, the East German secret police of the Ministry for State Security, and testimony of the athletes themselves, the government developed a program to make steroids a regular part of athletic training. As early as age 13, talented youngsters selected to attend special schools received both world-class training and special "vitamin" pills or injections that in fact contained steroids. Reports estimate that 10,000 young athletes received steroids, most without their knowledge or consent.[37] Some went on to win Olympic medals: Carola Nitschke, for example, broke the world breaststroke record at age 14, Ulrike Tauber broke the world record for the women's 400-meter individual medley, and Waldemar Cierpinski won the marathon gold medal in 1976 (finishing ahead of American Frank Shorter). However, most of the 10,000 athletes given steroids risked the dangerous side effects without the glory of victory.

One story illustrates both the success and tragedy of the doping program. Martina Fehrecke Gottschalt entered the East German national swimming program in 1972 at age six. After doing well in the program, she was invited to attend a special boarding school at age 10.[38] Along with intense training and special foods, she received in the years to come 40 pills a day, among them a steroid manufactured in East Germany. With newly muscular shoulders and arms and a deep voice that surprised her parents when she went home, Gottschalt won several junior championships. However, she had trouble adjusting psychologically to the training and never became an Olympic champion. She instead ended up with liver ailments and other health problems perhaps brought on by steroid use at a young age.

A scientific research program on steroid chemistry supported government sports efforts.[39] East Germans manufactured a steroid called Oral-Turinabol in a form attractive to teens—pink pills for small doses and blue pills for large doses. Less appealing to the athletes, another testosterone derivative, Depot-Turinabol, required injections to supplement the cycles of pills. Along with developing products, scientists learned how to mask steroid use from medical tests. For example, traces of Oral-Turinabol disappeared from the body after 14 days, allowing trainers to stagger steroid cycles to end shortly before competition. As soon as Olympic officials developed a more sensitive test, East German chemists tried to devise a new form of testosterone that tests would not detect. The athletes knew little about these experiments but felt they had to follow the recommendations of their trainers.

East German officials supervising the use of steroids became national heroes at first but criminals later. Manfred Ewald, the East German Minister of Sport, and Manfred Hoeppner, the Olympic Program's medical director, started the chemical road to sports success in the 1970s.[40] The need for secrecy and the political importance of Olympic victories for the government led Stasi to administer the program. In 2000, after the facts had come out, German prosecutors charged and convicted Ewald and Hoeppner for contributing to the bodily harm of minors. By that time, the abuse of steroids had ended, but the taint on the Olympics from past abuse remained.

Since the collapse of East Germany, another nation may have promoted drug abuse among its Olympic athletes.[41] In the early 1990s, women swimmers from China exhibited extraordinary progress in their performance times. The improvement coincided with increased test evidence of use of banned substances: More than 40 Chinese swimmers have failed drug tests since 1990, three times as many as any other nation's swim team during the same period. In 1998, one Chinese swimmer was found to be carrying human growth hormone in her luggage. Confirming suspicions that national authorities had established a program of drug use, an investigation alleged centralized control of doping and use of payoffs to coaches of medal winners. The program never reached the extremes of the one in East Germany but demonstrated the continued potential for cheating on a large scale.

Blood Doping

Along with steroids, trainers and athletes soon developed other, highly creative ways to enhance performances during the 1970s and 1980s. One strategy avoided taking chemical substances that are foreign to the body and instead used the athlete's own blood. Rumors started in the early 1970s that European distance runners, cyclists, and cross-country skiers had adopted a new method called blood doping to increase the oxygen-carrying capacity of their blood. Athletes allegedly would remove and store blood in a reduced and frozen form. In the meantime, the body naturally replaced the lost blood and the red blood cells that transport oxygen from the lungs to the muscles and organs. Before competition, a transfusion of the stored blood product would then increase the red blood cells in the body and the ability to deliver the extra oxygen needed for an exceptional performance.

The method had drawbacks that limited its use. Reducing and freezing the blood required special equipment; storing the blood inevitably degraded some of its contents; transfusing the blood caused infections. A related method overcame some of these problems. To avoid freezing and storage, a transfusion could come from the fresh blood of a match who had the same blood type. Using either one's own blood or that of a blood match would make it hard to detect. Since red blood cells occur naturally in the body, tests could not easily distinguish those produced by the body from those added externally.

Early studies made blood doping sound promising. In the late 1960s and early 1970s, Professor Bjorn Ekblom of the Institute of Physiology and Performance in Stockholm found that the process could increase oxygen use of the body by 9 percent and improve performance by 23 percent.[42] The procedure in principle simulated the benefits of high-altitude training, which over time deals with the lower levels of oxygen in the air by increasing red blood cells. Racing at sea level and in the presence of higher oxygen levels would then give the athlete a special advantage. Although other early studies did less well in replicating the gains from blood doping, more recent experiments have demonstrated decreased running time with blood infusions.[43]

Extensive publicity about the potential benefits of blood doping first emerged in 1976. During the Montreal Summer Olympics that year, television announcers mentioned rumors that Finnish long-distance runner Lasse Viren had used blood doping. Because the early studies of blood doping had come from Sweden, it made some sense that athletes from Scandinavia and nearby Finland might first adopt the procedures. In Viren's case, however, nothing more than his gold medal victories in two strenuous running events, the 5,000- and 10,000-meter races, led to the allegations. Despite the lack of documented evidence, the allegations and Viren's denial alerted others to the practice.

Better documentation of the use of blood doping came eight years later in the United States. In 1984, the American cycling team used blood doping to help win nine medals at the Summer Olympics in Los Angeles.[44] A team member revealed after the games that half the team received infusions of blood in a hotel room before their events. Although criticized for their actions, the cycling team members had not done anything illegal and received only minor punishment. After all, the athletes merely obtained blood rather than foreign drugs such as steroids or stimulants.

At first, the IOC did not ban blood doping because it had no way to test for it. It certainly seemed unethical and contrary to the spirit of the games, however. The IOC definition of doping banned the use of abnormal amounts of substances (including natural substances) and abnormal methods for the purpose of attaining an artificial and unfair performance advantage. Since it involved using abnormal amounts of blood, relied on transfusions, and aimed to help the athlete perform better, blood doping fit the definition.

In 1986, after the scandal involving the U.S. cycling team, the IOC banned blood doping—even though it had no test for the practice. Only those willing to admit to the practice faced punishment. For example, American Kerry Lynch won a silver medal in Nordic skiing at the 1987 World Championships. After admitting to blood doping, however, he lost his medal and was banned from competition for two years.

By the late 1980s, an alternative to transfusion of blood was developed, which athletes found more attractive than the traditional form of blood doping. The new method involved the use of a hormone that stimulates the production of red blood cells in the bone marrow of the body. The hormone, called erythropoietin or EPO, is produced by the kidneys, but in 1984 a biotech company licensed a synthetic form to help treat patients with anemia or low red blood cell counts. Athletes with normal counts found that EPO could boost their levels to a point that would help their performance. They had to receive an injection and wait a few weeks for new red blood cells to grow but otherwise could get the benefits of blood doping without the transfusion.

One suspected case of using EPO to enhance performance occurred in the 1988 Winter Olympics in Calgary, Canada, among cross-country skiers. There were also claims that EPO, called cycling's new wonder drug, was linked to the death of 18 cyclists between 1986 and 1991.[45] Just before the 1998 Tour de France, French border officials found more than 200 doses of EPO in a car driven by a Belgian employee of one of the leading teams. In these cases, however, the evidence did not come from testing. Since the hormone occurs naturally in blood and urine, tests could not easily distinguish natural from artificial levels.

The IOC first introduced tests for EPO in the 2000 Sydney Olympics. The tests were unsophisticated—they required positive results from separate examinations of both blood and urine. None of the samples tested reached this standard, perhaps implying that the test was too strict. Alternatively, the publicity about the tests, which were announced before the Olympics began, might have warned athletes from using EPO. Better tests emerged in later years, which appear to have helped control use of the artificial hormone.

Ironically, the availability of EPO tests may have encouraged a return to the older methods of blood doping. Most recently, U.S. cyclist Tyler Hamilton tested positive for blood doping at the trials for the 2004 Athens Olympics, but problems with the blood samples led to dropping of the charges. A few weeks after winning a gold medal in Athens, he again tested positive for an illegal blood transfusion during another race. A new test identified the likely presence of blood cells from another person and led to Hamilton's suspension from racing for two years.

Human Growth Hormone and Designer Steroids

While blood doping aids oxygen capacity, other performance-enhancing drugs help increase muscle and bone strength. These drugs have one key advantage over more common anabolic steroids: They are more difficult to detect with current tests.

One drug derives from a medicine used to treat children with abnormal growth problems. A deficiency in the human growth hormone (hGH), which the pituitary gland normally produces to regulate growth, results in dwarfism or lack of full body development. Along with helping poorly developed children grow taller, hGH might also help athletes of normal or large size grow stronger. Word spread in the 1980s of the benefits of hGH as an alternative or supplement to steroids.

Early on, the supply of hGH remained so limited that athletes could not get much access to it. Scientists had found they could extract the hormone from pituitary glands of cadavers. Although a difficult and expensive process, obtaining the extract could help children with low levels of the hormone grow to normal height. Athletes wanting to build muscle and able to get the scarce hormone could inject themselves with it but in effect deprived children of crucial medicine. In addition, the hormone taken from cadavers might be contaminated with the life-threatening Creutzfeldt-Jakob disease. As an alternative to hGH, some recommended taking a form of monkey growth hormone available on the black market.[46] Despite the implausibility of the idea that monkey hormones would help humans grow, some athletes and doctors believed that it helped build muscle mass.

Use of hGH in sports became more prevalent with the 1986 discovery of a new synthetic version. Advances in genetic technology allowed biotech companies to produce large amounts of hGH in the lab with recombinant DNA methods. Even if officially limited to use for children with a hormone deficiency and given only with a doctor's prescription, the synthetic hGH could be easily purchased by athletes on the black market. Although it inconveniently required injection, hGH had the crucial advantage that no means existed to detect it in urine or blood. Demand for the product grew among athletes.

Ironically, studies have not demonstrated clear benefits of hGH.[47] To the contrary, the risks of the hormone to adults with fully developed bodies include distortion of bone structure and problems of high blood pressure, heart problems, and diabetes. The hormone may cause growth in all body parts (including internal organs) rather than just the muscles most needed to compete. These drawbacks have not, however, prevented athletes from using the substance and claiming that it has benefits. One steroid advocate misleadingly praised hGH as "great stuff" and the "best drug for permanent muscle gains."[48]

Two famous champions in the 1988 Olympics, Canadian runner Ben Johnson and U.S. runner Florence Griffith Joyner, have been accused of using hGH along with steroids. After being banned from competition for using steroids, Johnson admitted that he also used hGH. Joyner always denied using hGH, as she always denied using steroids. However, another Olympic athlete said he bought the hormone for Joyner to use in the 1988 Olympics, and her early death and known heart problems make the accusations more plausible.

Perhaps in response to Johnson's disqualification for steroids, the popularity of hGH as an undetectable alternative grew in the 1990s. Without a way to test athletes for the drug, the 1996 Atlanta Summer Olympics were called the "growth hormone games" by one expert. The 2000 Sydney Olympics faced the same problem. For example, an Italian newspaper "claimed that five of their country's gold medalists had abnormally high hGH levels before the Olympic competition."[49] Athletes from other countries no doubt used the drug as well.

One famous Olympic champion, American Marion Jones, has faced accusations of using hGH. Jones won five medals at the 2000 Sydney Olympics, earning her the informal titles of fastest woman and best woman athlete in the world. Some years later, however, revelations about drug use tarnished her achievements. In December 2004, the founder of a lab under investigation for illegally distributing steroids and other drugs, Victor Conte, said on the television show *20/20* that he supplied hGH and watched her inject it. Jones disputed the claim and sued Conte for $25 million for defamation, but others said much the same, including her former husband, shot putter C. J. Hunter. Jones's later boyfriend and past world-record holder in the 100 meters, Tim Montgomery, has admitted to use of hGH— although he never directly implicated Jones.

Only in 2004 did testing for hGH begin. Despite beliefs of common use of hGH by top athletes, no positive tests for the hormone turned up at the 2004 Olympics. Authorities performed hundreds of blood tests at the 2006 Winter Olympics to check for hGH but again obtained no positive results.

Another new product called tetrahydrogestrinone (THG) created a scandal beginning in 2003. Some years earlier, a company called BALCO, founded by Victor Conte, had started to distribute a new steroid that common tests did not detect. Known as a designer steroid, THG differed just enough in chemical composition from known steroids that it would require new tests for detection. While distributing THG to selected athletes, BALCO managed for many years to keep the new steroid hidden from authorities. In 2003, however, a track and field coach tipped off the U.S. Anti-Doping Agency about the steroid and sent them a small amount of the drug.

The head of the agency, Terry Madden, reacted with anger to revelations about the designer steroid: "This is a conspiracy involving chemists, coaches and certain athletes using what they developed to be 'undetectable' designer steroids to defraud their fellow competitors and the American and world public who pay to attend sports events."[50] With samples of THG in hand, U.S. authorities quickly developed a new test for the steroid and began to reanalyze previously collected samples. International Olympic authorities added it to the list of banned substances.

Because of the reanalysis, several well-known athletes, including four Americans, ended up testing positive for THG. Other American athletes did not test positive but became implicated in the THG scandal. Marion Jones was accused by Victor Conte of using THG (as well as hGH), and Tim Montgomery admitted to a grand jury investigating Conte and BALCO that he used THG. Both ended up being suspended for two years, not because of a positive test but because of information obtained from the BALCO investigation about their use of banned substances. Otherwise, none of the athletes tested at the 2004 Athens Olympics showed evidence of THG, perhaps because publicity in America warned athletes away from the product. The worry remains, however, that chemists will continue to tweak the formulas for steroids in other ways for the sole purpose of hiding drug use from testers.

The 2004 Athens and 2006 Turin Olympics

U.S. Olympic officials declared that they did everything possible to make sure the 531 American athletes sent to Athens for the 2004 Summer Olympics were free from drugs. Following the damaging disclosure of use of hGH and TGH by former Olympic champions, authorities wanted badly to stay clear of any new scandals. It appears they succeeded—none of the U.S. athletes tested positive for drugs at the games. Some athletes from other nations had less success. A record 22 participants—mostly from Eastern European nations—tested positive in Athens. The high number likely does not signify greater drug use; rather, more thorough testing likely caught more users. As IOC president Jacques Rogge concluded, "These were the Games where it became increasingly difficult to cheat and where clean athletes were better protected."[51]

Rogge seems correct. Few track records were broken at the Athens Summer Olympics, and many world records have now stood for more than 10 years. If steroids and other drugs aided past performances, the weaker performances today indicates a change in drug use. Suspicions that track athletes still use drugs remain, but it appears likely that they used them more in the past. At the same time, concern remains that tests fail to capture some drug use. After all, the 22 athletes caught in the Athens Olympics make up only a tiny portion of all participants in the games. It is always possible that athletes and trainers have used their resources to come up with new drugs that can escape discovery.

For the 2006 Winter Olympics in Turin, Italy, new tests led to suspensions of members of several cross-country ski teams. The International Ski Federation announced the day before the Winter Games were to start that eight cross-country skiers, including two Americans, had shown unusually high levels of hemoglobin in the blood. Such levels can increase performance in endurance events like cross-country skiing. The federation suspended the skiers for five days, arguing not that they had proof of doping but that the high levels were a health risk. Fortunately, the events participated in by most of the skiers did not occur until after the suspension had ended. One U.S. skeleton slider, Zach Lund, also was suspended for testing positive for a masking agent that is an ingredient in an antibalding medicine he was taking—a suspension that led many to criticize the excess of the testing.

In taking a tough approach to enforcing antidoping policies, IOC president Jacques Rogge said that the Turin games would do something new. They would rely on tips from informants as a means to catch drug users. And indeed, a tip that banned Austrian biathlon coach Walter Mayer was present at the quarters of the Austrian Olympic team led Italian police to raid the quarters on the night of February 18. Despite efforts of at least one team member to throw used medical equipment out the window, the police discovered doping-related equipment. In a bizarre twist, Mayer escaped but was later found asleep in his car on a road in Austria and when awoken tried to escape police by crashing through a roadblock. Austrian authorities complained bitterly about being treated as criminals during the raid, and 10 Austrian athletes underwent and passed urine tests. Still, the IOC promised to investigate the use of drugs by the Austrian team more fully. Whatever the outcome, the incident emphasizes the renewed vigor of efforts to stop drug use.

Drug scandals have continued since the most recent Summer and Winter Olympics. In the United States, two track-and-field stars tested positive for drug use in 2006. Justin Gatlin, who shares the world record in the 100 meters, tested positive for steroids. Having tested positive several years earlier for stimulants, he faced a lifetime ban from racing. However, negotiations with the U.S. Anti-Doping Agency over the punishment led to a compromise: Gatlin will serve an eight-year ban, which will make him eligible to race competitively again at age 32. Marion Jones, after facing accusations of doping due to her association with BALCO and several steroid users, tested positive for EPO. She denied using the drug, and a second test supported her claim. Analysis of her backup sample proved negative and invalidated the first positive test. Now cleared, Jones can continue racing, but suspicions remain about her use of performance-enhancing drugs.

THE ENDURING STRUGGLE OVER TESTING

Although testing followed by punishment remains the most effective method of stopping the problem, it has limits that trainers and athletes well understand. While authorities strive for better and more complete testing, others strive to find drugs that can aid performance without being detected. The struggle between testers and users sometimes seems like a high-tech version of cops and robbers.

The problem has appeared most clearly in the Olympic Games. The IOC has led efforts for better testing, and its officials point with pride to the progress they have made with better and more thorough methods. The testing methods in fact represent the state-of-the-art and serve as a model for other sports. They have ended the use of most short-term stimulants, relaxants, and narcotics during competition and stopped the casual user from taking steroids and other longer-acting drugs to build muscle. Yet, sophisticated athletes can avoid detection with the help of trainers and physicians. In the careful words of one expert, "Use of performance-enhancing drugs is more widespread than drug-testing data indicates."[52] In the blunt words of another, an athlete has to be "either incredibly sloppy, incredibly stupid or both" to get caught.[53] To the detriment of most sports, the struggle over drug testing has become a key part of athletic competition.

New and Better Tests for Steroids

Although testing for a variety of banned substances among Olympic athletes began in the 1960s, the tests did not include steroids until the 1970s. Until then, authorities had not included steroids among the banned substances for a simple reason—they had no way to detect their use. That changed in the 1970s with discovery of crude steroid tests and in the 1980s with development of more sophisticated tests. The tests managed over the years to catch a small number of users but never became as effective as those opposed to drug use had hoped.

In articles published in 1973, British scientists first identified a way to find evidence of steroids in urine. The tests did not search for testosterone or steroids directly but looked for by-products excreted in the urine that came from the metabolism of steroids by the body. The method required expensive and complex equipment for chemical analysis that few labs had available. Given its concern about the growing problem of steroid use, the IOC adopted the testing procedures anyway. After some informal trials of the new test, officials used it to examine the urine samples of participants in the 1976 Montreal Olympics for steroid by-products.

Surprisingly, only eight of the 283 samples tested turned out positive—seven male weightlifters, including two Americans, and one female discus thrower. The small number appeared puzzling given informal reports of pervasive steroid use. Indeed, critics labeled the tests as incomplete and inconsistent. Reflecting a problem that would always detract from the tests, athletes knew that stopping the use of certain steroids a few weeks before the competition would leave time for the evidence to wash out of the body. Other kinds of steroids that stayed in the body for a longer time allowed easier detection, but athletes knew to avoid them. Throughout the 1970s, then, a few athletes at any particular competition had the bad luck of getting caught for steroid use.

To illustrate, tests during the 1980 Moscow Olympic Games—which the United States and many other countries boycotted—discovered no evidence of illegal drug use by athletes. Yet, one German scientist, Manfred Donike, had developed a new test to supplement the usual tests. Rather than search for the metabolites of anabolic steroids that disappear from the body quickly, his test screened for excessive testosterone that came from outside the body. Typically, the body produces equal amounts of testosterone and another hormone called epitestosterone, and if urine showed testosterone levels six times higher than epitestosterone levels, it almost certainly indicated steroid use. This more sophisticated test found a 20 percent failure rate. These experimental results could not be used to disqualify competitors, but they indicated the extent of the problem.

A turning point came when authorities first approved official use of the Donike steroid test at the 1983 Pan American Games in Venezuela. Word of the new method surprised many participants who had not prepared for the technology and its ability to examine testosterone levels more directly. After learning of the new test, a dozen U.S. athletes, seemingly worried that a positive result would disqualify them from more important future events, returned from Venezuela without having even competed. Among all those who stayed, 12 lost medals for testing positive.

Athletes responded quickly to the change. Even with the new test, only 12 of the 1,510 samples taken in the 1984 Los Angeles Olympics contained evidence of steroids. The number of positive tests for steroids fell to four in the 1988 Seoul Olympics, five in the 1992 Barcelona Olympics, and six in the 2000 Sydney Olympics. Positive tests occurred even less frequently in the Winter Olympic Games. The low counts may have come from weeding out the worst offenders with tests done before the Olympics. More likely, the low counts meant that athletes could hide their drug use from even the more sophisticated tests. After all, Ben Johnson, who admitted to continuous use of steroids before getting caught at the 1988 Olympics, passed 19 drug tests.

A 1997 article in *Sports Illustrated* summarized the worries of many experts: "What is surprising is that 25 years after the introduction of supposedly rigorous drug testing of Olympic athletes, the use of banned performance-enhancing substances has apparently become more widespread, and effective, than ever."[54] As one physician said, "There may be some sportsmen who can win gold medals without taking drugs, but there are very few."[55]

Tests for steroid use have continued to improve over the last decade, having now reached remarkable levels of sophistication. Expensive computerized machines for chemical analysis can uncover the tiniest amounts of a substance; dozens of accredited analysis labs have been established across the world; skilled scientists devote their careers to improving testing; and millions of dollars are spent on the task of detecting steroids and other banned substances. New tests developed for blood doping, EPO, and hGH represent advances in the technology. Despite these upgrades, questions remain about the effectiveness of drug testing.

Current Banned Substances and Methods

The IOC has built up a long list of banned substances.[56] The list changes as newly discovered drugs are added and reevaluated drugs are dropped. For example, THG and androstenedione have been added recently, while caffeine, once banned when above a high threshold, was removed. The 2005 list from the IOC includes the following:

I. Prohibited Substances In- and Out-of-Competition
    A. Anabolic Agents
        1. Anabolic Androgenic Steroids
        2. Other Anabolic Agents
    B. Hormones and Related Substances
        1. Erythropoietin (EPO)
        2. Human Growth Hormone (hGH)
        3. Gonadotrophins
        4. Insulin
        5. Corticotrophins
    C. Beta-2 Agonists
    D. Anti-Estrogens
    E. Diuretics and Masking Agents
II. Prohibited Methods In- and Out-of-Competition
    A. Enhancement of Oxygen Transfer (e.g., blood doping)
    B. Chemical and Physical Manipulation (e.g., tampering with samples)
    C. Gene Doping
III. Prohibited Substances and Methods In-Competition
    A. Stimulants
    B. Narcotics
    C. Glucocorticosteroids

Introduction to Drugs and Sports

IV. Prohibited Substances in Certain Sports
   A. Alcohol
   B. Beta Blockers

With some of these categories listing dozens of product names, athletes and trainers must take special efforts to avoid the banned substances and methods. However, the IOC notes that it may reduce sanctions when violations occur unintentionally or do little to enhance sports performance.

The list of banned substances and methods continues to change as experts identify new ones. In 2004, authorities added gene doping to the list. Gene doping, a variant on genetic therapies used to treat muscle-wasting disorders, has the potential to give athletes a synthetic gene that produces naturally occurring hormones such as insulinlike growth factor and promotes muscle growth. Since gene doping produces more of the body's naturally occurring hormones, existing urine or blood tests for foreign substances will not work. Effective uses of gene doping for sports have not been demonstrated yet, but the potential for misuse worries authorities. More recently, authorities considered banning hypoxic or hyperbaric chambers that some athletes use to simulate high-altitude conditions and increase red blood cells. Experts suggest that the chambers or tents can cause sickness and weaken the immune system. However, they decided in 2006 against a ban. Before taking any further action, the IOC Medical Commission was asked to evaluate the health effects of the training method.

Limits of Testing

Testing for a wide-ranging set of banned substances and methods will always have limits. The problem stems from the need to balance two contradictory goals: Testing must correctly identify real cheaters while not falsely identifying innocent athletes. On one hand, the more tests do to find cheaters and the smaller the amounts of banned substances they can identify, the greater the risk that they will misidentify nonusers. On the other hand, the looser the standards, the greater the risk that users will slip through. Errors in testing inevitably occur, and doing more to eliminate one kind of error increases another kind of error.

Given this dilemma, international figures on test results show that authorities have erred on the low side. Of the 117,314 urine tests done by IOC-accredited laboratories in 2000, only 1.9 percent uncovered drug violations.[57] Of these positive results, 38.1 percent came from anabolic steroids, 19.7 percent from beta-2 agonists (another type of anabolic agent), 18.3 percent from stimulants, and 11.9 from marijuana (a drug most always used recreationally). With other evidence of widespread drug use, these figures suggest that athletes can beat the tests.

Such problems in testing effectiveness have discouraged authorities. In April 1995, for example, Ralph Hale of the U.S. Olympic Committee said, "Our anti-doping campaign, I'm afraid, has been a failure to this point. Many countries have lost confidence in our anti-doping effort. I'm not sure we're doing the right job."[58] Since then, Olympic officials in the United States and elsewhere have reinvigorated their testing efforts but many problems remain.

Timing and Out-of-Competition Testing.   Many drugs like steroids can be used during periods of training between competitions and then stopped before the events and associated testing. Athletes and trainers learn about clearance time—the period needed to wash evidence of illegal drug use out of the body. Short clearance times allow users to stop taking drugs just before competition, while long clearance times require users to suspend their drugs earlier. In most cases, the clearance times remain short enough that benefits to muscle growth from steroids remain while evidence in the urine disappears. Drugs such as stimulants and narcotics bring no benefit once emptied from the body and need to be taken at the time of the event. As a result, tests have largely eliminated their use in competition. The same has not happened with steroids and associated drugs, however.

The best solution to the problem comes from year-round or out-of-competition testing. Some nations such as Norway and the United Kingdom started programs of random testing of athletes during the periods between events in the 1970s and 1980s. The U.S. Anti-Doping Agency now follows a similar process of randomly selecting athletes throughout the year and requiring them to give urine samples without advance notice. The samples undergo tests just as they would for Olympic events, and positive results lead to penalties ranging from warning to suspension.

Coordination and WADA.   Testing outside of competition has created a problem of coordination across nations. While most nations make sincere efforts to keep drug users from competing, others have resisted effective out-of-competition testing. Some nations may make only token efforts to test its athletes and then impose only mild punishments when they obtain positive results. Poorer nations may have trouble affording the cost of year-round testing. A few nations may even use their own testing to warn athletes of the need to better hide their drug use rather than to ensure they do not use drugs. Such inconsistency across nations creates resentment, as those with strict programs feel disadvantaged relative to those with lax programs.

One source of inconsistency comes from relying on national sports organizations to supervise testing. When governing bodies of individual sports—swimming organizations, weightlifting organizations, and track and field organizations—take responsibility for testing, it creates conflicting goals. The goal of producing champions and increasing popularity of their sport may make the governing bodies hesitant to declare its most famous athletes to be drug users. One solution has been to set up an organization devoted solely to doping control in Olympic sports, a task now done in the United States by the U.S. Anti-Doping Agency.

Ideally, all nations should follow the same set of high-quality standards for out-of-competition testing and avoid dual goals of both promoting and testing athletes. Toward that end, the IOC established the World Anti-Doping Agency (WADA) in 1999. The agency sets uniform standards for obtaining drug samples, analyzing the samples, and imposing punishments, and it helps coordinate national efforts to follow those standards. It also supervises testing at the Olympics and many international events. Before the 2002 Winter Olympics in Salt Lake City, WADA conducted more than 3,500 tests across 34 sports and on athletes from 75 different nations. In 2003, WADA collected 4,229 unannounced urine tests and 775 out-of-competition tests, which resulted in 25 adverse findings.[59] WADA also launched an athletic passport program that maintains on a secure web site the testing history of athletes competing in events sponsored by any variety of national and international organizations.

Testing Errors. Despite the best efforts of national and international doping agencies to ensure high-quality tests, errors inevitably result. Sometimes tests identify banned substances that athletes used for health reasons rather than to improve performance. Cough and cold medicines available without a prescription can occasionally lead to positive tests, as can nutritional supplements and herbal products that contain mild stimulants. Other types of errors may result. Mary Decker Slaney, a well-known American middle-distance runner, appealed her positive test for steroid use in 1996. She argued that menstruation or alcohol consumption could skew the steroid test among women. This flaw made her results invalid. Although experts disagreed, U.S.A. Track and Field eventually lifted her suspension and dropped the doping charges.

One anabolic steroid has presented special testing problems. Nandrolone is an anabolic steroid that has been the most common source of positive tests, in part because it is relatively easy to detect. However, eating meat products from animals given steroids to increase their growth or using certain legal dietary supplements in combination with intense training might cause positive tests for nandrolone. Oral contraceptives or pregnancy may also lead the bodies of women to produce nandrolone metabolites naturally, thus resulting in false tests for use of steroids. Linford Christie of Great Britain, the winner of the gold medal for the men's 100-meter race in the 1992 Olympics, tested positive for nandrolone in 1999 but was cleared of all charges. A disciplinary committee could not conclude beyond a reasonable doubt that the positive test actually came from using the steroid.

The problem of positive tests resulting from innocent behavior has led the IOC, in the eyes of some, to become overly cautious. In the 1996 Atlanta Olympics, for example, positive tests found from the use of an expensive, more sensitive high-resolution mass spectrometer were withheld until more experience and confidence in the machine could make sure no athletes were falsely accused. Given the harm to an athlete of a false accusation of drug use, the IOC decided it must be extra careful. To make certain of guilt before punishing athletes, the IOC sometimes set high levels needed to qualify for a positive test. The ratio of testosterone to epitestosterone in tests for steroids, initially set at six to one and then later reduced to four to one, well exceeds the normal ratio of one to one. As a result, athletes can use steroids in amounts sufficient to help their performance but still stay under the testing threshold.

Legal Challenges.   Athletes generally recognize the need for testing and favor rules against drug use, but many have also challenged the results with lawsuits. In 1990, the current world-record holder in the 400 meters, Harry "Butch" Reynolds of the United States, sued over a suspension resulting from a positive test for steroids. He contended that irregularities in the testing procedure might have allowed someone to tamper with his sample. He also claimed that the procedure violated his constitutional rights: Athletes testing positive must prove their innocence rather than, as in normal court proceedings, make authorities prove guilt. Reynolds eventually won his appeal of the suspension but failed in an effort to sue for damages.

In another case, Jessica Foschi, a U.S. swimmer in her teens, tested positive for steroids in 1995. She claimed to have never used steroids and that the drug must have been given to her without her knowledge in an effort to sabotage her career. That the test showed a large amount of the steroid in her urine, though she did not exhibit other symptoms of a steroid user, lent weight to her denials. In response to a suit, the U.S. Swimming Federation accepted her arguments and lifted her ban from competition, but the body governing international swimming did not. Eventually, an international court of arbitration ruled in Foschi's favor.[60]

These cases illustrate the vulnerable position of Olympic authorities in charge of testing. The courts have upheld the legality of testing and the authority of Olympic organizations to punish drug users, but legal challenges make the task more difficult. The more complex the tests, the more likely it is that a mistake could occur and that athletes will contest the result.

New Drugs.   Even if perfectly accurate, tests would still miss newly discovered drugs. Officials test for hundreds of substances but cannot test for those they do not know about. Designer steroids such as THG change the chemical structure of known steroids just enough to escape detection, and those intent on creating new designer products can find the expertise to do so. Hoping to discourage athletes from using substances such as THG, Olympic authorities plan to store samples for a long period. They can then retest the samples after the discovery of new designer drugs. Athletes who use new drugs in competition may risk losing their medals once officials find out about the new drug and test the old samples. Even so, development of new drugs creates a difficult enforcement problem.

Education

Given the limits of testing, some experts emphasize the need to educate athletes about the risks and unfairness of drug use. If educational programs begin with young athletes and then continue among professional athletes, they may diminish the desire to use steroids and make testing less important. Until such programs become more widely adopted, however, testing will remain the primary source of control for drug use in the Olympics and other sports.

AMERICAN FOOTBALL

Outside the Olympics, one popular American sport, football, seems particularly prone to abuse of drugs. Football requires bursts of speed and energy during plays that could be aided by amphetamines, high tolerance of pain that could be aided by painkillers, and strength in blocking, tackling, and running that could be aided by steroids. The growing popularity of the sport after the 1950s made for fame, high salaries, and intense competition, all of which encouraged players to look to drugs for extra help. Even the schedule of football games, held only once a week during the season, allowed for use of some drugs on a weekly rather than a more dangerous daily basis.

Drugs and Sports

Amphetamine use emerged in the National Football League (NFL) as early as the 1960s. Taking pep pills helped players get psyched up before a game and then helped mask fatigue with an extra lift during a game. Most experts deny that amphetamines bring physical benefits, and some suggest that they worsen performance by making players jumpy and unfocused. At the time, however, many athletes believed the drug helped them. In some cases, trainers and coaches thought so too, as they provided amphetamines to their players.

Exact figures on amphetamine use in the NFL are hard to come by, but drug use became common by the 1970s. Arnold Mandell, a psychiatrist who served as team physician for the San Diego Chargers from 1972 to 1974, observed the use of amphetamines firsthand. He also interviewed 87 players on 11 NFL teams, finding that two-thirds used amphetamines occasionally and one-half used them regularly.[61] Linemen tended to take the largest doses as a way to encourage fearlessness, while receivers and quarterbacks used lower doses as a way to encourage creativity and quick thinking on the field.

Some players went a step further, using cocaine rather than amphetamines during games. According to Vic Washington, a star running back with the San Francisco 49ers in the 1970s, "We were in a war out there. And using cocaine was seen as a way of getting psyched up to have an edge. I understood it at the time because we were out of reality. Pro football is not reality."[62] Use of cocaine during a game may have made players feel better but no doubt harmed rather than helped their performance and never became common. More worrisome, 40 percent of football players had, by the estimate of one player, used cocaine recreationally after games or in the off-season. The NFL was concerned enough about the problem to hire a drug adviser to identify and counsel players who used drugs socially.

Football players also relied on another set of medications to help them recover from injuries. Drugs normally used for medical therapy during a period of recovery and rehabilitation could also help injured players continue to play. Sometimes encouraged by NFL team physicians, trainers, and coaches, players used painkillers such as Novocain and anti-inflammatory drugs such as cortisone to enhance performance. If injuries and pain slowed the movement of players, then medications temporarily masked the problem. The problem, however, would come back after the medication wore off and might even end up getting worse. As one physician notes, "If you inject a joint, particularly on a game day, and anesthetize the injured area, the player is not going to know if he is injured worse."[63] In the short run, however, injured players could do things on these drugs they could not otherwise do, and pressures to perform, even in pain, led to potential abuse of painkillers.

Introduction to Drugs and Sports

Steroids in the NFL

Compared to amphetamines, cocaine, and painkillers, steroids present a more serious threat to the NFL today. The benefits of steroids to football players are both clear and long lasting. They add strength, size, and speed that in particular help large players on the offensive and defensive lines but also help those in other positions who need to fight off blockers, make tackles, and run through opponents. During the 1970s and 1980s, as coaches and trainers started to recognize the full benefit of weight training, the players began to recognize how steroids could enhance muscle growth obtained from weight training.

In testimony before Congress in 1989, two successful football players described the extent of the problem over the two previous decades. Bill Fralic, an offensive lineman with the Atlanta Falcons who did not use steroids, told senators, "Steroid use is rampant among the NFL, and that includes my own team. It is rampant in colleges, and it is rampant in high schools."[64] By his personal estimate, about 75 percent of linemen used steroids. The pressure to win and the desire to succeed were so strong that athletes at all levels felt they had to use the drug.

Steve Courson, former linebacker with the Pittsburgh Steelers and Tampa Bay Buccaneers, also opposed steroid use but spoke more of his personal experiences. "I would estimate conservatively 50% of the line of scrimmage positions have augmented or still periodically augment their training programs with steroids."[65] Those in other positions used steroids less commonly according to Courson but still enough to make for a serious problem. As a result, NFL players have reached unprecedented levels of size, strength, and speed. In Courson's words, "NFL football and Olympic sport cannot be played at present levels without steroids. This is the cruel but serious reality of the modern sports world."[66]

Reflecting the experience of many other football players, Courson first used steroids in college. When switched from linebacker to defensive lineman in 1974, he had to add 20–30 pounds to his frame and obtained steroids from the team physician to help. He again used steroids when reporting to his first training camp for the Pittsburgh Steelers, finding that they helped him compete with the top players. Steadily raising the dosage and number of steroids he took, Courson discovered in 1985 that he had an irregularity in his heartbeat. He then stopped using steroids and ended his football career soon after.

Lyle Alzado, a 15-year NFL player, who admitted taking steroids continuously during his career from 1969 to 1985 and then during the years of his retirement. The steroids increased his size and ferocity on the field. Over the years, he tried different, newer, and stronger forms of steroids to get more out of them. He injected himself so many times with steroids that he needed plastic surgery to cover up damage to the skin. He even helped teammates get steroids: "I wasn't a dealer, but if I was asked, I'd help other guys get steroids. Because they were doing for me what I wanted them to do, I hoped they would do the same for the other players."[67] When Alzado was stricken with brain cancer, he blamed the disease on his excessive use of the steroids. He died in 1992 at age 43.

Some believe that players have overstated the extent of steroid use. Former NFL commissioner Pete Rozelle pointed out that preseason testing in 1987 and 1988 found that only 6 to 7 percent of the players had positive results for steroid use. Although the low figures may merely indicate that players could effectively hide their steroid use, other coaches and players agreed with the commissioner. In testimony before Congress in 1989, Chuck Noll, the coach of the Pittsburgh Steelers, Marty Schottenheimer, the coach of the Cleveland Browns, and Gene Upshaw, the executive director of the NFL Players Association, all expressed concern about steroid use but did not believe it was as high as some players suggested.

Whatever the usage figures, NFL leader took action during the 1980s to stop drug use. Starting in 1983, a letter sent to all players by Commissioner Rozelle reminded them of the NFL policy against abuse of legal prescription drugs, including steroids. In 1986, a new drug policy flatly stated that "use of anabolic steroids and similar growth-enhancing substances is considered a violation of the NFL's drug program."[68] The new policy was followed by a program of urine testing during 1987 and 1988 preseason training camps, with those testing positive given counseling and education. In 1989, the NFL toughened its policy by punishing those who tested positive for steroids or masking agents and by suspending 13 players in the first year.

Testing only once a year, however, had obvious drawbacks. Users could easily avoid getting caught—they merely needed to stop taking steroids a few weeks before the preseason and then restart once the regular season began. Responding to this loophole in 1990—and to increasingly negative publicity about steroid abuse—the NFL announced another more stringent testing procedure. Besides facing preseason tests, randomly sampled players would undergo unscheduled testing during the regular season and off-season. The NFL Players Association had opposed additional random tests without cause but by the early 1990s came to agree to the testing plan.

According to the NFL, the year-round unscheduled testing has succeeded in lowering steroid use. Although the new policy led to suspension of four players in 1990, the numbers fell to one in 1991 and zero in 1992.

Testing almost certainly reduced the suspected high levels in the 1970s and 1980s, and the NFL took pride in having set up thorough drug testing before other professional leagues did. According to Commissioner Paul Tagliabue, the NFL currently conducts more than 9,000 unannounced tests every year on NFL players and suspends first-time offenders for four games.[69]

If players have found ways to use steroids without getting caught, however, the low suspension figures may be misleading. Such concerns were reinforced by a March 2005 report that three members of the Carolina Panthers had received prescriptions for steroids only two weeks before they played in the January 2004 Super Bowl. Yet, none of the three had tested positive for steroids. In May 2005, Minnesota Vikings running back Onterrio Smith was found during a routine airport check to be carrying a device called a whizzinator. Advertised as a way to pass drug tests, the device uses a plastic bladder to pass clean urine through a fake penis. In fall 2005, Bill Romanowski, a recently retired NFL linebacker and part of the 1996 and 1997 Super Bowl champion Denver Broncos, admitted to having used THG from 2001 to 2003. He also never tested positive for steroids. According to two experts, because of problems in testing and the ability of users to evade the tests, "performance-enhancing drug use remains a significant and widespread problem in the NFL."[70]

More recently, critics of the NFL voiced concerns about the use of hGH by players. Although the IOC has started taking blood samples to test for the growth hormone among Olympic athletes, the NFL has not adopted the test. Players can avoid a positive drug test by using hGH as an alternative to steroids. New Commissioner Roger Goodell defends the league's policy as effective but agrees with the need to consider new tests. The NFL Players Association opposes blood testing as too invasive. The league instead has invested in research to develop a more reliable urine test for hGH that it hopes to use in the future.

College Football

Stories of steroid use by college football players, though less common than those about the NFL also appeared. In 1985, a Nashville case involving the illegal sale and distribution of steroids listed 32 current and former Vanderbilt University football players as co-conspirators (but did not charge them). One current NFL player who took steroids in college said, "Vanderbilt is the straw that broke the camel's back. There are [players at] a bunch of other schools who are doing steroids, too. The whole college deal has gotten out of hand."[71] In a 1988 story in *Sports Illustrated*, a former college football player at the University of South Carolina, Tommy Chaikin, told of his steroid use and the psychological damage it caused.[72] Doing much the same as other athletes he knew, Chaikin used weightlifting and steroids to reach a weight of 250 pounds on his 6′ 1″ frame. By his junior year, he said that about half his teammates used steroids, with small groups sometimes helping one another with injections. His coaches never encouraged use of the drug but seemed to know of it and did nothing.

Two surveys of National Collegiate Athletic Association (NCAA) athletes confirmed the reality of the problem among college football players. From the first survey in 1985 to the second survey in 1989, steroid use averaged around 10 percent, amphetamine use about 7 percent, barbiturates/tranquilizers about 3 percent, and major pain medications about 37 percent. Steroid use in particular proved higher among college football players than among athletes in other sports. The surveys also found that fewer athletes got steroids from coaches or trainers in 1989 than 1985, but, given the lack of change in levels of use, they managed to get them elsewhere without too much trouble. Indeed, the surveys likely understated true usage. Despite the anonymous answers to the questions, some athletes may have attempted to hide their drug use.

In response to evidence of drug use, the NCAA began taking action in the 1980s. In testimony before Congress in 1990, Frank D. Uryasz, the official responsible for NCAA drug education and testing, noted that most (but not all) member schools had drug education and treatment programs for student-athletes. Testing took a variety of forms. First, random urine tests were required for teams playing in league championship or bowl games. Second, about 30 percent of member schools (60 percent of the largest Division I schools with the most competitive sports teams) operated their own testing programs. Third, schools could request off-season steroid testing by the NCAA. The program did not test all athletes during both the season and off-season but seemed to have some success. By 1997, steroid use by college football players had fallen to 2.2 percent from 8.4 percent in 1985.

Beginning in fall 2004, the NCAA has added year-round or off-season testing for Division I schools. Each member institution may be selected once a year for randomly selected testing of 18 football players and eight players from another sport. The testing program costs the NCAA millions to run but does more to catch drug users than its earlier programs. According to test results from August 2002 to June 2003, the latest reported on the NCAA web site, only 46 positive results for steroids occurred among the 4,713 tests of Division I football players.

Introduction to Drugs and Sports

BODYBUILDING AND PROFESSIONAL WRESTLING

Drug use appears especially common in bodybuilding and professional wrestling, two sports that formally or informally require a muscular physical appearance. Bodybuilding involves the development of large, symmetric, and well-defined muscles that, in the competitive form of the sport, are displayed in posing routines during contests. Bodybuilding depends on weight training, but it differs from Olympic weightlifting, where the goal is to lift heavy weights rather than to build and display muscles. Professional wrestling, a form of athletic entertainment, also emphasizes the muscular physiques of its athletes. By most accounts, athletes in both sports extensively use steroids and other drugs.

Bodybuilding in particular has become, in the words of a former power-lifter, "nearly synonymous with steroid use."[73] According to scholars who have studied the sport, nearly all professional or elite competitive body-builders have used steroids sometime in their lives. One expert said that bodybuilding "is the only sport I know of where nearly everyone contends that at the elite level, participation in the sport and illicit drug use are absolutely intertwined."[74] Like men, elite women bodybuilders also use steroids to help build muscle mass. One study reported that 70 percent of elite competitive female bodybuilders use steroids.[75] In the view of critics, competitive bodybuilding has become a form of chemical warfare among participants.

The world's most famous bodybuilder, Arnold Schwarzenegger, has admitted to past steroid use. Before becoming an actor, world-famous movie star, and governor of California, Schwarzenegger won bodybuilding's most prestigious title, Mr. Olympia, seven times (1970–1975 and 1980). Although he took steroids as a bodybuilder before they became illegal, he recommends now that bodybuilders not do the same. Still, his past use of steroids reflects the common reliance on the drug by bodybuilders.

Drug use by bodybuilders goes beyond steroids. Nonsteroid drugs help give large muscles a clearly defined (ripped, cut, or shredded) look. To increase definition of the muscles before competitions, bodybuilders use diuretics to release water from the body and the stimulant ephedrine to help eliminate fat. One other nonsteroid drug, clenbuterol, is normally prescribed to open the bronchial airways of asthma patients but also increases muscle mass and reduces fat. Bodybuilders use it as either a substitute for steroids (without the unpleasant androgenic side effects) or as a supplement to steroids that gives special help just before competitions.

Along with professionals, amateur and recreational bodybuilders also rely on steroids and other muscle-enhancing drugs, although likely not to the same extent. Figures on steroid use range from 20 to 50 percent for male bodybuilders and 3 to 10 percent for female bodybuilders.[76] The attraction of drugs to the wider bodybuilding community shows in dozens of internet web sites, easily found in a search, that offer to sell steroids and provide guidance for their use.

More than athletes in other sports, bodybuilders helped encourage the spread of steroids to nonprofessionals. The *Underground Steroid Handbook* by Daniel Duchaine, first distributed in 1981, cited the benefits of steroids for bodybuilders and encouraged their use. It contained details on a variety of steroids and explained how to give injections, determine proper doses, and maximize muscle growth. Duchaine ended up serving prison time for sale of drugs and died at age 47 in 2000, but his handbook allowed amateurs without trainers and medical guidance to learn about steroids.

Bodybuilders have come to recognize the image problem created by steroid use. Once a symbol of good health and concern with physical fitness, bodybuilding is now tainted by use of drugs that may harm rather than improve health. The public often views the large muscles of bodybuilders as the artificial creation of pills and injections. Stories of criminals arrested for distributing steroids, bodybuilders addicted to steroids, and users becoming violent worsen negative public views. Bodybuilders deny this image, viewing the proper use of steroids as a safe form of physical self-improvement. They believe that most users have sufficient knowledge of drugs to protect themselves from harm, and that bodybuilders who abuse steroids are not typical.

Bodybuilding organizations have responded to the negative images of steroid use by prohibiting performance-enhancing drugs in contests. The International Bodybuilding Federation (IBBF), the umbrella organization of national bodybuilding groups across the world, maintains that the random tests of athletes it started in 1986 have significantly reduced drug use among bodybuilders participating in its events. Hoping to make bodybuilding an Olympic sport, the IBBF more recently has adopted the drug guidelines of the IOC and WADA. Consistent with the claims of prohibiting drug use, Ronnie Coleman, the current champion and eight-time winner of Mr. Olympia, firmly denies having ever taken steroids.

Many remain skeptical of the testing. The discrepancy between the formal stance against drug use and the unevenness of actual testing allows drug use among bodybuilders to continue. The IBBF may require random testing, but national organizations and event sponsors are the groups expected to apply the testing guidelines, and they avoid rigorous use of the expensive tests. If drug tests eliminate the most famous bodybuilders, it would reduce the ability to attract large crowds to the events and harm the promoters who sponsor them. Even when facing thorough testing at events, most bodybuilders can—like those in other sports—adjust their drug use to avoid a positive test result.

Professional wrestlers, whose large and well-defined muscles help make for success, also appear to use performance-enhancing drugs regularly. Steroids help build muscles, and pain pills help to deal with injuries. Famous wrestlers Hulk Hogan and Rowdy Roddy Piper have admitted to using steroids, and many of the most famous stars have physiques that suggest steroid use. One other unpleasant piece of evidence points toward a drug problem: Wrestlers have a high rate of early death. According to one report, "Examination of medical documents, autopsies and police reports, along with interviews with family members and news accounts, shows that at least 65 wrestlers died in that time [since 1997], 25 from heart attacks or other coronary problems—an extraordinarily high rate for people that young, medical officials say."[77] The numbers indicate that professional wrestlers are 12 times more likely to die of heart disease at ages 25–44 than men in the general population. Although not caused directly by use of steroids and other drugs, the deaths document unexpected health problems consistent with drug use.

Professional wrestling has in the past done little to combat drug use, but this neglect may change. In part due to the negative publicity about the deaths and congressional hearings on drug use in sports, the major professional wrestling organization, World Wrestling Entertainment (formerly the World Wrestling Federation), announced in 2005 that it will begin testing its athletes.

BASEBALL

The use of steroids—and the associated negative publicity—came to baseball later than other sports. Baseball players had used amphetamines since at least the 1950s, but they felt little need for the large muscles that steroids brought to weightlifters, bodybuilders, and football players. That belief changed dramatically in the 1990s, when several well-known Major League Baseball (MLB) players apparently used steroids to improve their ability to hit home runs. Suspicions of drug use recently turned to fact when some players admitted to taking steroids. Unfortunately for baseball, the admissions created a scandal that continues to taint the sport.

Amphetamines First, Then Steroids

The use of amphetamines has a long history in MLB, but it has received only occasional attention. The current MLB commissioner, Bud Selig, said he first learned of amphetamine use by players in 1958, when he walked into the clubhouse of his hometown team, the Milwaukee Braves. In *Ball Four*, a 1970 best-selling book detailing his 1969 MLB baseball season, pitcher Jim Bouton wrote about the use by players of greenies—a slang term for amphetamine pills or speed. A 1985 federal trial involving recreational cocaine use by players on the Pittsburgh Pirates also discovered evidence of amphetamine use during games. One sports writer recently said, "Years ago—in the late 1970s and early '80s when I was in baseball clubhouses almost daily— the use of amphetamines was rampant."[78] Few fans knew of the extent of the problem, however.

Until recently, amphetamine use remained extensive—and largely hidden. By some accounts, 85 percent of players took some form of this illegal drug, leaving only a handful of players on a team who stayed clean. Players believe that the drug overcomes fatigue and improves their alertness, concentration, and quickness. The drug may in fact give a short-term psychological boost rather than actually improve physical performance, but either way players are convinced of the benefits. Indeed, they refer to going on the field without the boost of amphetamines as "playing naked," a condition viewed by some as the same as not trying to play one's best. One American League manager said that banning greenies would make it hard for players to keep going full strength during the long season.

Compared to amphetamines, the less common use of steroids would receive much more attention—perhaps because the performance benefits are so much more apparent. Yet the attention came only recently. Until the last few years, players kept their steroid use out of the public eye. One of the first to rely on the drug, Jose Canseco of the Oakland Athletics, amazed the public and other players with his speed, power hitting, and muscular physique. He brought steroids to MLB in 1985 and to some of his Oakland teammates later in the 1980s. While a player, Canseco denied steroid use but would later admit that steroids improved his performance: "If you're smart, and careful, and know what you're doing, you can use them to reach your true potential."[79]

Steroid use spread more widely in the 1990s. One team's general manager estimated in 1995 that 10 to 20 percent of players used steroids. One of the most successful users, Ken Caminiti of the San Diego Padres, admitted that steroids helped him win the Most Valuable Player Award in 1996. Taking steroids for the first time at age 33, Caminiti immediately made remarkable strides in his performance, increasing his previous home runs from 26 to 40. He remained unapologetic over his use of the drug, saying that at least half of the players used steroids at the time. After retirement, however, Caminiti faced other drug problems and died in 2004 at age 41 from a drug overdose of opiates and cocaine.

In the late 1990s, other players bettered the batting feats of Caminiti, again it appears with the aid of steroids. In 1998, Mark McGwire shattered the single-season record by hitting 70 home runs as a member of the St. Louis Cardinals, and Sammy Sosa of the Chicago Cubs followed close behind by hitting 66 home runs (the previous record of 61 by Roger Maris had been in place since 1961). McGwire's huge build, admitted use of a then legal steroid-related supplement called androstenedione, and record-setting performance raised suspicions of many that he used steroids. Jose Canseco would later claim that he introduced steroids to McGwire in 1988 and gave him steroid injections. Canseco also accused Sammy Sosa of using steroids but without firsthand evidence.

In 2001, Barry Bonds of the San Francisco Giants broke the record once more with 73 home runs, but like McGwire and Sosa did so under a cloud of suspicion. A 180-pound leadoff hitter when young, Bonds became one of the greatest home run hitters of all time after bulking up to 235 pounds during his record year. The weight and muscle change seemed consistent with steroid use, and Bonds's personal trainer, Greg F. Anderson, was indicted in 2004 (and later convicted) for illegal distribution of steroids. Anderson never said he provided steroids to Bonds, but Bonds admitted in 2003 grand jury testimony to unintentionally using steroids called "the cream" and "the clear." He said his trainer provided the substances without telling Bonds they contained steroids and denied ever taking any other performance-enhancing drugs. Even so, doubts remain about the legitimacy of his performance in the last few years.

These doubts increased with reports in March 2006 that Bonds had in fact been using high doses of steroids and performance-enhancing drugs since 1998. Mark Fainaru-Wada and Lance Williams, two reporters for the *San Francisco Chronicle*, made the accusations in an article in *Sports Illustrated* and then in a book, *Game of Shadows: Barry Bonds, BALCO, and the Steroid Scandal that Rocked Professional Sports*. Relying on sources and records from the BALCO investigation, the reporters claimed that federal agents found detailed records of Bonds's drug taking in their raid of BALCO. The drug taking involved injections as well as pills, cream, and liquid taken orally, and Bonds was using drugs in 2001 when he broke the home run record. In response, Baseball Commissioner Bud Selig appointed former Senator George Mitchell to lead an investigation into the allegations and past use of steroids by MLB players.

Given evidence of its benefits, steroid use spread well beyond a few stars during the late 1990s to the early 2000s. Pitchers found that steroids gave them extra strength needed for faster pitches and a longer career, while smaller and faster players who hit few home runs found that steroids improved their batting average. Many even started to use the more dangerous and less understood human growth hormone. Although no one knows the past prevalence of use with certainty, estimates ranged from 10 to 40 percent overall and 90 percent for power hitters.

Consistent with the estimates, statistics indicate that batting improved greatly in the 1990s and 2000s, when steroid use peaked. One sportswriter notes that, in part because of steroids, "Thirteen of the top 20 career slugging leaders have been active since 1993."[80] One writer summarizes the remarkable change: "In 1998 a 70-year-old man would have seen a major leaguer hit 60 home runs in a season only once in his lifetime. By the time the man was 74, the feat had occurred six more times, all by players accused in the court of public opinion of having used performance-enhancing drugs."[81]

Pressure for Drug Testing

Extensive drug use did not stay hidden for long, and two events helped inform the public of the behavior in baseball. The first involved the investigation of Victor Conte, the founder of a chemical supplement company named BALCO, for the illegal distribution of steroids. Federal agents started to look into the company in 2002, after it appeared Conte had provided steroids to Olympic athletes. The investigation later determined that BALCO had distributed the designer steroid THG to several athletes who used it to prepare for Olympic events. Conte had in addition many contacts with professional baseball players and, in particular, with Barry Bonds's personal trainer, Greg Anderson. Between the grand jury testimony of BALCO in fall 2003 and the guilty pleas of both Conte and Anderson in July 2005 for the illegal distribution of steroids, the case embarrassed baseball and highlighted the problem of steroids among players.

The second event, the February 2005 publication of the book *Juiced* by Jose Canseco, brought more bad publicity. Canseco did more in the book than admit to his own steroid use or discuss widespread steroid use in general—he also gave names of those he knew or believed he knew to use steroids, including Mark McGwire, Sammy Sosa, and another star player, Rafael Palmeiro. Although most of the named players denied using steroids (and some called Canseco a liar), the claims seemed plausible to fans. Canseco's often self-serving book hurt baseball's reputation but also presented an honest picture of its problems.

Concerned about the integrity of the sport, Congress held two initial sets of hearings: the Senate Committee on Commerce in March 2004 and the House of Representatives Committee on Government Reform in March 2005. In the Senate hearings, Senator John McCain (R-Arizona) told MLB Commissioner Bud Selig and executive director of the MLB Players Association (MLBPA) Donald Fehr that their sport "is about to become a fraud" and threatened legislation to enforce drug bans.[82] In the House hearings, Jose Canseco, Mark McGwire, Sammy Sosa, Rafael Palmeiro, and other stars testified before indignant representatives. In their widely reported testimony, most of the players denied using steroids themselves, said they may have unknowingly (though never intentionally) used steroids, or refused to talk about their past behavior. The press and the public greeted the denials with disbelief.

The accusations of steroid use in baseball, now given the backing of congressional hearings, made fans wonder about the honesty of the players and the legitimacy of recent records. Whether common or not, steroid use involved cheating in the view of many fans. Said one sportswriter, "Every writer and every player knows that using steroids to pump up your numbers is flat-out immoral, unethical and wrong."[83] Why then should the records of Mark McGwire and Barry Bonds, some might ask, stand above those of earlier stars such as Babe Ruth, Roger Maris, and Hank Aaron who never used drugs? Although nothing came of the proposal, newspaper articles discussed adding an asterisk next to the official listing of records reached by steroid users to indicate their drug-enhanced advantage.

MLB owners came under criticism as well. In the eyes of sportswriters and politicians, the league had failed in its duty to keep the sport clean from drugs. In 2001, MLB first required drug testing of minor league players but could not under the existing collective bargaining agreement with the MLB Players Association do the same for major league players. A new agreement with the union in 2002 allowed for preliminary, anonymous testing in the major leagues. The policy lacked penalties for offenders and off-season testing, however, which made it seem as more a public-relations ploy than a real step forward. A new agreement reached in 2005 went further: It included off-season random testing and suspension of 10 days for the first positive test, and then 30 days, 60 days, and one year for each subsequent positive test.

When the penalties went into effect in 2005, nine of the 1,400 tests turned out positive. In April 2005, Alex Sanchez of the Tampa Bay Devil Rays became the first MLB player suspended for a positive steroid test. Although he served the 10-day suspension, Sanchez denied having ever taken steroids and blamed unknown ingredients in some over-the-counter drugs he bought. Ironically, one of the players who also tested positive, Rafael Palmeiro, had denied steroid use in testimony given under oath before Congress only several months earlier. He also denied knowingly taking steroids, claiming they must have been part of a nutritional supplement given to him by a teammate. The denials led some writers to accuse players of lying as well as cheating.

Despite a few well-publicized cases, the small numbers of positive findings overall made the testing program look inadequate. Defenders of the policy viewed the low numbers as an encouraging sign of compliance with the anti-steroid policy, but Congress saw things differently. After harshly criticizing MLB owners and players, Senator John McCain and former ballplayer and current member of the Hall of Fame, Senator Jim Bunning (R-Kentucky), introduced legislation requiring strict testing for all the major professional sports—baseball, football, basketball, and hockey. The threat of federal control brought quick action from MLB. Commissioner Selig proposed a 50-game suspension, 100-game suspension, and a permanent ban after, respectively, the first, second, and third positive test. He also proposed extending the tests to include amphetamines—a gap in the current program—and to increase the number of tests administered over the year. On November 15, 2005, the players' union, which has been more reluctant to accept testing without first having probable cause of drug use, agreed to these conditions.

Did the new policy prove effective? It certainly represented a major change—baseball now has the harshest penalties for steroid use in pro sports. With strict punishments in place, tests should largely eliminate the use of amphetamines, off-season tests should reduce the use of steroids, and reliance on testing procedures recommended by the World Anti-Doping Agency should minimize use of a variety of other drugs. Of the 60 MLB players tested in the 2005–06 off-season, none came up positive. Many believe that the steroid era of baseball has ended. They look at the 2006 season as a fresh start that returned baseball to the days of honest and natural athletes, with star players now free of suspicions of steroid use. Still, as Olympic and football authorities recognize, athletes can find ways around the tests.

If use of performance-enhancing drugs declined during the 2006 season because of the new policies, investigations of past drug use continue. Responding to accusations that Barry Bonds used steroids, Commissioner Selig appointed former senator George Mitchell to investigate Bonds. Since Bonds refuses to discuss the topic any further, it remains unclear what result will come of the MLB investigation. In a separate development, federal agents raided the home of Arizona Diamondback pitcher Jason Grimsley in June 2006 following his admission of using hGH, steroids, and amphetamines. MLB suspended the pitcher for 50 days, and the Diamondbacks released him from the team. Rumors continue that Grimsely will name other players who used steroids.

OTHER PROFESSIONAL SPORTS

Besides football and baseball, several other popular professional sports have had to deal with doping.

Cycling

Among all major sports, professional cycling has had the most trouble with drug use. One expert has said, "Long-distance cycling has been the most consistently drug-soaked sport of the 20th century."[84] Cyclists used cocaine and strychnine early in the century, amphetamines in the 1960s and 1970s, steroids in the 1980s, EPO and hGH in the 1990s, and blood doping in the

2000s. The attraction to performance-enhancing drugs comes from the grueling nature of the sport. The world's most well known and prestigious race, the Tour de France, challenges even the fittest riders with three weeks to cover a course 2,000 miles long. Aiming to increase both their speed and endurance, riders have found it difficult to resist drugs.

The largely hidden drug use spilled out into the open in a 1998 scandal. Shortly before the Tour de France that year, French customs officials discovered prescription drugs, narcotics, EPO, hGH, testosterone, and amphetamines in the car of Willy Voet, an assistant for Festina, a team competing in the race. Voet, who had helped distribute drugs to the team riders and taught them how to avoid getting caught by drug tests, admitted the drugs were for use during the race. After the Festina director and medical officer also admitted to giving drugs to the riders, the Tour de France organizers expelled the team from the race. The confessions then led police to search hotel rooms of other riders, leading many to drop out of the race. Trials and testimony to come further documented the widespread reliance on drugs by racers. Affecting more than the riders disqualified from the event, the scandal, according to one source, "transformed the politics of doping by revealing that an entire athletic community—athletes, trainers, physicians, and officials—has been practicing and concealing comprehensive doping as a way of life."[85]

Part of the problem leading to the 1998 so-called Tour of Shame came from the organization in charge of the Tour de France and other racing events, the International Cycling Union (or UCI for Union Cyclist Internationale). Over the years, the UCI had done little to eradicate widespread drug use. In fact, the French police and government rather than the UCI used the arrest of Voet to start a thorough investigation of drug use on the tour. The UCI promised tougher policies, and the popularity and prestige of the race returned in the following years with the success of U.S. racer Lance Armstrong. Problems emerged again, however. In 2004, for example, members of the Cofidis team admitted using EPO and other banned drugs after police found evidence in the team offices.

Beginning in 2004, the UCI further toughened its testing procedures. Hoping to catch those using EPO and other drugs to prepare before the race, it began to take blood and urine samples from riders a month before the start. During the race, it randomly selected riders to give samples after each stage. And it used increasingly sophisticated tests to identify abnormalities in the blood due to doping or EPO. Owing either to ridding drugs from the race or the ability of riders to hide their use, the 2005 Tour de France found no positive tests. More recently, the UCI has demonstrated renewed commitment to punishing drug users and even punishing nondrug users who participate in unapproved events with banned riders.

Drugs and Sports

One more recent drug controversy in cycling goes back to the 1999 race and its winner, Lance Armstrong. The seven-time Tour de France champion had always denied using performance-enhancing drugs, but his amazing string of victories from 1999 to 2005 made his critics suspicious. In 2005, a French newspaper accused him of having used EPO to help win the 1999 race. To back up the accusation, the paper analyzed six-year-old urine samples that, through matching of numbers listed on the samples with other documents, appeared to belong to Armstrong. The urine samples had been taken before EPO tests existed, but reanalysis of the samples after discovery of new tests seemed to show the presence of the outlawed drug. Armstrong vigorously denied the accusation, claimed that the supposed positive tests had no validity, and likened the attack to a witch hunt. Recent admissions of EPO use in 1999 by two former teammates of Armstrong have kept the accusations in the news.

Drug use in the 2006 Tour de France has overshadowed news about Armstrong. Before the race started, Spanish police raided a Madrid clinic, where they seized 100 bags of frozen blood believed to be used for blood doping. The UCI then barred riders who had contact with the clinic from competing in the Tour, including the two favorites to win, German Jan Ullrich and Italian Ivan Basso. American Floyd Landis then won the race but shockingly tested positive for performance-enhancing testosterone. Landis denied using steroids, and all but one of the many samples he gave during the race came out clean. Still, he has already been fired by his cycling team. After deliberation by the U.S. Anti-Doping Agency and appropriate appeals, Landis faces more punishment, likely loss of his Tour de France title, and suspension from racing.

Basketball

Leaders of the National Basketball Association (NBA) say that use of performance-enhancing drugs, particularly steroids, is not a problem among their players. Positive tests for drug use, or even rumors of use, have been so rare that Antonio Davis, an NBA player and president of the NBA Players Association, said, "We are confident in our belief that the use of steroids and other performance enhancing drugs are virtually non-existent in the NBA."[86] Players give a simple reason for not using these drugs: They do not improve the skills needed for professional basketball players. They want to be long and lean, with agility, quickness, and a feathery touch in shooting the ball, and they believe that added bulk does little to aid these skills.

The NBA bolsters its point about low drug prevalence with statistics from its testing program. The NBA had first adopted a drug program in 1983 to counter well-publicized recreational use of cocaine and marijuana.

Introduction to Drugs and Sports

In 1999, the drug program added steroids and performance-enhancing drugs to its testing. It required random testing of rookie players once during training camp and three times during the season; it required testing of all veterans during training camp but not during the season (unless there was reasonable cause to suspect drug use). Of approximately 4,200 tests done under the policy, only three had confirmed positive results that led to a suspension. Not one of the 400 rookies tested positive.

Congressional representatives investigating steroid use in the sport viewed the statistics differently. They said that the weak testing policy made it impossible to know the true extent of steroid use. The policy tests veterans only during training camp, making it easy to stop steroid use during the short period of preseason testing, and included only a small number of substances. The few positive results may come from poor testing rather than from the lack of steroid use. Representative Henry Waxman (D-California) called the policy one of the weakest of the major sports; Representative William Lacy Clay (D-Missouri) called the policy a joke; Representative Stephen Lynch (D-Massachusetts) called the policy rather pathetic.

Stung by the criticism, the NBA implemented a stronger policy in 2005. Although believing that the policy aimed to fix something that was not broken, a new labor contract made several changes. All players must take randomly assigned tests four times during the season (from October 1 to June 30) and additional tests during the off-season if there is evidence to suspect drug use. Violators face a 10-game suspension for the first offense and a 25-game suspension, a one-year suspension, and dismissal from the NBA for each additional offense. The testing began without incident or protest. The worst problem to occur so far involved the delay of a starting player, Reggie Evans of the Seattle SuperSonics, in returning to the court after a halftime urine test; the NBA now prohibits tests during the game. Otherwise, the tests have not yet, as many players predicted, revealed incidents of drug use.

Hockey

Like the NBA, both owners and players of the National Hockey League (NHL) deny their sport has drug problems. NHL Commissioner Gary Bettman has said, "We don't think performance-enhancing drugs is much of an issue. If you look at the history of hockey players throughout the world being tested . . . you rarely ever get a positive test, and if you do, it's probably because it's been prescribed for therapeutic use. So we don't think, unlike possibly some of the other sports, that this is an issue."[87] Although the NHL lacked its own testing program until just recently, it could point to other programs to support its claims. Over the years, around 1,000 NHL players have undergone tests when playing in international competitions. Only three had positive results, and none for steroids.

With some qualifications, players interviewed agree on the rarity of steroid use. Comments include, "I've played for eight years and I haven't seen anything around our team"; "I'm only on one team and I don't see it"; and "We don't have troubles here [on my team]."[88] Players and owners say that the muscles brought on by steroids do little to help in the fast-paced game of hockey. They qualify that claim by noting that enforcers—players who intimidate the other team with fighting and physical play—can benefit from steroids. One enforcer, Dave (Moose) Morrissette, admitted using steroids to help him compete with others enforcers who, he believed, also used the drug. Still, the problem does not seem pervasive among the sport's best players.

Not everyone agrees. Dick Pound, the president of the World Anti-Doping Agency, located in Montreal, believes that about a third of NHL players use performance-enhancing drugs. When he made this allegation public, it brought a swift rebuttal. Ted Saskin, the executive director of the NHL Players Association, called Pound's comments "incredibly irresponsible and have no basis in fact."[89] Players also responded angrily, saying that Pound unfairly labeled them as cheaters. Furthering such controversy, newspapers reported that up to 20 percent of hockey players take the nonprescription cold medication Sudafed for the stimulant pseudoephedrine it contains.[90] The NHL denies such use, however.

Whatever the prevalence of drugs in hockey, the NHL has agreed to a new testing policy. Even if steroids remain absent from hockey, the league wants a testing program to assure the public of that fact. On July 15, 2005, NHL owners and the union reached a collective bargaining agreement that included drug testing. Players would undergo at least two unannounced, random drug tests during the season and face successively harsher punishments for positive tests: a 20-game suspension for the first offense, a 60-game suspension for a repeat offense, and a permanent ban for a third offense. The testing program began on January 15, 2006, but during the first season found no positive test results.

Boxing

Steroids and other drugs can do much to help boxers, but the structure of the sport makes it hard to know the extent of drug use. Professional boxers, who rely in good part on strength along with quickness and endurance, can gain more power in their punches from steroids. Perhaps more important, steroids during prefight training allow for harder work and quicker recovery. Boxers using steroids can enter the fight having prepared better than those not using steroids. Other drugs may also help: Diuretics promote water loss so that boxers stay within weight limits, and amphetamines may give boxers extra energy during the fights.

Although the benefits of steroids would suggest wide usage, no one knows for certain. Marc Ratner, chairman of the Nevada State Athletic Commission, says, "I don't think it's a widespread problem but we have to be vigilant. Of the hundreds of tests we've administered, we've only had a couple of positives."[91] Larry Hazzard, commissioner of the New Jersey Athletic Control Board, says much the same: "With all the years that this has been a problem in other sports, and it has been much more of a problem in other sports, we haven't seen a lot of it. We've had a few positive tests, but it's been a very small percentage."[92] A few isolated incidents make it clear that some use the drug. In April 2005, heavyweight James Toney tested positive for steroids after defeating his opponent, John Ruiz, in a championship match. Toney, who blamed the positive test on medication for an injured shoulder, lost his championship title, was banned for two years from competing for the title, and faced a suit from Ruiz for cheating. A few other famous boxers such as Roy Jones, Jr., and Fernando Vargas have tested positive for steroids, and Shane Mosley testified about use of THG in the BALCO investigation. Beyond these examples, however, statistics are lacking.

The limited information on use of steroids and drugs stems from the nature of professional boxing. The three competing organizations that run the sport—the World Boxing Association, the World Boxing Council, and the International Boxing Federation—have their own titles, fights, and champions. Rather than coming from a single national organization, responsibility for testing falls to state boxing or athletic commissions. Not all state commissions take testing seriously. Nevada, the most common location for boxing matches, conducts random drug tests of fighters. Other states such as California and New York do not go that far but require tests after title bouts. A recent bill in Congress to establish national control of boxing might have brought consistent policies to the sport, but it failed to pass. In the meantime, testing remains inconsistent and suspicions of steroid use remain.

YOUTH

Performance-enhancing drugs attract more than famous athletes in professional sports—they also reach down to affect high school youth. Teens imitate the look and behavior of sports stars, including those known or suspected to use steroids to better performance. They may naively hope that steroids or other drugs can help them become high school stars and perhaps even get scholarships to college and become professional athletes. High school coaches sometimes unintentionally fuel the desire by encouraging players to get bigger and stronger. Rarely do coaches suggest steroids, but teens using weight training to build muscle may, given the models of professional athletes, take the drug to speed their development. Those wanting to get bigger and faster will have little trouble getting hold of steroids.

Extensive use of steroids by high school youth began as early as the 1980s. A *Wall Street Journal* article in 1988 quoted a physical trainer who worked with athletes: "People think the cocaine issue is big. It's not as big as anabolic steroids. Among kids, it's epidemic."[93] One national survey of 3,400 male high school seniors in 1987 found that 6.6 percent had at one time taken steroids, a percentage that translates into hundreds of thousands of users. Another survey of high school football players in Oregon found that 38 percent said they knew how to get steroids.

Surveys since the 1980s indicate that the problem has worsened. According to figures from a national survey of high school drug use called Monitoring the Future, the percentage of 12th-grade students who said they have used steroids rose from 2.1 percent in 1991 to 4.0 percent in 2000. It fell to 3.4 percent in 2004 but stayed well above 1991 levels.[94] Another study of youth in grades 9 through 10, the Youth Risk Behavior Survey, found that use of steroids had risen from 2.7 percent in 1991 to 6.1 percent in 2003. Exact figures differ across surveys because of varied wording of the questions, but the upward trend worries school officials and health authorities.

The popularity of steroids may stem in part from the desire of teen boys to look "buffed." The highest use of steroids likely occurs among boys on football, wrestling, and track teams. However, about one-third of steroid users in the 1987 survey said they did not intend to participate in high school sports. Those devoted to bodybuilding and physical appearance, even without joining team sports, may still use steroids to imitate the build of muscular athletes and actors.

Usage figures remain much higher among boys than girls, but the gap has declined. The Monitoring the Future surveys find use of steroids by senior girls to have risen from 0.9 in 1989 to 1.7 in 2004. Based on these figures, Professor Charles Yesalis said there could be "as many as 300,000 to 400,000 high school aged girls in this country who have cycled on anabolic steroids!"[95] Growing prevalence of steroid use by high school girls involves more than sports. Since steroids help reduce weight by suppressing appetite and burning fat, girls may use the drug to look thin. Their desire to live up to glamorously thin models—rather than muscular athletes—contributes to the problem of steroid use.

Parents lay partial blame on professional athletes for use of steroids and drugs by teens. If famous sports stars, many of whom serve as models for youth, find it acceptable to cheat, purchase illegal drugs, and risk their health, then teens will do the same. Don Hooton of Plano, Texas, whose son Taylor committed suicide after secretly using steroids, says that athletes should take responsibility for the influence they have on teens. School authorities and public health officials have tried to educate high school students about the risks of steroids but with little success. Although one program managed to cut steroid use by half, most efforts do little to counter the influence of steroid use that occurs outside of schools.

Some coaches have tackled the problem more directly. Football coach Bobby Barnes of Buckeye High School in Arizona suspended 10 players from the team when he discovered their steroid use. Despite the attraction of high school athletes to steroids, no other such suspensions had occurred in the state. The loss of many of its best players hurt the team, which lost all of its initial games, and angered some of the community fans. Barnes argues, however, that severe punishments are needed to counter the problem.

One program, Athletes Training and Learning to Avoid Steroids (ATLAS), has received praise for its success in reducing steroid use among teen athletes. Indeed, the program has gained awards from the Center for Substance Abuse Prevention, Safe and Drug Free Schools, and *Sports Illustrated* (which came with $1 million in funds and publicity from the magazine). The program uses peer discussions to educate teen athletes about the risks of steroids. A related program called Athletes Targeting Health Exercise and Nutrition Alternatives (ATHENA) does much the same for recreational drugs and alcohol. Evaluations of the programs have found that they reduce use of steroids and other illegal substances.

THE EFFECTS AND SIDE EFFECTS OF DRUGS FOR SPORT

The long list of drugs banned from use in Olympic competition and other sports makes it hard to summarize the effects and side effects of them all. For the less commonly used drugs, studies are rare. For the more popular drugs—steroids, growth hormone, stimulants, and forms of blood doping—studies are common but often flawed. Users can describe the changes they observe but often have biased and selective insight. Studies of animals can demonstrate physical and behavioral effects of the drugs but may not apply to humans. Studies of humans are limited by ethical concerns that prevent giving high doses to healthy subjects for many months and by the tendency of most users to keep their illegal activities secret. And even the best studies can give conflicting results because of the variety of subjects and tests that can be used. These limitations leave room for disagreement in interpretation of the evidence, but most scientists and experts agree on some basic conclusions.

Drugs and Sports

PERFORMANCE EFFECTS

Steroids

At one time, the medical community denied that steroids delivered performance benefits. Athletes who tried the drug said that it had real effects, but scientific studies had trouble confirming these claims. In the 1970s, Dr. Allan J. Ryan, former president of the American College of Sports Medicine, called anabolic steroids "fool's gold" and labeled the belief that they enhanced performance a myth. He and others disputed the testimonials of athletes about the benefits of steroids, asserting that muscle gains came from working harder and feeling more confident while on steroids rather than from the drug itself. The American College of Sports Medicine reached much the same conclusion. According to the official position taken by the organization in 1977, "There is no conclusive scientific evidence that extremely large doses of ana-bolic-androgenic steroids either aid or hinder athletic performance."[96]

In fact, the early studies had flaws that new research would soon identify. For example, some early studies used untrained subjects who started learning to weight train at the same time they began using steroids. Because inexperienced athletes lack knowledge of how to train most effectively, these studies offered mostly negative results. Later studies based on subjects with experience in weight training showed clear gains from steroids. Not until the 1980s did the evidence convince the medical community of the performance changes brought on by steroids. Today, Charles E. Yesalis, a Penn State University professor, and Virginia S. Cowart summarize the consensus: "The truth is that anabolic steroids work. That is to say that anabolic steroids, especially when used in conjunction with intense strength training, increase muscle mass and strength well beyond what can be achieved with training alone."[97]

Used properly, steroids can help add 6.6 to 11 pounds of mostly muscle after several weeks of use.[98] The weight and muscle gains come ultimately from chemical processes at the level of the cell. Steroids increase the amount of testosterone that gets to muscle and other cells in the body. This extra testosterone in the blood travels to cell receptors, is transferred into the cell, and stimulates the production of enzymes for protein synthesis. The protein synthesis then contributes to the growth and repair of muscle cells. Both a good diet and intense exercise amplify the effects of steroids: Nutritious food provides the materials needed for muscle growth, and weight training stimulates the body to build muscles.

Along with building muscle, steroids have other physical effects that improve the performance of athletes in a wide variety of sports:

- They increase the blood volume and the amount of oxygen carried to the cells, a change that helps runners as well as those in strength sports.

- They increase the density and strength of bones and decrease body fat, again aiding performance.
- They speed the healing of muscle injuries, making it possible for athletes to train harder and longer and to require less time for recovery between workouts.
- They improve stamina and help players perform at top levels during a long season.

None of these effects can make up for lack of talent, hard work, and skill development. Steroids can give elite athletes an edge over competitors, however.

Steroids have associated psychological effects that can also improve performance. Users report feeling more aggressive, a trait they believe contributes to better training, greater motivation to win, higher pain tolerance, better mental focus, and improved sports performance. The psychological benefits may result from changes in the chemistry of the brain brought about by steroids. Alternatively, they may come from a newfound confidence of athletes who see their strength grow and speed improve with steroids. Either way, psychological changes accompany physical changes.[99]

Athletes who admit to taking steroids agree with the scientific evidence of physical and psychological improvement. Kelli White, a U.S. sprinter caught using steroids and now regretful about her actions, tells of the changes brought by the designer steroid THG: "In a relatively short period, I had gone from being a very competitive sprinter to being the fastest woman in the world!"[100] NFL star Lyle Alzado, who died of cancer at age 43, said that under steroids, "I was like a maniac. I outran, outhit, outanythinged everybody. . . . All along I was taking steroids, and I saw that they made me play better and better. I kept on because I knew I had to keep getting more size. I became very violent on the field."[101]

Other observations also point to the benefits of steroids. The amazing baseball records of those suspected of taking steroids, the poor showings of Ben Johnson in races after he stopped using steroids, the performance gains of East German and Chinese women swimmers after starting steroids, and the huge muscles of male and female bodybuilders who have relied on steroids—all lend credibility to the results of scientific experiments.

Steroid Use in Practice

Although steroids improve performance, the benefits occur only under certain conditions. Effective steroid use depends on proper products, doses, timing, and training methods, and even then, some users will benefit more than others. The choices available to athletes are many.

Steroids come in several types: oral, injectable oil-based, injectable water-based, and patches or gels. Oral forms have a chemical structure to prevent them from breaking down in the stomach or liver before they can get to muscle cells. They have a short half-life of only several hours and need to be taken often (half-life refers to the time it takes for a drug to fall to one-half of its peak concentration in the blood). Injectable oil-based steroids go into muscles of the buttocks or shoulders rather than veins to allow for slow release into the blood stream; they have a long half-life of several days and traces can remain in the body for weeks or even months. Injectable water-based steroids, less commonly used than the other forms, resemble oral steroids in terms of half-life but do not have to pass through the stomach and intestines. Patches continuously deliver steroids, while gels rubbed on the skin can be applied daily to slowly release the steroid into the blood.

Most steroids go by two names. The brand name comes from the company that manufactures a particular product, while the generic name refers to the chemical nature of the steroid and may overlap with several brand names. Common oral steroids include (listed by the generic name first and some selected brand names in parentheses):

- Methandrostenolone (Dianabol): once the most popular steroid but no longer manufactured in the United States. Still available from foreign countries, it has a short half-life and many side effects.

- Stanozolol (Winstrol, Stromba): also comes in an injectable form and is one of the most popular products used by athletes (Ben Johnson's positive drug test at the 1988 Olympics revealed use of stanozolol). Because it washes out of the system quickly, it needs to be taken regularly.

- Oxandrolone (Anavar): absorbed and concentrated in the blood quickly. It is known for increasing strength but not size and is often used in combination with other steroids. Its limited androgenic effects make it popular with women.

- Oxymetholone (Anadrol): considered the strongest oral steroid available, resulting in both anabolic and androgenic effects that many find hard to tolerate. Web sites suggest that it is best used in combination with other steroids.

Common injectable steroids include:

- Boldenone undecylenate (Equipoise): an oil-based steroid first developed for use in animals but later adopted by bodybuilders. It is thought to have fewer androgenic side effects than many other steroids and to produce rapid growth of muscle mass.

- Nandrolone decanoate (Deca-Durabolin): perhaps the most commonly used injectable steroid. It can be detected in the body for weeks or months, making it hard to mask before tests, but it has benefits for bulking up that attract users.

- Testosterone cypionate (Depo-Testosterone, Testacyp): a long-acting oil-based steroid that has strong androgenic effects but is known to produce dramatic gains in size and strength (testosterone enanthate is a similar steroid that tends to cause water retention).

Although less commonly used, patch and gel products have advantages over the oral and injectable steroids in releasing the chemicals more evenly and avoiding fluctuations in testosterone blood levels.

Users often cycle, pyramid, and stack steroids to maximize effects. Cycling refers to using steroids for specific time intervals. Taking a steroid for six to 12 weeks, then stopping for the same time span, and repeating the process allows the body and its hormone system to recover from the high amounts of testosterone. Pyramiding refers to beginning with low doses during the steroid interval, slowly building to a peak, and then slowly reducing steroids to zero before the off period. The slow buildup allows the body to adjust to the higher testosterone levels, and the builddown allows the body to adjust to the decline. Stacking refers to taking multiple steroids at the same time in the hope that the combination will build muscle better than one steroid alone.

Cycling, pyramiding, and stacking aim to overcome a problem called plateauing. The term refers to the point where users develop a tolerance such that steroids no longer seem to contribute to muscle development. The body may become so saturated with a chemical that receptors no longer transfer the testosterone into the cells. Going on and off the steroid, changing the doses, and stacking different forms of steroids may help avoid plateauing. Some guidebooks suggest that certain steroids work particularly well in combination: If one steroid no longer brings benefits, perhaps the other will; or if one helps to bulk up, perhaps the other will help to define muscle. Little scientific evidence backs up claims about cycling, pyramiding, and stacking, but the strategies have gained popularity among users.

Although each product has recommended doses for therapeutic purposes, users often exceed these amounts. Thinking that if recommended amounts help build strength, then excess amounts will do even more, some athletes abuse the products. More careful users limit the amounts they take and adjust the amounts depending on their sport and goals. Endurance runners, who do not need strength but want to help repair muscles after long workouts, generally take doses equal to the amount of testosterone typically produced by the body. Sprinters wanting more in the way of explosive speed take 1.5 to two times the replacement level, and lifters and strength sports that require muscle bulk take 10 to 100 times the replacement amount. Women can take lower doses because they benefit from smaller amounts of testosterone.

All users have to take care to ensure that they obtain only genuine steroids. The manufacturing of steroids in the United States is limited, and the sale of steroids without a prescription is illegal. Users often must rely on products manufactured elsewhere, smuggled into the country, and sold on the black market. Those with experience can spot crude fakes, but many products that look real may not contain the listed amount of steroids. One German study of products bought on the black market found that 37.5 percent contained no steroids or the wrong kind of steroid.[102] Worried that the product contains less than the amount listed on the label, users may take more than the recommended amount.

Less Effective Anabolic Drugs

Several anabolic products related to steroids have less clearly demonstrated advantages. Products known as steroid precursors or testosterone precursors such as androstenedione (or andro for short) and dehydroepiandrosterone (DHEA) have become a popular alternative to steroids. Andro gained publicity in 1998 when a reporter noticed a bottle in the locker of Mark McGwire, the baseball player on the way to breaking the home run record. McGwire admitted to using the product, which was legal at the time. Once considered a legal and safe alternative (or perhaps supplement) to anabolic steroids, andro became popular before its benefits could be evaluated.

Andro and DHEA occur naturally in the body and aid in the production of testosterone but differ from steroids. They are called precursors because the body uses them in creating natural testosterone and in this way may bring about the same benefits of steroids. Even if not testosterone, andro and DHEA should, critics argue, be classified as steroids because they have no purpose other than to enhance performance by artificially increasing testosterone. The IOC, NFL, and NCAA have banned the product, and the Anabolic Steroid Control Act of 2004 made the sale or possession of steroid precursors without a prescription illegal.

Although illegal, steroid precursors have not been demonstrated as effective by scientific studies. One review of the studies concluded that, "the effect of ingestion of oral androstenedione on muscle growth and strength levels has been inconsistent, and no direct evidence suggests that it is an effective anabolic agent."[103] By this and other accounts, the use of andro-stenedione for performance enhancement remains questionable.

Other nonsteroid products used for muscle growth also lack convincing evidence of effectiveness. Clenbuterol belongs to a group of beta-2 agonists used for the treatment of breathing problems and asthma (agonist refers to a drug that stimulates natural processes in the body, and beta-2 refers to a cell receptors). When given to livestock—its original purpose—clenbuteral increased muscle mass and decreased body fat. Working differently than steroids, it limited the breakdown of existing muscle rather than creating new muscle. Athletes, particularly those wanting to keep within weight limits, came to value the product as an aid to losing weight while maintaining bulk. Bodybuilders also found the product helped reduce fat before events and maintain muscles after steroid use. Despite the findings of animal research, however, human studies have shown less consistent effects. According to one scientific review, "Most recent evidence suggests that clenbuterol does reduce body fat and increase muscle mass, though whether this leads to a consistent increase in strength does not seem to have been demonstrated yet."[104]

Like clenbuterol, human growth hormone (hGH) has become popular among athletes with little scientific support for its advantages. Stories from users and a few studies suggest that it may help athletic performance by increasing nonfat body weight. Others note that under normal conditions, exercise releases small amounts of hGH to help build muscle; adding hGH to the body should logically intensify this process. Not all experts are convinced of these benefits, however. Since most hGH users take it in combination with steroids and other drugs, they can confuse the effects of hGH with the well-demonstrated effects of steroids. One scientific review concludes that even when combined with weight training, hGH "does not appear to augment muscle strength."[105] Some underground advocates of steroids also question the benefits of hGH.

Blood Doping and EPO

Blood doping and EPO offer ways to increase blood cells that transport oxygen throughout the body and help particularly in endurance sports. Studies of time trials in running and cycling demonstrate the benefits of blood doping, and studies of subjects participating in lab exercises demonstrate the benefits of EPO for the oxygen-carrying capacity of the body.

Stimulants

Stimulants have a long history of use in a variety of sports but may not help performance as much as athletes believe. Amphetamines increase the breathing rate, heart rate, blood pressure, and metabolism, all of which can improve performance. Yet, elite athletes already reach maximum levels of these physiological processes, making it hard for amphetamines to do much more. Similarly, amphetamines may merely mask fatigue rather than eliminate its effect on performance. Perhaps the real effects come from the feeling of euphoria brought on by amphetamines—even without improving performance, they make athletes feel better.

One other common stimulant, ephedrine, affects the central nervous system to reduce fatigue, increase alertness, dilate the bronchia, and speed the heart rate. It promotes weight loss by burning more calories and suppressing appetite. A variant form called pseudoephedrine is found in over-the-counter cold medicines. The IOC bans both products, as do the NFL and NCAA. Some athletes testing positive for ephedrine or pseudoephedrine claim it came from cold products, nutritional supplements, or asthma medication rather than the intent to cheat. In any case, an expert review says, "There are no documented ergogenic effects of ephedrine or pseudoephedrine when ingested alone."[106] To the contrary, they may hurt performance by causing anxiety and headaches. Like other stimulants, their attraction may come more from the pleasant feelings they create than the improvements in physical skills.

HEALTH EFFECTS

Nearly all drugs have unintended and undesired side effects. A drug will have a primary target or goal but also affect other parts of the body in unwanted ways. For medically approved drugs used in proper doses, beneficial effects greatly outweigh harmful side effects, while for unapproved drugs and those used in excess, the opposite may occur. Unlike legitimate medicines, performance-enhancing drugs used in sports have few medical uses to outweigh the many side effects. These side effects range from rare but life-threatening illnesses to more common but minor conditions. Although individuals respond differently to the same drug, taking high doses heightens the risk of serious side effects.

Physical Problems

The most dangerous threats to health come from the effects of drugs on the heart and blood flow. Sometimes the threats come suddenly, as in a heart attack, blood clot, stroke, or internal abdominal bleeding. Although rare, sudden deaths due to steroids can occur. Amphetamines taken in large doses can also harm the heart, as shown by the deaths of cyclists who combined these drugs with extreme exertion and dehydration. Most often, steroids and other drugs slowly and steadily contribute to heart and blood flow problems in the longer term by increasing fatty substances in the blood, promoting clotting in the blood, and straining the heart muscle. It is possible, thought not certain, that steroids also cause thickening of the heart muscle and ultimately weaken the pumping ability of the heart. By acting on internal organs as well as muscles, hGH can likewise enlarge the heart and thicken its muscle in ways that cause in heart failure.

Also in the long term, steroids can cause liver and kidney problems. The liver processes steroids, particularly those taken orally, to make them usable by the body, and the kidneys filter waste from the blood, including excess testosterone and its metabolites. One result is the formation of tumors in the liver and kidneys. Another is the development of several types of liver disease. Still further, steroids may enlarge the risk of prostate cancer among men and increase the risk of breast cancer among women. Although rare, these outcomes add to the risks faced by steroid users.

Several less dangerous but more common side effects relate to sexuality. Among men, excess steroid use shrinks the testes, reduces sperm production, and sometimes causes infertility. The hormone increases the sex drive (though not the ability to perform sexually) and, surprisingly, can lead to gynecomastia or the development of small breasts. Among women, excess steroid use can cause an irregular menstrual cycle and reduce breast size.

Steroids produce awkward, though not dangerous, changes in appearance. They lead to acne, oily skin, and balding among both men and women (which often persist after stopping steroid use) and a deepening of the voice and growth of excess body hair among women. Those who use steroids at a young age face the risk of stunted growth and shortness as an adult. Taking hGH can cause a thickening and coarsening of the skin, sometimes called elephant epidermis, and the unattractive enlargement of the fingers, toes, and jaw.

Steroids and related drugs are linked to a variety of other health problems. Anabolic substances can build muscles to such a size that tendons and cartilage cannot support them. Ruptured tendons and joint problems result, and athletes on steroids have a reputation in football and baseball as prone to injury. Amphetamines may cause damage among athletes by masking fatigue. The drug redistributes blood away from the skin and prevents cooling during intense exercise in hot temperatures, and amphetamine users who ignore or miss the symptoms of heat stroke during athletic events risk death. Sometimes the delivery of drugs rather than the drugs themselves causes sickness. For example, injection of steroids, hGH, or EPO with contaminated needles can spread dangerous infections such as HIV and hepatitis B and C.

Psychological Problems

The most widely reported psychological changes from drug use in sports relate to steroids. The drug increases aggressiveness, which can show up as an explosive temper (sometimes called "roid rage"), mood swings, and general hostility. These negative feelings may not begin right away. To the contrary, steroids at first may create positive feelings of self-esteem, well-being, competitiveness, and sexual desire. As users advance to larger doses, however, the psychological changes become more negative, exaggerating feelings of anger, irritability, hyperactivity, sadness, self-importance, and physical inadequacy. In most cases, these negative effects are not serious. However, with extremely high doses of steroids, more severe (and rare) psychological disturbance can produce violence, addiction, and personality disorders.

First, steroid use may occasionally spur criminal violence. A 1998 article in *Sports Illustrated* entitled "The Muscle Murders" reported on several bodybuilders who committed murder after using steroids to increase their testosterone levels to 500 times the norm.[107] The cases usually involved men killing their female partners, but one woman bodybuilder on steroids shot her husband after a quarrel. Incidents of domestic violence and assault among bodybuilders occur more frequently than murder and can come from steroid use. A former bodybuilder says, "When I was using 1,000 milligrams [of Anadrol], I dragged a guy out of his car for cutting me off in traffic, and I'm usually a calm man."[108]

Second, the use of drugs for sports performance can become addictive. Stimulants and narcotics have well-known addictive properties: After initial use, larger amounts of the drugs must be taken to get the same effect, which then makes it hard to stop without suffering from withdrawal symptoms. Similar, though less severe, addiction can occur with steroids. The drug may affect brain chemistry in a way that makes users depend on the continued delivery of the high levels of testosterone to feel well. The addiction to steroids takes a different form from addiction to stimulants and narcotics but nonetheless makes it hard to stop using the drug.

Third, steroid use can sometimes lead to personality disorders such as depression, delusions, and suicidal thoughts. One study found that 23 percent of 88 steroid users had major mood disorders, including serious depression. Another study found that 3.9 percent of 77 steroid users attempted suicide. Still another study found that of 34 deaths of steroid users, nine were victims of homicide. Steroids taken during adolescence, a period already prone to impulsive and risky behavior, worsen other troubles. Accidents (including motor vehicle accidents), homicide, and suicide are the three leading causes of death at ages 15–24, and use of steroids can add to the early deaths from these causes.

The tendency of steroid users to take other drugs can magnify the psychological harm. Performance-enhancing drugs such as hGH, amphetamines, and narcotic painkillers are sometimes added to stimulate muscle growth or counter the side effects of steroids. Sometimes steroid use occurs with binge drinking and use of recreational drugs such as cocaine, marijuana, hallucinogens, opiates, and ecstasy. Multiple drug use heightens the risk of crime, dependence, and psychological distress.

ETHICS

The consequences of drug use in sports go beyond the performance and health of athletes. They also relate to ethical and moral considerations. By giving some athletes an unfair and illegal advantage, drug use as a performance aid goes against essential values of sport. Goals of playing fairly, building character, enhancing self-discipline, learning from defeat, and fostering a spirit of even-handed competition get lost with the reliance on drugs. The decisions of individual athletes to use or not use drugs thus shape the ethical and moral foundation of sports. In the view of some, drug use has created an ethic of cheating and a moral crisis in sports.

Drug use may also magnify social pressures to win at all costs. Some believe that sports place too much value on commercialism and winning and too little value on doing one's best and maintaining personal integrity. Winning brings fame, money, and national, even worldwide celebrity, and drug use—regardless of the ethics involved—can improve the odds of winning. As a result, eliminating drug use in sports requires more than a technical fix such as better testing. It requires a change in the moral values of fans, coaches, owners, athletes, and national leaders that downplay the single-minded focus on winning.

MINORITY VIEWS IN FAVOR OF STEROID USE

Some question the widely accepted views about the health and ethical harm of steroids. Based on their own experiences, a few users accuse sports officials, politicians, physicians, and scientists of distorting and even lying about the risks. Users reason that if steroids have not harmed them, and, to the contrary, made them feel healthier and look younger, then opponents of steroids must be overstating their case and using scare tactics to end the use of the drug for sports. Although not large in number, those advocating steroids hold strong views.

Jose Canseco, now retired from baseball, has become a public advocate of steroid use. He started taking them more than 20 years ago and expresses no regret over his decision. In his view, the proper and intelligent use of steroids brings many benefits. They made him a better athlete and ballplayer, improved his health and confidence, and gave him a younger body and attractive appearance. They also made baseball a more exciting game for fans who enjoyed the home runs, new records, and star players. Canseco expresses contempt for owners who publicly criticized steroid use while at the same time taking the profits brought by the feats of players on steroids. A more honest approach would promote rather than ban steroids by athletes. He predicts that steroids will become an accepted part of sports in the future.

Many bodybuilders take much the same view as Canseco. They believe that proper use of steroids presents little risk for adults. Although dangerous side effects come from misuse and excessive doses, sophisticated users who take the time to learn about steroids know how to avoid adverse effects. Bodybuilders say that steroids help them feel better, remain physically fit, and live longer. They point to millions of users who have not experienced any health problems. After all, testosterone is a naturally produced hormone that has little in common with dangerous and addictive drugs like cocaine, heroin, and amphetamines.

Do steroids cause roid rage? Despite acts of temper and violence by steroid users, advocates answer no. Even without steroids, large and strong athletes tend to be competitive and aggressive. These traits get wrongly blamed on drug use. As Professor Charles Yesalis notes, "There's a certain degree of aggression that's not only acceptable but necessary in competitive sports. What's perhaps just the intensity that's common to many athletes gets perceived as steroid-linked outbursts."[109] Those already prone to violence and crime might see steroids as an excuse for their actions, but the vast majority of steroid users do not become violent or criminal. Do steroids lead to addiction? Only rarely, according to advocates. Like Arnold Schwarzenegger, most steroid users stop the drug when they finish competing. Athletes treat steroids as a tool to help them in sports rather than as a source of psychological dependence.

Those favoring steroid use recognize that the drug has some risks, but then so do most things in life. Rick Collins, a lawyer in favor of legalizing steroids says, "'What's 'safe?' Nothing is free of risk. Not swimming, not driving, not skiing. Certainly not scuba diving or hang gliding or thrill sports. Aspirin or Tylenol can be quite 'unsafe'—in fact, they can kill. Alcohol and tobacco can be, and all too frequently are, deadly."[110] Steroids fall within the range of legitimate risk and, in Collins's view, do not justify the hysteria created about the drug. Given the value of strong muscles and the enjoyment of bodybuilding, many willingly take the small risks.

In some ways, steroid use differs little from other medical procedures and medicines commonly accepted in sports. Writing in *Slate* magazine, William Saletan argues that laser eye surgery improved Tiger Woods's vision in a way that aided his golf score and contact lenses helped Mark McGwire see better than normal.[111] Since surgery and magnification lenses improve performance, Saletan asks why do people consider these aids acceptable but not steroids? Steroid users likewise see little difference. Adding testosterone to the body is no more unnatural than shaping the eye with a laser or placing objects on the eyes to improve vision.

Steroid users object most vigorously to criminalizing the drug. Making possession of steroids for nonmedical purposes a criminal act does not fit the seriousness of the offense. Steroids differ from cocaine, heroin, or LSD—they do not make users high or destroy their ability to hold jobs, raise families, and remain part of the community. Use of steroids by adults should remain an individual decision made with the advice of a physician. Criminalization instead keeps individuals from making informed choices about their athletic training and physicians from supervising use of the drug in a responsible way. By forcing those wanting to use the drug to go to illicit markets for more dangerous and unsupervised products, criminalizing steroids actually encourages misuse of the drug and results in more rather than fewer health problems. It also creates a social problem. Otherwise law-abiding citizens who merely want to improve their muscular appearance can face jail, fines, and an arrest record.

Advocates agree that steroids should not be used by teens who have yet to reach full development or without proper medical supervision. Sporting leagues and associations should also have the right to ban steroid use from the games or events they sponsor. For good or bad, athletes need to follow the rules laid down for sports competition. Otherwise, however, advocates want steroids and some other performance-enhancing drugs made legal. Rick Collins summarizes the case for legalization:

> *Hundreds of congressional transcript pages were devoted to promoting fair play at the elite and collegiate levels. Nobody ever mentioned the idea that the 35-year-old guy who's paving the road by day, feeding his family, and using a moderate amount of juice to enhance the effects of his training, would be arrested and prosecuted. No teens are looking up to him. He is cheating no other athletes. He's not bothering anybody.*[112]

THE FUTURE OF DRUGS AND SPORTS

As in past decades, future decades will likely see both better drugs to aid sports performance and better tests to stop use of those drugs. Although some hope that education of youth and adult athletes will lessen the desire to use drugs in sports, the effects of education so far appear meager. Change requires something besides knowing about the health risks of performance-enhancing drugs and the unfairness of using banned substances. Without a change in the ideals of the athletes, testing and punishment remain the main, though not an ideal deterrent.

In the area of testing, there have been several advances over the last five years. Most sports now require some form of out-of-competition testing, enforcement of real punishments on proven users, and employment of new tests for drugs such as EPO, hGH, and THG. Other improvements will certainly follow. For example, better technology can make testing faster, cheaper, and more reliable. Right now, the large number of banned substances and expensive equipment needed for testing place a strain on the time and finances of sports organizations. Better instruments for chemical analysis and new techniques to identify previously undetectable drugs can help overcome these obstacles.

Improvements in testing may also come from analyzing substances other than urine. Blood tests now done on Olympic athletes can find evidence of blood doping that does not appear in urine. Tests that analyze easily obtained hair samples also have a special feature. Although traces of a drug may wash out of the urine in a few days, they remain in the hair for longer periods and make testing for long-term drug use easier. Problems remain with the hair-testing method, as coloring, bleaching, and shampooing can affect the results. Still, this direction in testing seems promising.

For each advance in testing, however, a counter response in drug use will likely follow. If procedures allow for faster, cheaper, and more reliable tests of existing drugs, then taking drugs that are more complex may require slower, more expensive, and less reliable tests. If scientists discover new ways to test for existing drugs, then the adoption by athletes of new drugs will escape detection. If testers examine blood and hair along with urine, then users will learn tricks to hide the effects of drugs from new techniques. Innovations in drugs occur so quickly and unpredictably that experts cannot foresee what new tests they will need.

One source of likely innovation in performance-enhancing drugs is genetic technology. Based on discoveries about the makeup of human genes, scientists have started to learn how to transfer partial or whole genes from one cell into another. This kind of gene transfer has the potential to heal injured body parts, regenerate damaged heart tissue, produce insulin among diabetics, and increase resistance to HIV. Although focused on medical therapy, the new knowledge and technology may apply to sports performance. Consider two possible innovations that may become practical in the next decades—pharmacogenomics and gene therapy.[113]

Pharmacogenomics aims to tailor a drug to an individual's genes. Knowing how genetic makeup affects the response to a particular drug can help in the design of more effective drugs with fewer side effects. With such designs, persons can have their own customized or personalized medicines. In the area of sports, pharmacogenomics can help create a special form of a steroid that, for persons with particular genetic traits, maximizes muscle growth and minimizes androgenic side effects. If experts design drugs more precisely to fit the genetic needs of users, then athletes could choose from hundreds of modified forms of a drug to gain the most benefit for performance. All the possible variants of the drug will make comprehensive testing even more difficult.

Gene therapy works differently but has similarly original goals. It introduces new genes into the body as a way to fix genes that do not work properly or add new, beneficial genes. Inserting genes into body cells relies on delivery from a virus—a task that right now remains prone to error. Correctly done, however, the process promises to fix genetic diseases or repair worn-out organs. In the area of sports, genes introduced into specific parts of the body could promote growth of muscles or red blood cells. Elite athletes already have genetic makeup well suited to their sport, but gene therapy could remedy a specific weakness or make existing talent even better. Once able to help athletes, gene therapy would present new difficulties in detection and require new technologies for testing.

Some hope that changes in social values will make the battle between testers and users unnecessary in the future. If the "win at any cost" attitude would change, so might the desire to use drugs to better one's performance. If fans stop following sports prone to drug use and cheering athletes known to use drugs, it would diminish the attraction to drugs. However, the deeply entrenched value placed on winning and the money given to successful athletes makes such changes unlikely. The struggle over testing during the last several decades will likely continue. Also as in the past, future testing will likely moderate but not end the use of performance-enhancing drugs in sports.

---

[1] Patrick Zickler, "NIDA Initiative Targets Increasing Teen Use of Anabolic Steroids," *NIDA Notes*, vol. 15, no. 3, August 2000, p. 1. Also available online URL: http://www.drugabuse.gov/NIDA_notes/NNVol153/Initiative.html. Posted in August 2000.

[2] Peter Lawson, quoted in Terry Todd, "A History of the Use of Anabolic Steroids in Sport," in Jack W. Berryman and Roberta J. Park, eds., *Sport and Exercise Science: Essays in the History of Sports Medicine*. Urbana: University of Illinois Press, 1992, p. 319.

[3] Robert Voy with Kirk Deeter, *Drugs, Sport, and Politics*. Champaign, Ill.: Leisure Press, 1991, p. 5.

[4] Thomas Hicks, quoted in David Wallechinsky, *The Complete Book of the Olympics*. New York: Penguin Books, 1984, pp. 44–45.

[5] Charles E. Yesalis and Michael S. Bahrke, "History of Doping in Sport," in Michael S. Bahrke and Charles E. Yesalis, eds., *Performance-Enhancing Substances in Sport and Exercise*. Champaign, Ill.: Human Kinetics, 2002, p. 6.

[6] Jan Todd and Terry Todd, "Significant Events in the History of Drug Testing and the Olympic Movement: 1960–1999," in Wayne Wilson and Edward Derse, eds., *Doping in Elite Sport: The Politics of Drugs in the Olympic Movement*. Champaign, Ill.: Human Kinetics, 2001, pp. 67–69.

[7] Yesalis and Bahrke, "History of Doping in Sport," p. 6.

[8] Jacques Anquetil, quoted in Bil Gilbert, "Something Extra on the Ball," *Sports Illustrated*, vol. 30, June 30, 1969, p. 32.

[9] William N. Taylor, *Anabolic Steroids and the Athlete, 2nd Edition*. Jefferson, N.C.: McFarland, 2002, p. 175.

[10] Pat Lenehan, *Anabolic Steroids and Other Performance Enhancing Drugs*. London: Taylor and Francis, 2003, p. 7.

[11] Taylor, *Anabolic Steroids and the Athlete, 2nd Edition*, pp. 177–178.

[12] Yesalis and Bahrke, "History of Doping in Sport," p. 4.

[13] Taylor, *Anabolic Steroids and the Athlete, 2nd Edition*, p. 181.

[14] Paul de Kruif, *The Male Hormone*. Garden City, N.Y.: Garden City Publishing, 1945, p. 226.

[15] Lenehan, *Anabolic Steroids and Other Performance Enhancing Drugs*, p. 9.

[16] Todd and Todd, "Significant Events in the History of Drug Testing," pp. 66–67.

[17] Yesalis and Bahrke, "History of Doping in Sport," p. 7.

[18] Todd and Todd, "Significant Events in the History of Drug Testing," p. 69.

[19] Todd, "A History of the Use of Anabolic Steroids in Sport," p. 330.

[20] Yesalis and Bahrke, "History of Doping in Sport," p. 7.

[21] Ken Patera, quoted in Terry Todd, "A History of the Use of Anabolic Steroids in Sport," pp. 327–328.

[22] Bil Gilbert, "Athletes in a Turned-On World," *Sports Illustrated*, vol. 30, no. 25, June 23, 1969, p. 71.

[23] Charles E. Yesalis, Stephen P. Courson, and James E. Wright, "History of Anabolic Steroid Use in Sport and Exercise," in Charles E. Yesalis, ed., *Anabolic Steroids in Sport and Exercise*. Champaign, Ill.: Human Kinetics, 2000, p. 56.

[24] Gilbert, "Athletes in a Turned-On World," pp. 64–72; Gilbert, "Something Extra on the Ball," pp. 30–42; Bil Gilbert, "High Time to Make Some Rules," *Sports Illustrated*, vol. 31, no. 1, July 7, 1969, pp. 30–35.

[25] Quoted in Todd and Todd, "Significant Events in the History of Drug Testing," p. 69.

[26] Voy and Deeter, *Drugs, Sport, and Politics*, p. 79.

[27] Voy and Deeter, *Drugs, Sport, and Politics*, p. 79.

[28] William N. Taylor, *Macho Medicine: A History of the Anabolic Steroid Epidemic*. Jefferson, N.C.: McFarland, 1991, p. 1.

[29] Tom Donahoe and Neil Johnson, *Foul Play: Drug Abuse in Sports*. Oxford, U.K.: Basil Blackwell, 1988, pp. 11–12.

[30] Todd and Todd, "Significant Events in the History of Drug Testing," pp. 73–83.

[31] "Ben Johnson (Athlete)," Wikipedia: The Free Encyclopedia. Available online. URL: http://en.wikipedia.org/wiki/Ben Johnson (athlete). Accessed in December 2005.

[32] Charles L. Dubin, *Commission of Inquiry into the Use of Drugs and Banned Practices Intended to Increase Athletic Performance*. Ottawa: Canadian Government Publishing Centre, 1990, pp. 260–269.

[33] Michael Janofsky and Peter Alfano, "Drug Use by Athletes Runs Free Despite Tests," *New York Times*, November 17, 1988. p. A1.

[34] Steven Ungerleider, *Faust's Gold: Inside the East German Doping Machine*. New York: St. Martin's Press, 2001.

[35] Ungerleider, *Faust's Gold*, pp. 166–167.

[36] Quoted in Alexandra Hudson, "East German Kids Bred on Steroids," Rediff. com. Available online. URL: http://www.rediff.com/sports/2004/nov/01dope. htm. Posted on November 1, 2004.

[37] Canadian Broadcasting Corp. "The East German Medal Machine," CBC Archives. Available online. URL: http://www.archives.cbc.ca/IDC-1-N41-N1409-8965/sports/drugs_sport/clip1. Posted on June 18, 1999.

[38] Alan Maimon, "Doping's Sad Toll: One Athlete's Tale from East Germany." *New York Times*, February 6, 2000, sec.1, p. 1.

[39] Ungerleider, *Faust's Gold*, pp. 36, 93.

[40] Hudson, "East German Kids Bred on Steroids."

[41] John Leonard, "Doping in Elite Swimming: A Case Study of the Modern Era from 1970 Forward," in Wayne Wilson and Edward Derse, eds., *Doping in Elite Sport: The Politics of Drugs in the Olympic Movement*. Champaign, Ill.: Human Kinetics, 2001, pp. 226, 233–234.

[42] Donahoe and Johnson, *Foul Play*, p. 117.

[43] David J. Armstrong and Thomas Reilly, "Blood Boosting and Sport," in David R. Mottram, ed., *Drugs in Sport, 3rd Edition*. London: Routledge, 2003, p. 215.

[44] Donahoe and Johnson. *Foul Play*, p. 118.

[45] Lenehan, *Anabolic Steroids and Other Performance Enhancing Drugs*, p. 85.

[46] Voy and Deeter, *Drugs, Sport, and Politics*, p. 58.

[47] Lenehan, *Anabolic Steroids and Other Performance Enhancing Drugs*, p. 84.

[48] Quoted in Voy and Deeter, *Drugs, Sport, and Politics*, p. 59.

[49] Quoted in Alan J. George, "Peptide and Glycoprotein Hormones and Sport," in David R. Mottram, ed., *Drugs in Sport,. 3rd Edition*. London: Routledge, 2003, p. 197.

[50] Terry Madden, quoted in Sara Brunetti, "THG: The Hidden Steroid," CBC News Indepth. Available online. URL: http://www.cbc.ca/news/background/steroids. Updated on November 26, 2003.

[51] Jacques Rogge, quoted in CTV.ca News Staff, "Song, Spectacle Bring 2004 Olympics to a Close," Athens 2004. Available online. URL: http://www.ctv.ca/servlet/ArticleNews/mini/CTVNews/1093810737985_31?s_name=athens2004&no_ads=. Posted on August 29, 2004.

[52] Taylor, *Anabolic Steroids and the Athlete, 2nd Second Edition,* p. 147.

[53] Quoted in Michael Bamberger and Don Yaeger, "Over the Edge," *Sports Illustrated,* vol. 86, April 14, 1997, pp. 60–64.

[54] Michael Bamberger and Don Yaeger, "Over the Edge," p. 60.

[55] Quoted in Michael Bamberger and Don Yaeger, "Over the Edge," p. 60.

[56] World Anti-Doping Agency, "The 2005 Prohibited List," The World Anti-Doping Code. Available online. URL: http://www.wada-ama.org/rtecontent/document/list_2005.pdf. Downloaded in December 2005.

[57] David R. Mottran, "Prevalence of Drug Misuse in Sport," in David R. Mottram, ed., *Drugs in Sport, 3rd Edition.* London: Routledge, 2003, p. 358–361.

[58] Ralph Hale, quoted in Jere Longman, "Olympics: U.S.O.C. Experts Call Drug Testing a Failure," *New York Times,* April 9, 1995, sec. 8, p. 11.

[59] World Anti-Doping Agency, "Introduction," Doping Control. Available online. URL: http://www.wada-ama.org/en/dynamic.ch2?pageCategory.id=338. Downloaded in December 2005.

[60] Jim Ferstle, "Evolution and Politics of Drug Testing," in Charles E. Yesalis, ed., *Anabolic Steroids in Sport and Exercise.* Champaign, Ill.: Human Kinetics, 2000, p. 402.

[61] Yesalis and Bahrke, "History of Doping in Sport," p. 11.

[62] Vic Washington, quoted in Brian Hewitt, "Playing at Any Cost; NFL Players Reveal They Took Cocaine, Drank Before Games," *Chicago Sun Times,* September 20, 1993, p. 100.

[63] Quoted in Hewitt, "Playing at Any Cost," p. 100.

[64] Bill Fralic, "Statement," *Steroids in Amateur and Professional Sports—The Medical and Social Costs of Steroid Abuse. Hearings before the Committee on the Judiciary, United States Senate, One Hundred First Congress, First Session, April 3, 1989, and May 9, 1989.* Washington, D.C.: U.S. Government Printing Office, 1990, pp. 179–180.

[65] Steve Courson, "Statement," *Steroids in Amateur and Professional Sports—The Medical and Social Costs of Steroid Abuse. Hearings before the Committee on the Judiciary, United States Senate, One Hundred First Congress, First Session, April 3, 1989, and May 9, 1989.* Washington, D.C.: U.S. Government Printing Office, 1990, p. 188.

[66] Courson, "Statement," p. 189.

[67] Lyle Alzado, "I'm Sick and I'm Scared," *Sports Illustrated,* vol. 75, no. 2, July 8, 1991, pp. 20–25.

[68] Quoted by Paul Tagliabue, "Statement," *Abuse of Steroids in Amateur and Professional Athletics. Hearing before the Subcommittee on Crime of the Committee on the Ju-*

diciary, House of Representatives, One Hundred First Congress, Second Session, March 22, 1990. Washington, D.C.: U.S. Government Printing Office, 1990, p. 7.

[69] Paul Tagliabue, "Testimony," Hearings before the Committee on Government Reform, U.S. House of Representatives, April 27, 2005. Available online. URL: http://reform.house.gov/UploadedFiles/NFL%20-%20Tagliabue%20Testimony. pdf. Downloaded in December 2005.

[70] Yesalis and Bahrke, "History of Doping in Sport," p. 12.

[71] Quoted in William Oscar Johnson, "Steroids: A Problem of Huge Dimensions," *Sports Illustrated*, vol. 62, May 13, 1985, pp. 38–54.

[72] Tommy Chaikin with Rick Telander, "The Nightmare of Steroids," *Sports Illustrated*, vol. 69, October 24, 1988, pp. 83–102.

[73] Todd, "A History of the Use of Anabolic Steroids in Sport," p. 334.

[74] Quoted in William Nack, "The Muscle Murders," *Sports Illustrated*, vol. 88, no. 20, May 18, 1998, p. 98.

[75] Maria R. Lowe, *Women of Steel: Female Body Builders and the Struggle for Self-Definition.* New York: New York University Press, 1998, p. 78.

[76] Charles E. Yesalis and Virginia S. Cowart, *The Steroids Game.* Champaign, Ill: Human Kinetics, 1988, p. 14.

[77] Jon Swartz, "High Death Rate Lingers behind Fun Facade of Pro Wrestling," *USA Today*, March 12, 2004, p. 1C. Also available online. URL: http://www.usatoday.com/sports/2004-03-12-pro-wrestling_x.htm. Posted on March 12, 2004.

[78] Hal Bodley, "Positive Test: Amphetamines Make Banned List," On Baseball. Available online. URL: http://www.usatoday.com/sports/baseball/columnist/bodley/2005-11-15-bodley-amphetmines_x.htm. Posted on November 15, 2005.

[79] Jose Canseco, *Juiced: Wild Times, Rampant 'Roids, Smash Hits, and How Baseball Got Big.* New York: HarperCollins, 2005, p. 225.

[80] Tom Verducci, "Is Baseball in the Asterisk Era?" *Sports Illustrated*, vol. 100, no. 11, March 25, 2004, pp. 36–39.

[81] Tom Verducci, "Pure Hitters," *Sports Illustrated*, vol. 104, no. 14, April 3, 2006, pp. 40–43.

[82] John McCain, quoted in Thomas Heath, "Senate Warns Baseball on Steroids Testing," *Washington Post*, March 11, 2004, p. A1.

[83] Rick Reilly, "Gutless Wonders," *Sports Illustrated*, vol. 103, no. 6, August 15, 2005, p. 124.

[84] John Hoberman, "How Drug Testing Fails: The Politics of Doping Control," in Wayne Wilson and Edward Derse, eds., *Doping in Elite Sport: The Politics of Drugs in the Olympic Movement.* Champaign, Ill.: Human Kinetics, 2001, p. 264.

[85] Hobeman, "How Drug Testing Fails," p. 264.

[86] Antonio Davis, "Testimony," Hearing on Steroid Legislation, U.S. Senate Committee on Commerce, Science, and Transportation, September 28, 2005. Available online. URL: http://commerce.senate.gov/pdf/davis.pdf. Posted on September 28, 2005.

[87] Gary Bettman, quoted in Associated Press, "Commissioner Meetsmeets with Davis, Waxman," ESPN NHL. Available online. URL: http://sports.espn.go.com/nhl/news/story?id=2214308&campaign=rss&source=NHLHeadlines. Posted on November 4, 2005.

[88] Canadian Press, "NHL Denies Steroid Allegations," SportingNews.com. Available online. URL: http://www.sportingnews.com/nhl/articles/ 20051124/677244-p.html. Posted on November 25, 2005.

[89] Ted Saskin, quoted in Associated Press, "Doping Official Says NHL Has Steroids Problem." MSNBC NBC Sports. Available online. URL: http://msnbc.msn.com/id/10196507. Posted on November 24, 2005.

[90] Michael Farber, "Hockey's Little Helpers," CNNSI. Available online. URL: http://sportsillustrated.cnn.com/features/1998/weekly/980202/nhlstory.html. Posted on January, 28, 1998.

[91] Marc Ratner, quoted in Robert Cassidy, Jr. "Boxing and Steroids." The Sweet Science. Available online. URL: http://www.thesweetscience.com/boxing-article/1819/boxing-steroids. Posted on March 20, 2005.

[92] Larry Hazzard, quoted in Cassidy, "Boxing and Steroids."

[93] Marj Charlier, "Among Teen-Agers, Abuse of Steroids May Be Bigger Issue Than Cocaine Use," *Wall Street Journal*, October 4, 1988 p. A20.

[94] Lloyd D. Johnston, Patrick M. O'Malley, Jerald G. Bachman, and John E. Schulenberg, *Monitoring the Future National Results on Adolescent Drug Use: Overview of Key Findings 2004.* Bethesda, Md.: National Institutes of Health, U.S. Department of Health and Human Services, 2004, p. 44.

[95] Charles Yesalis, "Testimony," Committee on Government Reform Hearings: Eradicating Steroid Use Part IV. Available online. URL: http://reform.house.gov/GovReform/Hearings/EventSingle.aspx?EventID=28694. Posted on June 15, 2005.

[96] Quoted in Taylor, *Macho Medicine*, p. 28.

[97] Yesalis and Cowart, *The Steroids Game*, p. 27.

[98] Michael S. Bahrke and Charles E. Yesalis, "Anabolic-Androgenic Steroids," in Michael S. Bahrke and Charles E. Yesalis, eds., *Performance-Enhancing Substances in Sport and Exercise*. Champaign, Ill.: Human Kinetics, 2002, p. 33.

[99] Taylor, *Anabolic Steroids and the Athlete*, pp. 68–69.

[100] Kelli White, "Statement," Committee on Government Reform Hearings: Eradicating Steroid Use Part IV. Available online. URL: 2005.http://reform.house.gov/UploadedFiles/White%20Steroids%204%20Testimony.pdf. Posted on June 15, 2005.

[101] Alzado, "I'm Sick and I'm Scared," pp. 20–25.

[102] George, "Peptide and Glycoprotein Hormones and Sport," pp. 149–150.

[103] William J. Kraemer, Martyn R. Rubin, Duncan N. French, and Michael R. McGuigan, "Physiological Effects of Testosterone Precursors," in Michael S. Bahrke and Charles E. Yesalis, eds., *Performance-Enhancing Substances in Sport and Exercise*. Champaign, Ill.: Human Kinetics, 2002, p. 84.

[104] George, "Peptide and Glycoprotein Hormones and Sport," p. 164.

[105] William J. Kraemer, Bradley C. Nindl, and Martyn R. Rubin, "Growth Hormone: Physiological Effects with Exogenous Administration," in Michael S. Bahrke and Charles E. Yesalis, eds., *Performance-Enhancing Substances in Sport and Exercise*. Champaign, Ill.: Human Kinetics, 2002, p. 69.

[106] Eric S. Rawson and Priscilla M. Clarkson, "Ephedrine As an Ergogenic Aid," in Michael S. Bahrke and Charles E. Yesalis, eds., *Performance-Enhancing Substances in Sport and Exercise*. Champaign, Ill.: Human Kinetics, 2002, p. 292.

[107] Nack, "The Muscle Murders," p. 96–100.

[108] Quoted in Nack, "The Muscle Murders," p. 98.

[109] Charles Yesalis, quoted in Dayn Perry, "Pumped Up Hysteria," Reason Online. Available online. URL: http://www.reason.com/0301/fe.dp.pumped.shtml. Posted in January 2003.

[110] Rick Collins, quoted in John Romano, "An Interview with Legal Muscle Author, Rick Collins, JD." Steroid.com. Available online. URL: http://www.steroid.com/interview.php. Posted in December 2002.

[111] William Saletan, "The Beam in Your Eye: If Steroids Are Cheating, Why Isn't LASIK?" Slate. Available online. URL: http://www.slate.com/id/2116858/. Posted on April 18, 2005.

[112] Rick Collins, *Legal Muscle: Anabolics in America*. East Meadow, N.Y.: Legal Muscle Publishing, 2002, p. 279.

[113] Will Carroll with William L. Carroll, *Juice: The Real Story of Baseball's Drug Problems*. Chicago, Ivan R. Dee, 2005, pp. 149–156.

CHAPTER 2

THE LAW AND DRUGS
AND SPORTS

Drug use in sports is subject to federal and state laws but also comes under control of the administrative rules of sports leagues and organizations. The federal and state laws restrict the possession and distribution of most performance-enhancing drugs, while administrative rules ban the use of the drugs before or during sporting events. Few people dispute the meaning of these laws and rules, but many object to drug tests as a way to identify law and rule breakers. Testing raises constitutional issues of individual rights, due process, and the authority of sporting organizations, issues that in some cases have worked their way up to the Supreme Court.

Adding to the legal complexities, some disputes between U.S. athletes and international organizations raise issues of national control. It is not always clear when and if international groups can force an athlete to follow their rules and accept their punishments. One lawyer writes, "The existing patchwork of inconsistent—and all too often contradictory—treaties, statutes, regulations, and case law creates so many exceptions to general rules one might draw concerning PES [performance-enhancing substances] regulation that the exceptions swallow the rules."[1] Still, a review of the major laws and court cases involving drug use and testing highlights some key issues.

LAWS AND REGULATIONS

FEDERAL LAW

For more than half a century, federal laws have defined which sports-related drugs are legal and illegal. Under the Food, Drug, and Cosmetic Act of 1938, the Food and Drug Administration (FDA) received the power to

78

regulate the sale of drugs. That same year, the FDA classified synthetic testosterone as a prescription drug and, as it did for other prescription drugs, worked with states to determine who could legally prescribe and dispense it. By the late 1960s, however, the explosion of drug use made it clear that the drug laws needed revision.

The Controlled Substances Act of 1970

A major recasting of federal drug laws came in 1970 with the Controlled Substances Act (CSA), a law that still guides drug enforcement today. The CSA managed to place a wide variety of drugs into a single scheme while at the same time distinguishing among the drugs based on their potential for abuse, addiction, and injury. Merging the many separate and inconsistent laws and rules that existed for particular drugs gave enforcement agencies clear guidance on what drugs were the most serious threats and deserved the harshest punishments. The law initially did not include many performance-enhancing drugs, but new laws in the years to come would fix this gap.

The CSA placed all drugs regulated by the federal government into one of five schedules.

- **Schedule I** drugs have no medical uses, present the greatest potential for abuse, and include heroin, LSD, and marijuana. Lacking medical value, these drugs cannot be prescribed and are illegal under nearly all circumstances.

- **Schedule II** drugs such as morphine, cocaine, methadone, amphetamines, and methamphetamines have high abuse potential but also have some medical uses. They are illegal without a prescription, and prescriptions are tightly controlled.

- **Schedule III** drugs have medical uses and, compared to Schedule I and II drugs, less potential for serious abuse. The category includes drugs such as codeine with limited quantities of narcotics.

- **Schedule IV** drugs have moderate potential for abuse. The category includes mild sedatives and tranquilizers such as Valium used mostly for medical purposes.

- **Schedule V** drugs have a low potential for abuse and include medicine with diluted narcotic mixtures prescribed for coughs and diarrhea.

Some drugs used in sports such as amphetamines were named as schedule II drugs, but steroids had not become well known enough by 1970 for the CSA to include them.

All the drugs included in the schedules are controlled. That means manufacturers must keep records of how much they make and where they send it, and pharmacists must keep records of how much is prescribed. With these records, the government can track the drugs and make sure they get used only for legitimate medical reasons. Since all but Schedule I drugs are legal with a prescription, the amounts of drugs manufactured should not exceed the amounts prescribed. Record checks can prevent excess manufactured drugs from being diverted for illegal purposes. The Drug Enforcement Agency (DEA) has the authority to enforce the law and to examine records of companies that make controlled substances.

Amateur Sports Act of 1978

Responding to conflicts over the selection of team members for the Olympic Games created by competing amateur sports organizations, Congress passed legislation in 1978 that reorganized amateur sports. The Amateur Sports Act named the U.S. Olympic Committee (USOC) as the governing body for the many individual amateur sports organizations that existed. The legislation allowed the USOC to

> exercise exclusive jurisdiction, either directly or through its constituent members of committees, over all matters pertaining to the participation of the United States in the Olympic Games and in the Pan-American Games, including the representation of the United States in such games, and over the organization of the Olympic Games and the Pan-American Games when held in the United States.[2]

The USOC would also

> provide for swift resolutions of conflicts and disputes involving amateur athletes, national governing bodies, and amateur sports organizations, and protect the opportunity of any amateur athlete, coach, trainer, manager, administrator, or official to participate in amateur athletic competition.[3]

By defining clear lines of authority for the many separate sporting organizations, the act put in place a more effective, logical, and fair system for governing amateur athletics. The new authority would, many hoped, improve the selection and training of athletes for the Olympic Games.

The law had, in addition, implications for drug testing of athletes. Although it said nothing about doping, the clause giving jurisdiction (or authority) to the USOC over all matters pertaining to participation in the games could be interpreted to include control over drug testing. If the USOC and associated sports organizations set rules for deciding who would make the Olympic team, they could also set rules for drug use. Amateur sports organizations would then have the right to ban certain drugs and suspend athletes who used those drugs.

One other implication followed. The clause requiring procedures for resolving disputes seemed to give still more control to the USOC and related agencies. They could, under the legislation, handle disputes on their own rather than deal with athletes in state and federal courts. Athletes would consequently have fewer options in appealing drug tests and penalties.

Anti-Drug Abuse Act of 1988

This short piece of legislation addressed the growing problem of steroid use. It amended the Federal Food, Drug, and Cosmetic Act (but not the Controlled Substances Act) to make it illegal to distribute anabolic steroids or possess anabolic steroids with the intent to distribute for purposes other than treatment of disease. Violators could be punished by up to three years in prison and a fine. However, violators who distribute or intend to distribute to persons under 18 years of age could get six years in prison and a fine. All 50 states had already made possession of steroids without a prescription illegal, but the federal law supplied a consistent standard that states could adopt or use to supplement their own laws.

The act did not, however, make steroids controlled substances that required manufacturers and sellers to keep careful records of where the products went. It also left enforcement responsibility with the Food and Drug Administration, an agency less well prepared than the DEA to catch major steroid dealers.

More practically, the act also required the government to study the use of anabolic steroids and human growth hormone among high school students, college students, and other adults. As summarized in a DEA document, the completed report found a problem that would greatly concern federal legislators:

> A Government Accounting Office (GAO) study of the problem, published in 1989, reviewed 15 separate studies and reported one which showed that more than six percent of male high school seniors, mostly athletes, used or had used steroids. Another survey indicated that 20 percent of athletes in five colleges surveyed used steroids. It also reported on the significant side effects of steroid use. The GAO supported federal and state efforts to exercise greater control over steroid distribution and use. A 1990 study by the Inspector General of Health and Human Services reported that over a quarter of a million adolescents used steroids.[4]

Another approach to anabolic steroid legislation, one that better addressed the teen drug use, soon followed.

Drugs and Sports

The Anabolic Steroid Control Act of 1990

Legislation in 1990 amended the CSA to add anabolic steroids to the list of Schedule III drugs. Along with applying CSA penalties to the possession and distribution of steroids, the new act added two extra years of jail for coaches, trainers, or advisers who persuade or induce an individual to possess or use anabolic steroids. When the individual persuaded or induced to use steroids has not attained the age of 18 years, the punishment rises to five extra years. Perhaps most important, making steroids a controlled substance directed manufacturers to account for the products they made and help prevent their use for nonmedical purposes. The CSA allowed prescription of steroids by physicians for medical problems but not for performance or cosmetic reasons. The DEA now had responsibility for enforcing the law.

Not all groups supported the change. The American Medical Association (AMA) shared the concerns of Congress about the abuse of steroids and their health risks for athletes. At the same time, however, the AMA did not believe steroids had the same risks as other controlled substances. The research had not shown steroids to lead to the severe psychological and physical dependence that, say, amphetamines and cocaine did. Making steroids a controlled substance without this research would bypass current rules for adding new drugs to the schedules and replace professional and scientific judgment with political views. The AMA's desire to keep steroids under the authority of other laws did not, however, prevent Congress from passing the act.

Under the new law, the DEA made 283 arrests, recovered 6 million steroid units, and seized assets worth $2.5 million between 1991 and 1994.[5] Most of those arrested were involved in national and international distribution. Experts Charles E. Yesalis and Virginia S. Cowart describe some examples of the enforcement efforts: Agents seized two million dosage units (both legitimate and counterfeit) in Detroit; prosecutors indicted a former Mr. Universe in Boston who had become a major East Coast distributor of steroids; and a judge sentenced a Miami gym owner who had been found with more than 100,000 dosage units to eight years in prison.[6]

No doubt more could have been done, but the DEA concentrated most on dangerous Schedule I drugs such as heroin and Schedule II drugs such as cocaine. The task of stopping steroid trafficking was made more difficult because many nations had not outlawed the drug at the time. Although drug enforcement agencies worked with other countries to stop trafficking of heroin and cocaine, they could not cooperate in the same way to stop trafficking of steroids. Still yet, catching steroid distributors did not bring the kind of punishment to justify use of public resources. Juries hesitated to give stiff sentences to steroid distributors, seeing their crime as less serious than those of other drug dealers.

Despite limitations, the act reduced the supply of steroids. A 1994 conference on the impact of the Anabolic Steroid Control Act concluded that federal enforcement "had significantly affected the illicit anabolic steroid market by making the steroids harder and more expensive to obtain."[7] Where most supply once came from drugs legally manufactured in the United States but diverted to illegitimate uses, the new law stopped this diversion. Most steroids now had to be made in secret factories or come into the country through smuggling. Some users traveled to Mexico where they could buy steroids without a prescription (but violated the law by bringing them into the United States). Still other users obtained illegal prescriptions, ordered and received steroids through the mail, or relied on friends and gym mates for products. With these black market sources, however, buyers had little assurance of the quality of the products.

Two recent prosecutions illustrate the continuing, though still incomplete efforts to limit access to steroids under the 1990 law. On December 15, 2005, the DEA announced that it had made the largest steroid bust in history. After a 21-month investigation, the agency arrested the owner of the world's largest steroid manufacturing plant and four others who helped distribute the drugs. It also indicted and requested extradition of the owners of five other Mexican companies that manufacture steroids. The U.S. sales of all these companies reached $56 million, and the DEA had identified more than 2,000 people who bought steroids from these companies over the Internet. Authorities hope the arrest will slow the smuggling of steroids from Mexico into the United States and scare users from buying the products.

Another recent case involved smaller amounts of drugs but brought more publicity. The target of the prosecution, Victor Conte, built a company called BALCO by getting athletes to publicly endorse his legal nutritional supplements but also by providing steroids to athletes (particularly the designer steroid THG). Federal investigation of BALCO began in 2002 and followed with a raid of the headquarters in September 2003. Later that fall, a grand jury questioned many famous athletes, including Barry Bonds, Marion Jones, and Bill Romanowski, about their association with BALCO and Conte. A 42-count indictment against Conte and three others brought in February 2004 added to the publicity, as did the leaking of grand jury testimony to California newspapers. In the end, the BALCO defendants pled guilty to charges of steroid distribution and received probation or short prison terms.

Dietary Supplement Health and Education Act (DSHEA) of 1994

This act had little to do with steroids but did affect the legality and sales of steroid-related products. The DSHEA set up measures to approve dietary supplements that differed from those used to approve new drugs and foods.

Dietary supplements come in the form of a pill, capsule, tablet, or liquid, are not used as a sole item of a meal or diet, and are labeled as dietary supplements. Examples include vitamins, minerals, herbs, and amino acids (the components of proteins). Under the law, manufacturers of new dietary supplements must submit information to the Food and Drug Administration (FDA) that any new ingredient will reasonably be expected to be safe. They must also include accurate lists of ingredients on the labels of the supplements. By not having to go through the long and expensive testing done for new drugs and food, manufacturers could bring supplements to market more quickly and offer consumers a better choice of products.

After passage of the DSHEA, companies began to market nutritional supplements that, they claimed, would aid sports performances. One of these supplements, the steroid precursor androstenedione, had similarities to steroids. Since andro occurs naturally in the body and has similarities to vitamins and other supplements, it fell within the DSHEA (testosterone also occurs naturally in the body, but unlike andro, steroids had been declared controlled substances in 1990). Another stimulant used in sports, ephedra, is found in certain herbs that the law treated as supplements. The law gave legitimacy to these products that they would not have otherwise had. In fact, the death of Steve Bechler, a pitcher with the Baltimore Orioles, has been linked to ephedra. Companies can nonetheless advertise that their supplements would make athletes better, faster, and stronger or safely build muscles.

The growing marketing and sales of andro and other performance-related products since the late 1990s led to a FDA crackdown in 2004. The agency sent letters to 23 companies asking them to stop distributing dietary supplements containing andro and threatened punishment if they did not respond. The FDA justified its action by noting that andro can lead to excess testosterone and associated health problems. The dangers of steroid precursors had in fact been the subject of recent congressional hearings. Yet, manufacturers had not abided by DSHEA requirements to list safety concerns on the labels of their andro products.

Nutritional supplement companies appeared to have done more than misstate the risks of legal steroid precursors—they also included illegal steroids as ingredients in some products. In October 2005, an article in the *Washington Post* reported on the Internet purchase of five nutritional supplements that claimed to build muscle quickly. When tested, four of the five contained steroids, including the designer steroid THG. As the article reported, "Two officials with prominent U.S. dietary supplement companies, who spoke on condition of anonymity, said it is easy for companies to outwit drug testers. 'There's an unlimited pool of steroids,' one official said. 'You could do this for the next 100 years. . .' The longer they don't pay attention the [more rampant] it gets."[8]

The report led the chairman of the House Committee on Government Reform, Tom Davis (R-Virginia), to request information from the FDA on how it regulates nutritional supplements. Since the FDA has responsibility for the safety of nutritional supplements and the accuracy of labeling, Davis suggested that the agency failed to fulfill its oversight duties. He suggested that control of steroid precursors should come under the authority of other enforcement agencies, ones now responsible for control of steroids.

Anabolic Steroid Control Act of 2004

Given that athletes and teens could easily and legally purchase steroid precursors in stores or over the Internet, the next piece of legislation restricted access to these substances. Experts argued that steroid precursors brought the same health risks as anabolic steroids but were openly advertised and sold. In response, the Anabolic Steroid Control Act of 2004 added about two dozen steroid precursors such as androstenedione to the list of Schedule III controlled substances. The evidence of the benefits of these precursors to athletes is less clear than for anabolic steroids, but concern about unrestricted access to dietary supplements with steroidlike ingredients grew along with widespread advertising to encourage use of the supplements. As a result, groups such as the AMA, the Major League Baseball Players Association, and the U.S. Anti-Doping Agency supported the legislation.

After considerable debate, Congress excluded one steroid precursor called dehydroepiandrosterone (DHEA). Representatives of the supplement industry argued that DHEA differed from andro and other steroid precursors in a crucial way. The body naturally limited its effects by ignoring excess levels and prevented it from contributing to high testosterone levels and related health problems. It also had benefits such as maintaining immune function, cognitive ability, and sleep patterns for elderly persons who no longer produced sufficient amounts of the hormone on their own.

With the support of the DEA, the legislation included another provision. Under the Anabolic Steroid Control Act of 1990, the agency had authority to add a new steroid drug to the Schedule III list if (1) it was chemically related to steroids and (2) it promoted muscle growth. With steroid precursors, however, scientists could not certify that steroid precursors promoted muscle growth. The DEA believed precursors presented real dangers and expected findings to eventually prove its effects on muscle growth but had to wait for the results of long-term studies. The 2004 act overcame this dilemma by declaring steroid precursors as Schedule III drugs without evidence of their muscle-building effects. Under the new law, the attorney general and the DEA no longer have to wait for proof that a new steroid-related substance builds muscles before adding it to the list of controlled drugs.

STATE LAWS

State laws have generally followed the lead of federal laws in defining schedules for controlled substances and defining harsher punishments for distribution than possession. However, state laws can still vary. They differ in the drugs defined as illegal, punishments given for violations, and rules for giving legal prescriptions. For example, California, Kansas, and New York treat the first offense for personal use of steroids as misdemeanors; Florida, Nebraska, and Washington treat first possession as a felony; and Alaska and Vermont do not include steroids as a scheduled substance.[9] Punishments may differ as well. California increases the penalty for unlawful possession of steroids from a misdemeanor without prison time for the first offense to prison time for additional offenses. Illinois makes simple possession of steroids punishable by probation, while New York reduces first-offender cases to noncriminal violations. Given such diversity in state laws, federal law provides the best summary of the legal treatment of performance-enhancing drugs across the country.

ADMINISTRATIVE RULES

The use of steroids, steroid precursors, and other performance-enhancing drugs by athletes for sports performance falls under the control of administrative rules of sports organizations and leagues more than federal and state laws. Although laws make possession and distribution of the drugs illegal without a prescription, authorities most often prosecute large-scale distributors rather than individual athletes. Since most professional athletes rely on trainers, teammates, and friends for drugs, they face little risk of arrest and prosecution as distributors. In the BALCO case, for example, prosecutors charged company executives but not any of the athletes using the company's drugs. In contrast, the administrative rules of sports organizations and leagues that ban performance-enhancing drugs apply directly to athletes who use the drugs.

Administrative rules vary by sport. The most comprehensive rules come from the International Olympic Committee (IOC) and the national organizations for swimming, track and field, gymnastics, and other Olympic sports. With aid from the World Anti-Doping Agency, international and national organizations for Olympic sports clearly list banned substances, specify procedures for getting urine and blood samples, perform first-rate drug tests on the sample, and enforce consistent penalties. The rules developed slowly but now offer a model for other sports. The National Football League (NFL) began adding rules to prohibit performance-enhancing drugs in the 1980s and improved their policy and procedures in the 1990s. Baseball, basketball, hockey, boxing, and professional wrestling formed administrative rules for drug use more slowly. Only recently have they banned performance-enhancing drugs, set up comprehensive testing procedures, and strictly enforced bans on drugs. Bodybuilding and long-distance cycling have had rules in place for longer but started to strictly enforce their rules only recently.

National Rules

Sports organizations and leagues have authority to ban drugs and punish violators because of their status as private organizations. Athletes participate in events and games sponsored by private organizations as a privilege rather than as a right. As long as they follow existing law and protect constitutional rights, organizations and leagues can set up their own administrative rules. No one has disputed the right of the IOC, the NFL, or Major League Baseball (MLB) to ban performance-enhancing drugs, even those that are legal outside the sport. The IOC, for example, bans alcohol from use during some events and at one time banned high levels of caffeine.

Administrative rules for testing have, in contrast, come under more criticism. Sports organizations and leagues can ban performance-enhancing drugs but can only enforce the ban with mandatory testing. All participants or a random sample of participants must undergo tests, even without any evidence of drug use. Yet such tests might violate constitutional rights for due process and protection from unreasonable searches. Under the Fourth Amendment of the Constitution, police and government agents must have reasonable grounds to believe a crime has been committed to make a lawful search or arrest. Testing an athlete without suspicion of drug use does not meet the usual requirements for a search.

Two grounds exist for sports organizations and leagues to justify blanket testing. First, courts have viewed the Fourth Amendment as protecting citizens from unreasonable searches by the government rather than private organizations. Since sports associations and professional leagues are private organizations, drug testing becomes an issue for collective bargaining between athletes and officials rather than an issue of constitutional protection. If a players' union accepts testing as part of the collective bargaining agreement, players are bound to undergo testing and accept the punishment for a positive test. Most such agreements seek to ensure the fairness of the tests and give athletes the opportunity to appeal the test results. Otherwise, professional athletes have little recourse other than to accept league rules.

Second, courts have ruled that even schools that are public rather than private entities can test for drugs without violating the constitutional rights of athletes. In a case involving drug tests of sports participants in an Oregon school district *(Vernonia School District v. Acton)*, the Supreme Court concluded that the benefits of the program outweighed the threat to personal liberty. The testing did more, according to the ruling, to promote the general interest of keeping drugs out of sports and protecting the health of athletes than it did to inconvenience athletes. Applied more generally, the ruling allows for legal testing of athletes without individual suspicion of drug use.

Despite the opportunities for testing afforded by collective bargaining and court rulings, some professional sports delayed taking action against drug use. MLB accepted compulsory testing only after the scandals about player steroid use and even then resisted having multiple off-season tests and severe punishments. It took several congressional hearings that further embarrassed MLB for it to set up effective policies. Basketball and hockey leagues also set up stringent policies only after being pressured by the government.

The resistance of major sports to adopting drug policies angered some politicians. They argued that if the leagues did not take proper action, then perhaps the government should force them to do so. In 2005, several bills in Congress proposed to regulate drug use and testing in professional sports. The House Committee on Government Reform, the House Committee on Energy and Commerce, and the Senate Commerce Committee all offered similar legislation. The House bills covered baseball, football, basketball, and hockey; required random testing several times a year; and set punishments that would apply to all athletes. One bill proposed to permanently ban players after two positive tests and the other after three positive tests. The Senate bill also proposed to standardize testing procedures and punishments for the four major professional sports. It would require five tests a year, three during the season and two in the off-season, a two-year suspension for the first offense, and a permanent suspension for the second.

While applauding the antidrug goals of Congress, representatives from all the sports leagues opposed the legislation. They believed that a single policy would not fit all four sports. Each league should instead develop policies best suited to its sport and based on agreements between players and owners. For example, opponents of the legislation did not want punishments as harsh as those proposed by the legislation. A lifetime ban for two positive tests could destroy the career of young players who made youthful mistakes. The threat of the legislation did, however, prod the leagues to implement stronger testing procedures. Still not satisfied, the sponsors of the bills continue to work for their passage.

The Law and Drugs and Sports

International Rules

The Olympics and other international competitions face special legal problems because they lack the authority for drug testing that comes from national law or collective bargaining. The authority must instead come from other sources. It comes indirectly from the authority given to the national Olympic committees that make up the IOC. If U.S. law, for example, allows the U.S. Olympic Committee (USOC) to test its athletes for drugs at national events, then the IOC can do the same to U.S. athletes at international events. In addition, international authority for testing comes from the agreement of individual athletes who want to participate in Olympic events. Athletes allowed to participate must accept the rules and policies of international organizations that sponsor events. Refusing to give a urine sample for drug testing is thus treated the same as a positive test result and brings suspension.

Despite these claims to authority, international organizations face the risk that national courts will not recognize them. A suit brought by an athlete in a national court might lead to a decision that overturns Olympic rules. International sports organizations cannot deal easily with laws and procedures of the more than 200 nations that send athletes to international competitions. Yet, they might be forced to do so if national courts reject the right of the IOC or other organizations to require drug tests or impose penalties. To avoid battles in national courts, all nations participating in the Olympic Games or other international competitions could sign a treaty to allow for drug testing and punishment. The possibility of such a treaty seems remote for the near future, however.

One approach to resolving international disputes over drug use involves the Court of Arbitration for Sport (CAS). Established as part of the IOC in 1984 and headquartered in Lausanne, Switzerland, the CAS later became an independent agency. It settles disagreements between athletes and sports organizations by relying on high-level jurists from countries around the world and with experience in legal matters. They reach decisions based on a CAS code, national laws that apply to the contesting parties, or Swiss law if no other laws take precedence. Those bringing a dispute to the court must first agree to accept the court decision, but by doing so can avoid the time and expense of a trial in a national court. The arbitration process usually takes six to nine months—much less than might be expected otherwise.

Over the years, the CAS has come to decide many cases related to drug use and testing. For example, British skier Alain Baxter lost his bronze medal from the 2002 Winter Olympics when he tested positive for a banned stimulant. He appealed the decision to the CAS, claiming that the drug appeared in such a small amount that it could not have aided in his performance. The CAS sided with the IOC and refused to restore the medal. In another case, U.S. sprinter Jerome Young tested positive for the steroid nandrolone in 1999, but USA Track and Field cleared him after another test six days later came up clean. Allowed to compete in the 2000 Olympics, he won a gold medal as part of the U.S. 400-meter relay team. When other groups found out about the earlier positive test, however, they protested. The IOC claimed that Young should not have been eligible for the Olympics and that his victory was illegitimate. The CAS agreed, allowing the IOC to strip Young of his medal. More recently, the CAS ruled against an appeal from cyclist Tyler Hamilton over his two-year suspension for blood doping. The CAS cannot deal with all potential disputes but, as in these cases, can help avoid appeals to national courts.

COURT CASES

Most of the major court decisions relating to sports and drugs address disputes over the legality of mandatory drug testing and the authority of sports organizations to suspend athletes for doping. Some cases have worked their way up to the Supreme Court, but most others have been decided in appeals, district, or state courts.

Supreme Court Decisions

VERNONIA SCHOOL DISTRICT 47J V. WAYNE ACTON, 515 US 646 (1995)

Background

In 1989, the Vernonia School District in Oregon, concerned about student drug use, adopted a new drug-testing policy for student-athletes. Approved by parents who attended an open meeting on the problem, the policy required student-athletes to give a urine sample for drug testing. Students wanting to play competitive sports had to sign a form consenting to the drug testing, as did the parents of the students. The student-athletes would then undergo a test at the start of the season, and a 10-percent random sample would undergo another test during the season. The school board expected that the policy would remedy an apparent increase in drug use over the past several years. Despite having offered antidrug classes, teachers and administrators observed growing disciplinary problems during the 1980s that, they believed, came from drug use. Student-athletes, who served as models for other students, could play a key role in controlling drug use; if testing stopped the athletes from using drugs, it could indirectly lead other students to do the same.

The testing followed the careful procedures used with professional athletes. Monitors watched or listened to make sure the student-athletes gave a real urine sample and did not tamper with the vial. Once labeled with coded ID numbers rather than names, the samples went to an independent laboratory for analysis. The lab searched for amphetamines, cocaine, and marijuana (but not steroids). A positive result led to an additional test, and only if it also produced a second positive result did the lab inform the school. Unless the drug came from a legitimate prescription, the offending student would have to agree to counseling and weekly urinalysis or be suspended from athletics.

In 1991, a seventh-grade student, Wayne Acton, was not allowed to join the football team when he and his parents refused to sign the consent form. In response, the Actons sued to end the policy. The school district could not, they said, rightfully exclude students from sports merely because they did not agree to the tests. They argued that drug testing without reasons to suspect drug use violated the constitutional rights of students. The district court ruled in favor of the school district by dismissing the action. An appeals court later reversed the district court decision, and the Supreme Court agreed to hear the case.

Legal Issues

The Actons' suit argued that the school district policy violated the Fourth and Fourteenth Amendments to the U.S. Constitution and parts of the Oregon Constitution, but the Supreme Court focused on issues involving the Fourth Amendment. This amendment reads: "The right of the people to be secure in their persons, houses, papers, and effects, against unreasonable searches and seizures, shall not be violated, and no warrants shall issue, but upon probable cause, supported by oath or affirmation, and particularly describing the place to be searched, and the persons or things to be seized." To meet the demands of the amendment, the government in most cases must have a signed warrant to search a suspect or have probable cause to believe a crime is either in progress or likely to follow.

However, courts had allowed exceptions to the general rule. Sometimes special law enforcement needs made it impractical to get a warrant or clearly define probable cause. A search might then be permissible under two conditions: The subjects face only a modest intrusion from the search, and the government has compelling and legitimate interests in the outcome of the search. For example, the Supreme Court had allowed drug testing of railroad employers because it did little to inconvenience the workers and helped prevent deadly train accidents.

Vernonia v. Acton thus addressed a key question: Should the testing policy be considered an exception to the general rule against searches without a warrant or probable cause? The drug testing certainly involved a kind of search that the Fourth Amendment usually protected against. Taking and analyzing a urine sample may differ from the search for a gun in someone's clothes or for drugs in someone's car trunk, but it still involved looking for illegal substances that otherwise remain hidden. When applied to all student-athletes, this kind of blanket search lacked evidence of suspected drug use by specific students. To be allowed, then, the drug testing would have to meet the conditions of low intrusiveness and high importance.

According to the plaintiffs, the Vernonia testing policy did not meet these conditions. First, the plaintiffs argued that observation of the highly personal activity of urinating clearly interfered with the privacy of students. Perhaps a test given before technicians in an independent lab would preserve privacy. Yet urination done in a locker room in front of teachers or coaches and with other athletes nearby did not. The policy also demanded that, before the test, students report any medications they take (even those not examined in the test). Since this information should remain private, the demand again violated student rights.

Second, the plaintiffs argued that tests had little value to the school or the state. The school board offered only vague and scattered evidence of drug use to justify the tests. Rather than relying on direct observation of students taking or under the influence of drugs, the evidence consisted of a few complaints about the problem. The situation did not appear serious enough to violate student rights. Even if it did, the assumption that testing athletes would prevent nonathletes from using drugs made little sense. Having overstated both the extent of the problem and the value of the solution, the school district had, according to the plaintiffs, little to gain from the blanket drug tests. Overall, high intrusiveness outweighed the state interest in the tests, and the policy did not justify an exception to the Fourth Amendment.

Third, the plaintiffs argued that including all athletes rather than a selected few did not make the policy any more acceptable. Subjecting all athletes to the indignity of a search without any evidence of unlawful or suspicious behavior sent the wrong message. It implied that all students were presumed guilty until found innocent. Only with outside evidence or clear suspicions of drug use should schools select students for a test. Indeed, the school district might have used defiance of authority, disorderly or disruptive behavior, foul language, fighting, tobacco use, and weapon possession as grounds for drug tests. Under the policy, however, even student-athletes who behave properly must undergo a test. Such a solution, according to the plaintiffs, is too broad and sweeping for the problem it addresses.

The school board defendants argued the opposite: The intrusiveness of the test was minor while the gain was substantial. Students in general have privacy rights that protect them from unreasonable searches at the hands of teachers and administrators, but the conditions of the testing in this case overrode those rights. First, the defendants argued that giving a urine sample differed little from going to the restroom in a locker room, places already devoted to undressing and showering with other teammates. It took only a few minutes and allowed students to stay fully clothed and avoid exposing private body parts. Since athletes already expected little privacy in this setting, urine tests did not seem highly unusual, awkward, or intrusive.

Second, the defendants argued that preventing drug use among students and athletes had the utmost importance to the school district and state. School officials viewed the spread of drugs as a crisis that undermined teacher authority, risked serious injury of athletes, and damaged teens later in life. Much as drug testing of railroad workers helped avoid train accidents, drug testing of student-athletes helped avoid the dangers of a drug epidemic. The state thus had a compelling interest in drug testing of the student-athletes that outweighed the minor intrusion on their privacy.

Third, the school board noted in its favor that not all students were tested. Limiting the policy to students choosing to participate in sports allowed those wanting to avoid the testing to simply not join the teams. Voluntary participation in athletics already subjected students to special rules such as undergoing physical exams, maintaining a certain grade point average, and following practice, dress, and behavior codes set by the coaches. Adding drug tests to this list did not place an undue burden on students.

Decision

By a vote of 6-3, the Supreme Court sided with the defendants in letting the school district's testing policy stand. The decision vacated (set aside) the previous appeals court decision and remanded (sent back) the case for reconsideration by the lower court. Writing for the majority, Justice Antonin Scalia concluded that the drug testing did not violate the student's right to be free from unreasonable search and seizure. Given the reduced expectation of privacy of student-athletes and the unobtrusive nature of the test, the procedure intruded little on privacy rights. At the same time, the critical need to control drug use in schools through drug tests made the minor inconvenience of a search acceptable. The decision warned against applying the same kind of testing to all students but found it acceptable when limited to those voluntarily choosing to join a sports team.

In a dissenting opinion, Justice Sandra Day O'Connor wrote that the school board policy did not reach the standard of a reasonable search. Throughout history, courts had limited suspicionless searches to situations when the normal course of action would not work. In this case, however, methods other than testing all athletes could have helped stop drug use. She also denied that a sufficient case had been made for the seriousness of drug problems among athletes to justify the crude method of selecting them all for drug tests. Indeed, when the school blocked Wayne Acton from joining the football team, he was only in seventh grade—not a grade considered to have a major drug problem. If schools wanted to eliminate drugs and discipline problems, it could do so in many other ways that do not violate student rights.

Impact

The *Vernonia v. Acton* ruling did not directly address drug testing done in most professional sports. It actually involved some special circumstances: The drug testing occurred in a school responding to a growing problem of drug abuse, dealt with students under the authority of teachers and administrators, and involved the actions of a public school and elected school board. Even so, *Vernonia v. Acton* gave Supreme Court approval to blanket tests of athletes that might apply to other contexts. Those sports leagues and associations that require drug testing could argue, as in this case, that the intrusiveness of the test is modest compared to the importance of fair, honest, and drug-free competition in sports. Because Congress has passed no legislation on drug testing in sports, this case and the reasoning behind the decision have stood as a legal defense of current policies.

Federal Appeals Court Decisions

HARRY L. REYNOLDS, JR., V. INTERNATIONAL AMATEUR ATHLETIC FEDERATION, THE ATHLETICS CONGRESS, ET AL., 23 F.3D 1110 (1994)

Background

Harry "Butch" Reynolds held the world record in the 400-meter race and had won gold and silver medals at the 1988 Seoul Olympics. After participating in an international meet in August of 1990, he underwent a drug test, which found traces of nandrolone, a steroid banned by the International Amateur Athletic Federation (IAAF). Following its rules, the IAAF suspended Reynolds from competition for two years, thus preventing him from participating in the 1992 Barcelona Summer Olympics. Headquartered in London, the IAAF regulates track and field competitions throughout the world and works closely with national track and field groups. The governing organization in the United States, the Athletics Congress (TAC) of the United States (later renamed as USA Track and Field), belongs to the IAAF.

Reynolds immediately sued the IAAF in the District Court of Southern Ohio. The case was dismissed because Reynolds had not exhausted all administrative remedies offered by the IAAF and TAC. Reynolds then appealed his suspension to the TAC, claiming that the test was done carelessly and produced a false positive result. The TAC found reason to doubt the result and cleared Reynolds of the drug use charge. The IAAF, however, overruled the TAC. An IAAF arbitration board concluded the test was valid, and it imposed the two-year suspension. After about eight months, Reynolds succeeded in getting the suspension lifted so he could compete in the U.S. Olympic trials, but the IAAF did not allow him to participate in the Olympics.

Reynolds again sued the IAAF in the Southern District of Ohio for breach of contract, breach of due process, defamation, and interference with business relations. This time he sought monetary damages rather than the right to compete. The IAAF refused to respond, claiming that this court did not have legal authority over the international organization. With no case from the defense, the district judge ruled in Reynolds's favor, awarding him damages of $27,356,008. Only when the court started to collect the award from four corporations associated with the IAAF did the federation submit a motion to quash the award. After the district court denied the motion, the IAAF appealed the decision.

Legal Issues

In one sense, the key legal issue concerned the jurisdiction or legal authority of an Ohio court over an international sports association. At the same time, however, it also concerned the ability of an international sports organization to ban a U.S. athlete from competition. Since the American governing organization had cleared Reynolds, the ban by the IAAF exerted control by an international organization over American selections for the Olympic Games. Reynolds, a U.S. citizen who lived in Ohio, claimed that U.S. courts should limit the actions taken by the IAAF. The court could not overturn his suspension, which he had already completed, but it could set a precedent and award damages.

To make his case against the IAAF, Reynolds had to prove that a U.S. court should have jurisdiction over a foreign association. He argued that the

IAAF, despite its London location, is in principle an organization in all states where its members reside. Because of Reynolds's residence, the IAAF in essence had a presence in Ohio. He also noted that Ohio law applies to parties transacting business in the state, and the IAAF had in fact transacted business with Reynolds through the mail. The relationship between Reynolds and the IAAF thus allowed Ohio courts to properly hear the suit. The courts could then address the core allegation: The IAAF acted improperly in suspending Reynolds, publicly announcing his drug test results, and interfering with his business dealings.

In its defense, the IAAF focused on the jurisdictional issues rather than the substance of the allegations. It argued that there had been no intent to transact business in Ohio. Merely sending letters to the plaintiff at an Ohio address did not represent the kind of substantial contact that would make the IAAF subject to the laws of Ohio. The IAAF did release a statement to the press reporting the results of the test but did not single out Ohio for the announcement. Otherwise, the key activities involving Reynolds took place elsewhere: The urine test was taken in Monaco, the sample analyzed in Paris, and the hearing held in England. Giving legal power to an Ohio court in this case would override international sports agreements and make international associations subject to the laws of thousands of local courts.

Decision

The appeals court sided with the defendants in concluding that the IAAF should not be subject to an Ohio suit. The decision cited Supreme Court precedent that contact between a local and an out-of-state party did not by itself give the local court jurisdiction. Rather, some degree of past negotiation and expectation of future cooperation are needed, something absent in the dealings between Reynolds and the IAAF. Perhaps, for example, a race sponsored by the IAAF in Ohio that included Reynolds as a participant would make for "substantial contact," but sending letters did not. The ruling allowed Reynolds to bring suit in London, the location of the IAAF, but it overturned the district court decision awarding Reynolds damages.

Impact

Along with depriving Reynolds of a rich financial award, the case affirmed the power of sports organizations to punish athletes. It gave international sporting organization at least partial independence from judicial decisions within individual countries. Another case, *Barnes v. TAC*, gave national sporting agencies the opportunity to resolve disputes under its own rules before going to court. The Reynolds case similarly gave international sporting agencies some freedom from U.S. courts in dealing with disputes. The ruling did not consider the disagreement over the validity of the drug test or the fairness of the punishment. In practice, though, it allowed the IAAF and the IOC more generally to set their own rules for drug testing and punishment.

Federal District Court Decisions

ELIZABETH O'HALLORAN AND ALAN BURCH V. THE UNIVERSITY OF WASHINGTON, ET AL., 679 F. SUPP. 997 (1988)

Background

While a member of the University of Washington track team, Elizabeth O'Halloran successfully sued the university in state court over its drug-testing program. Because the NCAA required universities to test athletes, it became one of the defendants and the case moved to federal district court. The original verdict in the state court against the University of Washington was then dismissed, but the university remained as a defendant with the NCAA in the federal court case. According to NCAA policy, athletes competing in intercollegiate sports must sign a statement agreeing, among other things, to be tested for banned drugs. At the time, the testing typically occurred only at championship events, but signing the consent form allowed for testing at other times.

When the plaintiff refused to sign the form, University of Washington athletic administrators did not let her compete with the track team. Her suit in federal court asked for an injunction—a legal ruling to prevent the University of Washington from enforcing the drug-testing policy. O'Halloran had not been suspended for a positive test or even asked to take a test, but she objected to having to sign the consent form and agree to a possible future test. A University of Washington rower, Alan Burch, later joined in the action. The university felt forced to follow NCAA rules about signing a consent form, as it would otherwise face NCAA punishment. The NCAA opposed the motion for an injunction on more substantive grounds.

Legal Issues

The case for an injunction depended on the answers to two questions. First, did the plaintiff face undue hardship in being suspended while the case was being considered? Second, did the plaintiff's claim that the testing requirement was unconstitutional have merit? Relief from the suspension should be allowed if the hardship was severe and the merit was strong. The plaintiff made a case for both points.

In terms of hardship, the plaintiff argued that without an injunction, the wait for a trial would make her miss the sophomore year of eligibility for the track team. The time lost from training under the guidance of her coach would permanently harm her career. The University of Washington and the NCAA responded that they would face the greater hardship from an injunction. Even while suspended from competing in track events, O'Halloran could still practice with the team, work with the coach, and use the facilities. With an injunction, however, the NCAA could do little to enforce its current drug policy. If the plaintiff could compete without consenting to take drug tests, then so could other athletes. Freedom to opt out of the testing would compromise the ability to keep drugs out of college athletes.

In terms of merit, the plaintiff argued that the drug-testing program interfered with her Fourth Amendment rights to be free from government interference in her privatelife. Signing the consent form would allow the university to interfere with her privacy in several ways: by observing urination to obtain a sample, by requiring information on legal but privately taken drugs such as birth control pills and depression medications, and by searching for illegal drugs in the urine without probable cause. According to the plaintiff, the drug testing program violated Fourth Amendment protection against unreasonable searches.

The NCAA denied that the Fourth Amendment had bearing on its program. While the amendment protects citizens against state searches, previous court decisions had designated the NCAA as a private rather than a government entity. Because the NCAA is not part of the government, its requirement for preseason consent to perform drug tests does not violate the U.S. Constitution. Even if viewed as acting on behalf of the government, the NCAA still argued that its program did not violate the Constitution. The drug tests did not involve highly personal family matters like abortion and were not required of all students. Those who wanted to avoid the test could simply withdraw from college athletics.

Decision

In denying the request for an injunction, District Court Judge Walter T. McGovern ruled in favor of the defendants. He found the hardship faced by the NCAA from an injunction would exceed that faced by O'Halloran and other athletes from suspension. Even if suspended from competition for not signing the consent form, O'Halloran could still train in ways that would help her athletic career. Under an injunction, however, the ability of the NCAA to control drug use by all athletes—a goal of broader importance than the plaintiff's participation in athletic events—would be impaired. More important, the judge ruled that the NCAA policy was not a state action that involved the Fourth Amendment. Even if it were, the judge did not find the claim that the search violated O'Halloran's privacy a convincing one. The inconvenience of giving a urine sample was minor compared to the compelling interest of the NCAA and the university in protecting athletes from the harm of drug use, ensuring fair competition, and creating an environment opposed to drug use in sports. As a result, the decision concluded that the merit of the plaintiff's case did not justify an injunction.

Impact

Setting the stage for other cases to come, this decision gave the NCAA and college sports teams the right to test athletes for drugs. The judge fully accepted arguments presented by the NCAA about the importance of drug testing to the integrity of college sport. By removing the debate over drug testing in colleges from constitutional issues, the decision allowed the NCAA to keep its current policies in place and expand them in years to come.

NATIONAL FOOTBALL LEAGUE PLAYERS ASSOCIATION V. NATIONAL FOOTBALL LEAGUE, 724 F. SUPP. 1027 (1989)

Background

In 1989, the National Football League Players Association (NFLPA) sought to block enforcement of the National Football League (NFL) drug testing policy. At the time, the policy involved urine tests that, if positive, led to a 30-day suspension. After publicly announcing the results of its most recent tests, the league suspended several players for the 30-day period. The NFLPA filed a grievance, requesting that the court reinstate the players and stop the league from further suspending players based on the test results.

Legal Issues

In claiming that the NFL drug policy violated the contract between owners and players, the NFLPA brought its case against the policy to arbitration. However, the existing arbitration process for dealing with disputes would take months. In the meantime, the NFLPA wanted the court to delay enforcement of the policy and reinstate the suspended players. The union worried that suspending players before the arbitration decision would unnecessarily and permanently harm their careers. A 30-day absence during the season would make it hard for a player to return successfully to the team and resume his career. If the suspension could in essence end a player's career, it should not begin until an arbitrator had declared the policy and punishment to be fair. If the arbitration ruled against the NFL policy, the suspended player would have been wrongly punished. Such a ruling might be a victory for a player but would have little value once he had already served the punishment.

In opposition to the motion, the NFL pointed to a U.S. law that restricted courts from interfering in private labor disputes such as this one between players and owners. The law allowed exceptions in rare cases in which a court order would correct flaws in the arbitration process. However, the plaintiffs presented no evidence of the unfairness of the ongoing process involving NFL players and owners. The NFL believed it had the right to settle the dispute on its own.

Decision

Judge Aubrey E. Robinson, Jr., of the U.S. District Court of the District of Columbia rejected the request to stop enforcement of the NFL drug-testing policy. He concluded that the plaintiffs did not make a sufficiently strong case of irreparable harm to suspended players that would justify an exception to U.S. law. Players suspended for 30 days, even if the arbitrator ended up siding with the players, would not be permanently harmed—they routinely returned to play without much trouble after missing more than 30 days from injury. If arbitration favored the players, then they would receive back pay and reinstatement to make up for their suspension. If arbitration favored the league, the players would have rightfully served their punishment. Under these circumstances, the judge agreed with the NFL that courts should not interfere in the ongoing dispute.

Impact

As illustrated by this case, courts have been reluctant to enter into disputes between athletes and sports leagues over drug testing. The ruling did not consider the fairness of the drug-testing policy or approve the suspensions. It instead left the issue to private arbitration and negotiation rather than to the courts. With the decision, the NFL and players union would agree in years to come on more stringent testing policies and could do so without worrying that the courts would overturn the agreement.

The Law and Drugs and Sports

ERIC RANDOLPH BARNES V. INTERNATIONAL AMATEUR ATHLETIC FEDERATION, THE ATHLETICS CONGRESS OF THE UNITED STATES OF AMERICA, AND WEST VIRGINIA ASSOCIATION/TAC, 862 F. SUPP. 1537 (1993)

Background

On August 7, 1990, world-record holder in the shot put, Eric "Randy" Barnes, tested positive for a banned steroid. Based on their policies, three major track and field organizations—the International Amateur Athletic Federation (IAAF), the Athletics Congress of the United States (TAC), and the West Virginia Association of the Athletic Congress (WVA/TAC)—suspended Barnes from competition for two years. In a West Virginia state court, Barnes sued to block the suspension and to compete in the 1992 U.S. Olympic trials. The state court agreed, ordering the organizations to allow Barnes to compete in the upcoming trials.

Along with having requested relief from the suspension, Barnes sought monetary damages. He claimed that the track and field organizations violated his rights to due process by acting arbitrarily and capriciously, failing to follow procedures for drug tests and punishments, and preventing him from disputing the drug findings. He also alleged libel because the IAAF and TAC released news to the media of, in his view, a false positive drug test. The negative publicity interfered in his business dealings and caused loss of income.

The TAC successfully filed a petition to shift the case from the state to the federal district court. In taking the case, the U.S. District Court dissolved the restraining order approved earlier by the state court. This decision in effect reinstated Barnes's suspension and kept him from trying out for the 1992 Olympics until the case was resolved. It further dismissed the claims against the IAAF, leaving the TAC and WVA/TAC as defendants. Given its status as an international organization and location in London, the IAAF did not fall under the authority of U.S. courts.

Legal Issues

The TAC and WVA/TAC asked to dismiss the plaintiff's complaint on two grounds. First, they argued that Barnes had failed to exhaust all the remedies available to him through the TAC. The suit should not jump to a state or federal court without first following procedures offered by the sports association to deal with disputes over drug tests. In support of this claim, the Amateur Sports Act (ASA) of 1978 gave exclusive control over eligibility of athletes to the U.S. Olympic Committee (USOC) and its governing bodies

101

such as the TAC. The USOC constitution and TAC bylaws spelled out steps to resolve disputes, including binding arbitration. According to the defendants, the courts had no legal power to overturn the TAC decision until Barnes first went through these steps. If the court intervened before the agencies had completed all appeals, it would give parties little reason to follow association rules. Unless Barnes convinced the appeals board or an arbitrator of the errors in his tests, he violated rules about drug use and deserved suspension.

Barnes argued in opposition that the ASA did not prevent him from using all possible means to resolve his dispute. In fact, sometimes the courts rather than the TAC can best decide a case. Barnes believed the TAC had shown bias against him that would make an administrative hearing unfair and an appeal almost certain to be rejected. Worse, a negative decision made by the TAC might make it harder to get a fair trial later.

The legal dispute thus hinged on interpretations of the ASA. The act gave exclusive jurisdiction or authority over participation of U.S. athletes in the Olympics to the USOC and affiliate groups such as the TAC. As required by law, the USOC then set up procedures to resolve disputes within its administrative structure and offered arbitration when outcomes did not satisfy the parties. Given the law, courts must have strong reasons to take priority over an agency. For example, an athlete could go to court rather than follow the appeals procedures within an organization when the procedures appeared biased or inadequate. Otherwise, the courts must try to balance the need to maintain the authority of sports organizations with the need to protect the rights of individual athletes. The plaintiff needed to show that he had good reason to question the authority of the TAC.

Decision

The district judge, John T. Copenhaver, Jr., ruled in favor of the defendants, TAC and WVA/TAC, by dismissing the complaint Barnes made against the organizations. The ruling stated that athletes had the opportunity to resolve disputes through several channels offered by the TAC. According to the ASA, these channels should be used first. Under special circumstances, the judge could override the normal process, but the plaintiff failed to prove the conditions existed to justify this action. He did not demonstrate that the TAC and WVA/TAC had already reached a decision on a possible appeal or that the process was pointless. Nor did the plaintiff give evidence that going through existing procedures would cause an unacceptable delay. Since Barnes failed to exhaust other procedures, the ASA prevented the court from hearing the case.

The Law and Drugs and Sports

Impact

The details of this particular dispute—whether Barnes used steroids, the governing sports bodies acted improperly, or Barnes deserved to participate in the Olympics—had little importance for the decision. In fact, the court did not even consider the merits of Barnes's accusations about the drug test. Rather, the decision gave priority to the governing sports bodies rather than the courts in evaluating the claims. Like other decisions, this one reaffirmed the authority of sports organizations to set rules for drug use, require testing of athletes, and punish violators with suspensions. Even if courts reached decisions different from sports organizations on issues of privacy, due process, and fairness of testing, they needed to give sports organizations a chance to deal with disputes first. Athletes might prefer going to court rather than to an administrative hearing, but under this ruling they have little choice in the matter.

TERRY LONG V. THE NATIONAL FOOTBALL LEAGUE, PAUL TAGLIABUE, PITTSBURGH STEELERS SPORTS, THE CITY OF PITTSBURGH, 870 F. SUPP. 101 (1994)

Background

While a member of the NFL Pittsburgh Steelers, Terry Long tested positive for steroids. Based on its policy, the NFL suspended him. Long then sued the NFL, the Pittsburgh Steelers, and the city of Pittsburgh on the grounds that the test violated his constitutional rights under the Fourth Amendment, Fourteenth Amendment, and the Pennsylvania Constitution. The defendants presented a motion to dismiss the complaint because it lacked facts to support its claims. The judge considered the motion to dismiss.

Legal Issues

The relevance of drug testing to the Fourth Amendment, which prohibits the government from unreasonable searches, raises some complex legal issues (see *Vernonia v. Acton*). In this case, however, the issue was more specific and straightforward: Does the Fourth Amendment apply to the NFL? The amendment limits the action of government or state agents rather than private parties. When done as part of an agreement between employers and employees, searches without a warrant or cause are constitutional. In deciding on Long's complaint, then, the court needed to consider whether the NFL policy took the form of a state action. Previous courts had ruled that action by a private organization might involve the state when (1) a condition of interdependence existed between the two, or

(2) the government had control over the actions of the private organizations. Without such interdependence or control, professional athletes could not appeal to the Constitution for relief from testing. They would instead have to resolve the disputes within the private organization through arbitration or collective bargaining.

Long argued that the interests of the NFL and Pittsburgh Steelers were closely linked to the city of Pittsburgh. The city collected taxes on Steelers tickets, provided municipal services to the team, issued bonds for construction of the stadium, and appointed stadium board members. According to the plaintiff, the financial gain to the city from the team and the financial gain to the team from the city defined interdependence. Through its control over the stadium, the city also had control over actions of the Steelers and their drug testing.

The defendants argued that despite business relationships with the city, the team did not depend on the city or become subject to control by the city. Merely having a relationship does not translate into control and dependence in sports any more than a relationship between a building owner and a business renting space does. To the contrary, the city had little if any influence on the decision making of the Steelers or the NFL. The league developed the drug testing policy without consulting the city of Pittsburgh, and the lab tests done for the league had no connection to the city.

Decision

The judge dismissed the plaintiff's complaint alleging violations of the Fourth and Fourteenth Amendments and the Pennsylvania Constitution. Judge Donald E. Zigler concluded that the plaintiff failed to show drug testing and player suspension done by private parties could be attributed to the state. The constitutional protections from unreasonable search and seizure therefore did not extend to NFL players.

Impact

Like the *National Football League Players Association v. the National Football League*, the district court affirmed the right of league owners and players to set up mandatory drug tests. Although the government must have probable cause before requiring certain drug tests, private organizations such as the NFL do not. The issue falls under the negotiations that occur between players and owners, and players had for many years opposed comprehensive testing. Yet, after collective bargaining led to an agreement between the league and the union, individual players could not dispute the legality of drug tests on constitutional grounds. Once again, the courts affirmed the rights of professional sports leagues to perform suspicionless drug tests.

United States of America v. Victor Conte, James Valente, Greg Anderson, and Remi Korchemny, No. CR 04-0044 SI (2004)

Background

The four defendants in this case were indicted on February 12, 2004, by federal investigators for several charges: conspiracy to distribute and to possess with intent to distribute anabolic steroids, conspiracy to defraud through misbranded drugs, and money laundering. The investigation and indictment of defendant Conte received much publicity because of his relationship with famous athletes such as Barry Bonds, Marion Jones, and Bill Romanowski. Suspicions that his company, Bay Area Laboratory Cooperative, (BALCO), gave undetectable steroids such as THG to sports stars raised awareness about drugs in sports. Of those prosecuted under the 1990 Anabolic Steroid Control Act by the government for distributing steroids, Conte had become the most famous. The other defendants included a BALCO executive (Valente), a track coach (Korchemny), and trainer (Anderson).

Legal Issues

The defendants moved to dismiss the charges against them on a variety of grounds. Conte, Valente, and Anderson alleged outrageous government conduct when information about the investigation was released to the media. Valente and Conte alleged that excessive pretrial publicity about the case made it impossible for them to get a fair hearing. And all defendants alleged in one form or another that the government gathered evidence in illegal ways. The motions said that the government agents had invalid search warrants, used excessive force in the searches, and wrongly obtained statements from the defendants. The U.S. government lawyers prosecuting the case denied the allegations. Before the case could go to trial, the judge would have to rule on the motions to dismiss the indictments.

Decision

Clearing the way for a trial, U.S. District Judge Susan Illston denied all motions to dismiss the indictments (but did allow for hearings on the acceptability of some of the evidence). Concerning the allegation of outrageous government conduct, she found no evidence that government prosecutors released private grand jury testimony to the public. One former state law enforcement officer wrote an article about the case that may have contained sensitive information, but the government did not approve that action. The defendants thus failed to demonstrate outrageous conduct.

Concerning the allegation of excessive pretrial publicity, the judge could not justify dismissal of the indictments merely because they attracted considerable media interest. Even if the government had, as wrongly alleged by the defendants, caused the pretrial publicity, it still would not justify dismissal. Instead, a change in location of the trial, a continuation until the publicity receded, or careful interviews of possible jurors about negative media coverage would be appropriate remedies.

Concerning the allegations that government agents obtained information improperly, the judge again rejected requests to dismiss charges. The defendants claimed that searches made of their e-mail and BALCO offices lacked probable cause, but the judge found the warrants for the searches to be accurate and properly approved. The defendants claimed that the agents used excessive force in entering with their guns drawn, but the judge ruled such action was appropriate until the offices had been secured. The defendants claimed they were not informed of their Miranda rights to remain silent when questioned during search of the offices, but the judge ruled that such rights are required only after suspects are taken into custody. A hearing could determine if the agents actually had taken the defendants into custody at the time of questioning and if some of the evidence should be suppressed. This provided no justification to dismiss charges.

Impact

With the motion to dismiss charges against the BALCO defendants rejected by the judge, the case could go forward (and hearings about appropriate evidence could proceed). Given the strong case against them, the defendants decided to plead guilty to reduced charges rather than risk harsher sentences from a jury trial. In return for guilty pleas, Conte was sentenced to four months in jail and four months in house arrest, Valente to probation, and Anderson to three months in jail and three months in house arrest. Korchemny has been sentenced to one year of probation.

On one hand, these sentences represent a step toward stopping use of drugs in sports. Imprisoning dealers who distributed steroids to professional and Olympic athletes should discourage others from doing the same. On the other hand, the sentences are short and exclude the athletes who used the steroids. The punishment may not be severe enough to scare those wanting to sell and take performance-enhancing drugs.

State Court Decisions

JENNIFER HILL ET AL. V. NATIONAL COLLEGIATE ATHLETIC ASSOCIATION, BOARD OF TRUSTEES OF LELAND STANFORD JUNIOR UNIVERSTIY, 7 CAL. 4TH 1; 865 P.2D 633; 26 CAL. RPTR. 2D 834 (1994)

Background

Jennifer Hill and other student-athletes at Stanford University challenged the university's drug-testing policy in 1987 by suing the NCAA. The drug-testing program required students to sign a form consenting to tests for banned drugs at the time of a championship event or post-season football game. A minimum 90-day suspension followed from a positive test or refusal to consent to a test. The plaintiffs contended that these drug-testing procedures violated the right to privacy guaranteed by the California Constitution. They asked for an injunction to make the NCAA and Stanford University stop the testing (although Stanford University later joined the plaintiff in the suit against the NCAA). The state court ruled in favor of the plaintiffs, finding that the NCAA policy invaded the privacy of the students and requiring that the NCAA end mandatory testing. After an appeals court upheld the lower court decision, the California Supreme Court considered the case.

Legal Issues

As listed in Article I, section 1 of the California Constitution, "All people are by nature free and independent and have inalienable rights. Among these are enjoying and defending life and liberty, acquiring, possessing, and protecting property, and pursuing and obtaining safety, happiness, and privacy." The last phrase "and privacy" was added to the constitution on November 7, 1972, by California voters concerned about potential loss of privacy rights. Based on this wording, the court needed to decide if the article governed the conduct of a private organization such as the NCAA and if the drug testing invaded the privacy of the athletes.

The plaintiffs argued that the California Constitution aimed to protect state residents from invasion of privacy by both public and private entities. Although the Fourth Amendment to the U.S. Constitution prohibits unreasonable search and seizure by state agents, the California Constitution extends that protection. When adding the right to privacy to their constitution, Californians had worried that private businesses might misuse information obtained from credit cards, banking records, and computers. The NCAA similarly had access to a variety of personal information on students and, like other businesses, should not abuse the constitutional right to privacy.

According to the plaintiffs, drug testing was just the kind of interference with personal privacy from which citizens needed protection. It required athletes to disrobe and urinate in front of monitors, answer embarrassing questions about use of birth control pills, and possibly reveal confidential medical information. If the NCAA wanted to stop drug use, they should do something other than to test athletes who have given no sign of using performance-enhancing drugs.

The NCAA disagreed, first arguing that the article in the California Constitution did not apply to the activities of private organizations. Even if the right to privacy did protect citizens from its actions, the NCAA argued that drug testing brought many benefits to athletics and athletes. It helped safeguard the integrity of the sport from unfair competition and from increased health risks of athletes who used drugs. In this way, preventing drug use was a compelling public need that must be balanced with other needs for individual privacy.

In return for these benefits, the drug test imposed only modestly on the athletes. Participation in sports already requires loss of privacy since athletes undergo special physical exams, share locker room space, and are observed closely by coaches and trainers. Advance notice of the rules against use of substances on the banned list and the nature of the test to come helped athletes know what to expect. The test itself would come as less of a surprise and less of an intrusion on their privacy. If athletes, despite the special conditions that lessen their expectation of privacy on sports teams, still object to the test, they need not participate in college athletics. Such participation is not a legal right, and it is reasonable to follow rules set up by a democratically governed agency that governs college sports.

Decision

By a vote of 4-3, the California Supreme Court sided with the defendants in overturning the lower court rulings. The decision agreed with the plaintiffs that the constitutional right to privacy applied to private entities such as the NCAA but otherwise sided with the NCAA defendant. It concluded that drug testing did not involve a major violation of privacy because athletes already expected reduced privacy when participating in sports. If some athletes felt otherwise, the advance notice reduced the intrusion and gave them the option to withdraw from sports. Given that the tests contributed in important ways to the integrity of college sports, the requirement seemed reasonable under California law. The dissenting judges disagreed with the majority, but the close vote still allowed drug testing to continue at Stanford University and other colleges in California.

Impact

The failure of this challenge to athlete drug testing in California meant that other legal challenges would likely fail as well. The nature of the case gave the plaintiffs advantages in making their claims that they would not have in federal court or other state courts. Unlike the U.S. Constitution, the California Constitution has an explicitly stated right to privacy that applies to private organizations. This provision made it more difficult for the NCAA to prove its case than elsewhere, and the NCAA had in fact lost in two lower court rulings. However, the California Supreme Court ruling in favor of NCAA drug testing, along with other federal rulings such as the *O'Halloran v. the University of Washington*, makes drug testing a permanent part of college athletics.

---

[1] Charles E. Petit, "Form Over Substances: The Legal Context of Performance-Enhancing Substances," in Michael S. Bahrke and Charles E. Yesalis, eds., *Performance-Enhancing Substances in Sport and Exercise*. Champaign, Ill.: Human Kinetics, 2002, p. 341.

[2] "United States Amateur Sports Act." Available online. URL: http://www.whitewaterslalom.org/rules/asa-1978.html. Downloaded in January 2006.

[3] "United States Amateur Sports Act."

[4] Drug Enforcement Administration, "Steroids," 1990–1994. Available online. URL: http://www.dea.gov/pubs/history/1990–1994.html. Downloaded in January 2006.

[5] Carol Cole Kleinman and C. E. Petit, "Legal Aspects of Anabolic Steroid Use and Abuse," in Charles E. Yesalis, ed., *Anabolic Steroids in Sport and Exercise*. Campaign, Ill.: Human Kinetics, 2000, p. 346

[6] Charles E. Yesalis and Virginia S. Cowart, *The Steroids Game*. Champaign, Ill.: Human Kinetics, 1998, p. 107.

[7] Quoted in Kleinman and Petit, "Legal Aspects," p. 346.

[8] Amy Shipley, "Chemists Stay a Step Ahead of Drug Testers," *Washington Post*, October 18, 2005, p. E1.

[9] Rick Collins, *Legal Muscle: Anabolics in America*. East Meadow, N.Y.: Legal Muscle Publishing, 2002, pp. 400–401.

CHAPTER 3

CHRONOLOGY

This chronology of significant events in the relationship between drugs and sports lists scientific discoveries, new testing policies, and instances of performance-enhancing drug use that have shaped the current state of the problem in the United States and internationally.

1849

- German professor A. A. Berthold finds that castrating roosters and surgically implanting the testes into their abdomens maintains male sex characteristics such as the size and color of the red combs on their heads. He correctly reasons that male hormones from the testes are released into the blood.

1865

- Swimmers in an Amsterdam canal race are accused of taking unnamed drugs to improve performance.

1887

- Chemists synthesize the first amphetamine, a drug that stimulates the brain and central nervous system to increase energy and alertness. After improvements are made over the next several decades, the drug would become popular among athletes trying to perform better in sporting events.

1889

- The term *dop*, referring to the use of a narcotic mixture to improve the performance of racehorses, first appears in an English dictionary. *Doping* would later come to refer to the use of drugs by humans to improve sporting performance.
- French scientist Charles Edouard Brown-Sequard injects himself with a mixture of substances extracted from the testicles of dogs and guinea pigs.

He claims, wrongly as it turns out, that the extract improved his physical and mental energy.

1896

- The first modern Olympic Games are held in Athens, Greece.
- Two Austrian scientists, Oskar Zoth and Fritz Pregl, inject themselves with the extract of bull testicles and then observe the consequences. They conclude that the extract increased muscular strength and suggest that athletes adopt it as a training tool.

1904

- Thomas Hicks, the U.S. winner of the marathon at the Olympic Games, collapses at the finish of the race. He survives, but his handlers admit to giving him strychnine and brandy during the race to keep him going.

1926

- Two U.S. scientists at the University of Chicago, Fred C. Koch and Lemuel C. McGee, isolate a small amount of a hormone from 40 pounds of bull testicles that, when injected in small amounts, returns atrophied male sex characteristics (such as the red comb) to castrated roosters. The experiment documents the existence of a male sex hormone.

1935

- Dutch professor and scientist Ernst Laquer determines the chemical structure of the male hormone found in bull testicles and names it testosterone.
- A Yugoslav chemist, Leopold Ruzicka, and a German chemist, Adolf Butenandt, independently synthesize human testosterone, for which they both will receive the 1939 Nobel Prize in chemistry. Testosterone created in the lab will be used to treat men with inadequate testosterone and, ultimately, to improve athletic performance.
- Scientists discover ways to chemically change synthesized testosterone so that it can be administered via pills or injection. Pure testosterone breaks down in the body and is excreted before getting to the muscles, bones, and organs. Synthetic and chemically modified forms of testosterone become known as anabolic steroids.

1938

- Synthetic testosterone is classified as a prescription drug that comes under control of the Food, Drug, and Cosmetic Act and the Food and

Drug Administration (FDA). As with other prescription drugs, the FDA begins working with states to determine who can legally prescribe and dispense anabolic steroids.

1945

■ In his book, *The Male Hormone*, U.S. writer Paul de Kruif claims remarkable performance benefits, including the growth of muscle, from using synthetic testosterone.

1952

■ At the Winter Olympics in Oslo, Norway, several speed skaters become ill and need medical care to recover from excess amphetamine pills. The incident represents one of the first documented uses of the drug in sports competition.
■ At the Summer Olympics in Helsinki, Finland, Soviet weightlifters win seven medals, creating suspicions that their accomplishments somehow came from use of artificial hormones.

1955

■ Five of 25 urine samples taken from participants in a bicycle race test positive for stimulants.

1956

■ At the World Games in Moscow, the team physician for U.S. weightlifters, Dr. John Zigler, witnesses Soviet athletes taking steroids.

1960

■ In the Summer Olympics in Rome, Knut Jensen, a Danish cyclist, collapses, fractures his skull, and dies during the road race. Tests disclose the presence of amphetamines in his blood.
■ Dr. John Zigler gives a new anabolic steroid product called Dianabol (manufactured by Ciba Pharmaceutical Company) to three U.S. weightlifters, who will become national champions.

1961

■ The International Olympic Committee (IOC), a nonprofit organization that supervises the Summer and Winter Olympic Games, sets up a medical commission to investigate doping among athletes and make recommendations on the steps needed to stop the problem.

Chronology

1964

■ At its meeting in Tokyo, the IOC condemns doping, agrees to have athletes sign a pledge of no drug use, asks national organizing committees to make their athletes available for drug tests, and threatens to punish those committees found to promote drug use.

1967

■ Tommy Simpson, a British cyclist in the Tour de France, dies during the race due to complications related to amphetamine use.
■ Jacques Anquetil, a five-time winner of the Tour de France, admits to the long-standing and widespread use of stimulants by bicycle racers. He says, "Since we are constantly asked to go faster and to make even greater efforts, we are obliged to take stimulants."
■ The IOC Medical Commission begins making plans for drug testing at the next Olympic Games (the 1968 Olympics in Mexico City).

1968

■ Contributing to publicity about the dangers of stimulants, a French soccer player and French cyclist both die from amphetamine complications.
■ The IOC Medical Commission begins taking urine samples of randomly selected participants in the Summer Olympics in Mexico City. The banned substances that the tests seek to find include alcohol, stimulants, cocaine, hashish, vasodilators (that cause the blood vessels to expand), and opiates such as morphine, heroin, or opium (but not steroids).
■ Swedish entrant in the modern pentathlon Hans-Gunnar Liljenwall tests positive for excessive alcohol and becomes the first Olympic athlete disqualified for drug use.

1969

■ Journalist Bil Gilbert brings the growing problem of drug use in sports to the attention of the public with three articles published in *Sports Illustrated*. Among many other examples, he writes that almost every team in the National Football League (NFL) and American Football League (AFL) has players who take steroids.

1970

■ At the Weightlifting World Championships held in Columbus, Ohio, tests of the medal winners reveal that several had used stimulants, but the International Weightlifting Federation decides to reject the tests and reinstate the medals for the winners. The incident illustrates the difficulties of enforcing drug policies.

- The Controlled Substances Act (CSA) classifies all drugs regulated by the federal government into one of five schedules. The act includes amphetamines as a dangerous Schedule II drug but does not define steroids and many other performance-enhancing drugs as controlled substances.

1971

- U.S. weightlifting champion Ken Patera publicly discloses his steroid use. After having lost to Russian Vasily Alexeev the previous year, he accuses his competitor of having used steroids and promises to do the same in the 1972 Olympic Games.
- With the publication of *Ball Four,* a best-selling book detailing his 1969 Major League Baseball (MLB) season, pitcher Jim Bouton tells of the use by players of greenies—a slang term for amphetamine pills or speed.

1972

- U.S. swimmer and gold medal winner at the Munich Olympics, 16-year-old Rick DeMont, tests positive for ephedrine, a drug legitimately used to treat asthma but banned for its stimulating properties. After having his medal revoked, DeMont unsuccessfully appeals the decision, arguing that he used the medicine for his asthma.
- At the Munich Olympics, East Germany wins 66 medals, a stunning improvement from the 25 medals it won in 1968 and a step toward winning 90 medals in 1976. The remarkable Olympic success of East German competitors and the mannish characteristics of some of its female athletes lead to accusations of steroid use.

1973

- English scientists identify ways to find evidence of steroids in urine. The tests do not search for testosterone or steroids directly but look for byproducts excreted in the urine that come from the body's metabolism of steroids. However, the method requires expensive and complex equipment for chemical analysis that few labs have available.

1976

- At the Olympic Track and Field Trials in Eugene, Oregon, 23 U.S. athletes fail drug tests.
- At the Montreal Olympics, tests for steroid byproducts in urine samples of athletes are done for the first time. Eight athletes out of 275 tested show positive results for steroids.

Chronology

- At the Montreal Olympics, television announcers mention rumors that Finnish long-distance distance runner Lasse Viren had used blood doping. Nothing more than his gold medal victories in two strenuous running events, the 5,000- and 10,000-meter races, led to the allegations, but the publicity alerts others to the practice.

1977

- The American College of Sports Medicine states, "There is no conclusive scientific evidence that extremely large doses of anabolic-androgenic steroids either aid or hinder athletic performance." The organization would later change its position, but not until after it had created distrust among steroid users who saw clear evidence of the benefits of steroids.

1978

- Congress passes the Amateur Sports Act to restructure amateur sports and designate the U.S. Olympic Committee (USOC) as the governing body for the many separate amateur sports organizations that selected Olympic participants. Although the act states nothing about drug use, it gives the USOC authority to resolve disputes, which the committee will use to handle problems with drug testing.

1979

- The International Association of Athletics Federation, the world governing body for track and field, bans seven women athletes from Eastern European countries for positive drug tests.

1980

- At the Moscow Olympics, a new and informal test for steroid use developed by German scientist Manfred Donike reveals that 20 percent of those tested would fail. Rather than searching for the metabolites of anabolic steroids that disappear from the body quickly, his test screens for excessive testosterone that comes from outside the body.

1981

- The *Underground Steroid Handbook* by Daniel Duchaine begins to circulate among bodybuilders wanting to know more about how to use steroids. It cites the benefits of steroid use for bodybuilders, describes a variety of steroid products, and explains how to give injections, determine proper doses, and maximize muscle growth.

Drugs and Sports

1983

- At the Pan American Games in Venezuela, 15 athletes from 10 nations test positive for steroids. After hearing about a new steroid test used at the games, many other athletes leave before participating and undergoing the test.

1984

- At the Los Angeles Olympic Games, Thomas Johansson of Sweden, winner of the silver medal in Greco-Roman wrestling, becomes the first medal winner to test positive for steroids. Martti Vainio of Finland loses the silver medal he won in the 10,000-meter race because of a positive steroid test. However, only 15 of the 1,510 samples taken in the 1984 Los Angeles Olympics contain evidence of steroids, leading to the conclusion that athletes can hide their drug use from even the more sophisticated tests.
- As disclosed later by a team member, the U.S. cycling team uses blood doping to help win nine medals at the Los Angeles Olympics. About half the team received infusions of blood in a hotel room before their events. Although criticized for their actions, the cycling team members had not done anything illegal and received only minor punishment.
- The biotech company Amgen receives approval to manufacture a synthetic form of the hormone erythropoietin (EPO) to help treat patients with anemia or low red blood cell counts. The hormone, which stimulates the production of red blood cells in the bone marrow of the body, boosts levels in healthy athletes to a point that it helps their performance.
- The Court of Arbitration for Sport (CAS) is established as part of the IOC to resolve national and international athletic disputes without long and expensive legal battles in national courts. In years to come, it will deal with many disputes over the fairness of drug testing and punishment.

1985

- A Nashville court case involving the illegal sale and distribution of steroids lists 32 current and former Vanderbilt University football players as coconspirators (but does not charge them). The case points out the spread of steroids from professional sports to college sports.
- A survey done by the National Collegiate Athletic Association (NCAA) of college athletes (and then redone in 1989) finds football players to have the highest levels of drug use. They report usage of steroids at about 10 percent, amphetamines at about 7 percent, barbiturates and tranquilizers at about 3 percent, and major pain medications at about 37 percent.

- A federal trial involving recreational cocaine use by players on the Pittsburgh Pirates baseball team also uncovers evidence of amphetamine use during games.

1986

- After the 1984 Olympic scandal involving the U.S. cycling team, the IOC bans blood doping, even though it has no test for the practice. Only those who admit to the practice face punishment.
- A synthetic form of the human growth hormone (hGH) is produced using genetic technology. Although officially limited to use for children with a hormone deficiency and given only with a doctor's prescription, the synthetic hGH is purchased by athletes on the black market to build muscle.
- A new NFL drug policy states that "use of anabolic steroids and similar growth-enhancing substances is considered a violation of the NFL's drug program." A program of urine testing during preseason training camps will follow in the next year.
- The International Bodybuilding Federation (IBBF), the umbrella organization of national bodybuilding groups across the world, starts a program to randomly test bodybuilders who participate in competitions for drugs. Critics claim that the tests are done haphazardly and do little to eliminate use of steroids and other drugs from the sport.

1987

- After admitting to blood doping, American Kerry Lynch, a silver medal winner in Nordic skiing at the World Championships, loses his medal and is banned from competition for two years.
- A national survey of 3,400 male high school seniors finds that 6.6 percent had at one time taken steroids, a percentage that translates into hundreds of thousands of teen users. By all accounts, teens who want access to the drug have little trouble finding it.

1988

- The first suspected use of EPO to enhance performance occurs at the Winter Olympics in Calgary, Canada, among cross-country skiers.
- Canadian Ben Johnson, winner of the 100-meter race at the Seoul Summer Olympics, tests positive for the steroid stanozolol and is stripped of his medal. An investigation to follow finds that he has used steroids for many years. The incident publicizes the problem of steroid use in the Olympics, but Johnson is one of only four athletes to test positive for steroids at the games.

Drugs and Sports

- American Florence Griffith Joyner wins three gold medals at the Seoul Olympics, reaching a record time in the women's 100-meter race once thought impossible. Although many believe that she must have used steroids to run that fast, she consistently denies the accusation and passes all her drug tests.
- In a story in *Sports Illustrated*, a former college football player at the University of South Carolina, Tommy Chaikin, tells of his steroid use while on the team and the psychological damage it caused. He estimates that about half his teammates used steroids.
- The Anti-Drug Abuse Act makes it illegal to distribute anabolic steroids or possess steroids with the intent to distribute for purposes other than treatment of disease. Violators face up to three years in prison and a fine. However, the act does not make anabolic steroids a controlled substance.

1989

- The popular television show *60 Minutes* devotes a story to the spread of steroids and the risks they present to sports.
- At Senate hearings on steroid use in amateur and professional sports, NFL players and coaches testify—and disagree—about the extent of drug use in their sport. Their testimony and that of experts on steroid use among high school and college football players help publicize the problem and lead to anti-steroid legislation.
- The NFL toughens its drug policy by punishing those who test positive for steroids or masking agents. It suspends 13 players in the first year.

1990

- The current world-record holder in the 400 meters, Harry "Butch" Reynolds is suspended for a positive test for steroids. He claims that irregularities in the testing procedure might have allowed someone to tamper with his sample and the punishment violates his constitutional rights to due process. Although Reynolds sues and eventually wins his appeal of the suspension in U.S. courts, international authorities block him from participating in the Olympics.
- NFL player Lyle Alzado dies of brain cancer at age 43. Prior to his death, he attributed the disease to his use of steroids and hGH during his NFL career from 1969 to 1985.
- The Anabolic Steroid Control Act amends the CSA to add anabolic steroids to the list of Schedule III drugs. Manufacturers must now account for the products they make and prevent the diversion of the drug for nonmedical uses. Physicians can prescribe anabolic steroids for medical problems but not for performance or cosmetic reasons. The act makes

steroids harder to obtain and leads buyers to search out sources of the drugs from foreign countries.

1994

- The Dietary Supplement Health and Education Act (DSHEA) sets up procedures for the regulation of dietary supplements. Companies take advantage of the new law to manufacture and market steroid-related products such as androstenedione (or andro for short) as diet supplements rather than as performance-enhancing drugs.

1995

- An investigation into the extraordinary progress made by Chinese women swimmers in their performance times and the coinciding increase in positive tests for banned substances alleges that Chinese national authorities had established a program of drug use that includes use of payoffs to coaches of medal winners.
- Discouraged by the widespread use of drugs by athletes, Ralph Hale of the USOC says, "Our anti-doping campaign, I'm afraid, has been a failure to this point. Many countries have lost confidence in our anti-doping effort. I'm not sure we're doing the right job."
- Jessica Foschi, a U.S. swimmer in her early teens, tests positive for steroids but claims that the drug must have been given to her without her knowledge, perhaps as a way to sabotage her career. The U.S. Swimming Federation lifts her ban from competition, but the international swimming governing body refuses to do the same until an international court of arbitration rules in her favor.

1996

- Experts call the Atlanta Summer Olympics the "growth hormone games" because of suspicions of widespread use of hGH by athletes and the lack of a test for its presence in urine.
- Positive drug tests found from the use of an expensive, more sensitive high-resolution mass spectrometer at the Atlanta Olympics are not used. Officials want to have more experience with and confidence in the machine so that no athletes are falsely accused. Critics see the decision as a failure of will to eliminate drugs from the games.
- Mary Decker Slaney, a well-known U.S. middle-distance runner, tests positive for steroids but appeals her suspension. She argues that menstruation or alcohol consumption can skew the steroid test among women. Although experts disagree, USA Track and Field eventually lifts her suspension and drops the doping charges.

- Ken Caminiti of the San Diego Padres baseball team wins the Most Valuable Player Award after, as he later admits, taking steroids to improve his performance.

1998

- Florence Griffith Joyner dies unexpectedly from an epileptic seizure at the young age of 38, restarting rumors about past steroid and hGH use and how it harmed her health.
- Baseball player Mark McGwire shatters the single-season record by hitting 70 home runs as a member of the St. Louis Cardinals, and Sammy Sosa of the Chicago Cubs follows close behind by hitting 66 home runs (the previous record of 61 by Roger Maris had been in place since 1961). Although never proven, accusations suggest steroids have aided the record-setting performances.
- Mark McGwire admits to using andro, which at the time was legal and not banned by Major League Baseball (MLB), to improve his strength.
- French custom officials discover prescription drugs, narcotics, EPO, hGH, testosterone, and amphetamines in the car of Willy Voet, an assistant for Festina, a team competing in the Tour de France cycling race. The discovery leads to an investigation by French police that includes numerous riders from several teams. The discovery documents the widespread reliance on drugs by racers.
- Chinese swimmer Yuan Yuan is found to be carrying hGH in her luggage during travel to the world championships. The discovery indicates continued use of drugs by Chinese swimmers, a problem that had concerned Olympic authorities for many years.

1999

- The IOC establishes the World Anti-Doping Agency (WADA) to set up uniform standards for obtaining urine and blood samples, analyzing the samples for drugs, and imposing punishments on athletes who test positive. The agency also helps coordinate national efforts to follow those standards.
- Linford Christie of Great Britain, winner of the gold medal in the 100-meter race at the 1992 Barcelona Olympics, tests positive for nandrolone but is later cleared of all charges. Reflecting concerns about tests for this steroid, a disciplinary committee concludes that the positive test might actually have come from sources other than the drug.

2000

- *July 18:* Manfred Ewald, former East German Minister of Sport, and Manfred Hoeppner, former medical director of the East German Olympic program, are found guilty by a German court of contributing to the bodily harm of minors. The two set up a program of training for young East German athletes that included giving steroids, often without the knowledge of the athletes.

- *September:* The IOC first introduces tests for EPO at the Sydney Summer Olympics. The tests require positive results from separate examinations of both blood and urine, and none of the samples tested reach this standard, perhaps implying that the test is too strict.
- *September:* American Marion Jones wins five medals at the Summer Olympics in Sydney, earning her the informal titles of fastest woman and best woman athlete in the world. According to accusations that follow the games, however, her performance benefited from use of steroids and hGH.

2001

- *Spring:* MLB first requires drug testing of minor league players. Under the existing MLB collective bargaining agreement with the players association, however, it cannot do the same for major league players.
- *October 7:* Barry Bonds of the San Francisco Giants baseball team hits his 73rd home run of the season, breaking the record but doing so under suspicion that he has used steroids.

2002

- *August 7:* A new agreement between MLB owners and the players allows for preliminary, anonymous testing in the major leagues. Because the policy lacks penalties for offenders and off-season testing, critics say it is more a public-relations ploy than a real step forward.

2003

- *Summer:* A track and field coach anonymously tips off the U.S. Anti-Doping Agency about a new and, at the time, undetectable designer steroid called tetrahydrogestrinone or THG. With a sample of the drug in hand, U.S. authorities quickly develop a new test for THG and begin analyzing old urine samples for its presence.
- *July 15:* Taylor Hooton, a high school student who played for the school baseball team, commits suicide after secretly using steroids. His father, Don, blames the steroids for the unexpected death. He also blames famous athletes who influence teens by their use of steroids.
- *December 4:* In grand jury testimony, Barry Bonds admits to unintentionally using steroids called "the cream" and "the clear." He said his personal trainer provided the substances without telling him that they contained steroids and denied using any other performance-enhancing drugs.

Drugs and Sports

2004

- **January 20:** In his State of the Union Address, President George W. Bush criticizes the use of steroids and other performance-enhancing drugs in baseball, football, and other sports. He says it is dangerous and sends the wrong message to young people, and he calls on team owners, union representatives, coaches, and players to rid their sports of steroids.
- **March 10:** The Senate Commerce Committee holds hearings on use of steroids in major league baseball. In response to criticisms made by senators at the hearings, owners and players will propose a new testing policy and set of punishments.
- **March 12:** A published report documents an extraordinarily high death rate among professional wrestlers. Although not attributable precisely to use of steroids and other performance-enhancing drugs, the deaths and unexpected health problems are consistent with use of these drugs.
- **July:** The International Cycling Union toughens its testing procedures at the Tour de France. It now takes blood and urine samples from riders a month before the start of the race and from randomly selected riders after each stage of the race. It also uses increasingly sophisticated tests to identify abnormalities in the blood due to doping or EPO.
- **August:** Tests for hGH begin at the Summer Olympics in Athens. Despite beliefs about the common use of hGH by top athletes, no positive tests for the hormone turn up.
- **August:** A record 22 athletes—mostly from Eastern European nations—test positive for drug use at the Athens Olympics. Although the number seems low relative to suspected drug use, the increase encourages IOC officials about the effectiveness of their testing.
- **Fall:** The NCAA adds year-round or off-season drug testing for Division I schools. Each member institution may be selected once a year for randomly selected testing of 18 football players and 8 players from other sports.
- **September:** A few weeks after winning a gold medal in Athens, cyclist Tyler Hamilton tests positive for an illegal blood transfusion. The test leads to Hamilton's suspension from racing for two years.
- **October 22:** Passage of the Anabolic Steroid Control Act adds about two dozen steroid precursors such as androstenedione to the list of Schedule III controlled substances. Previously treated as dietary supplements that could be sold with few restrictions, the steroid precursors are made illegal without a valid prescription for medical purposes.
- **December 4:** Victor Conte, founder of BALCO, says on the television show *20/20* that he supplied steroids and other drugs to Marion Jones, American Tim Montgomery, and other Olympic athletes.

Chronology

2005

- *January 13:* A new agreement between MLB owners and the players union includes off-season random testing and suspension of 10 days for the first positive test, and then 30 days, 60 days, and one year for each subsequent positive test.

- *February 14:* Publication of the book *Juiced* by Jose Canseco creates a storm of publicity. The author names baseball players he knew or believed he knew to use steroids, including stars Mark McGwire, Sammy Sosa, and Rafael Palmeiro.

- *March 17:* The House Committee on Government Reform holds a hearing on steroid use in baseball that includes testimony from Jose Canseco, Mark McGwire, Sammy Sosa, Rafael Palmeiro, and other stars. Most of the players deny use of steroids or refuse to talk about their past behavior but still manage to hurt the image of professional baseball.

- *March 30:* A report comes out that three members of the NFL Carolina Panthers had received prescriptions for steroids only two weeks before they played in the January 2004 Super Bowl. None of the three had tested positive for steroids, at least for any known variants.

- *April 3:* Alex Sanchez of the Tampa Bay Devil Rays becomes the first MLB player suspended for a positive steroid test. Although he accepts the 10-day suspension, Sanchez denies having ever taken steroids and blames unknown ingredients in some over-the-counter drugs he bought.

- *April 21:* Minnesota Vikings running back Onterrio Smith is caught carrying a device called a whizzinator during a routine airport check. Advertised as a way to pass drug tests, the device uses a plastic bladder to pass clean urine through a fake penis.

- *April 30:* Heavyweight boxer James Toney tests positive for steroids after defeating his opponent John Ruiz in a championship match. Toney, who blamed the positive test on medication for an injured shoulder, loses his championship title, is banned for two years from competing for the title, and faces a suit from Ruiz for cheating.

- *May 19:* During a hearing of the House Committee on Government Reform, representatives criticize the National Basketball Association (NBA) for its weak drug testing policy. Stung by criticism, the NBA begins to require all players to take randomly assigned tests four times during the season and additional tests during the off-season if there is evidence to suspect drug use. The policy also increases the punishments for positive tests.

- *July 15:* Victor Conte, the owner of BALCO, a nutritional-supplement company that also deals in performance-enhancing drugs, pleads guilty to the illegal distribution of steroids and is sentenced to four months in jail and four months in house arrest. Greg Anderson, the former trainer of Barry Bonds, also pleads guilty to the same crime and receives a sentence of three months in jail and three months in house arrest.

- *July 15:* National Hockey Leagues (NHL) owners and the players' union reach a collective bargaining agreement that includes drug testing. Players will undergo at least two unannounced, random drug tests during the season and face successively harsher punishments for positive tests: a 20-game suspension for the first offense, a 60-game suspension for a repeat offense, and a permanent ban for a third offense.
- *August 1:* Rafael Palmeiro of the Baltimore Orioles baseball team, who had denied steroid use in testimony given under oath before Congress only several months earlier, receives a 10-day suspension for a positive steroid test. He denies knowingly taking steroids, claiming they must have been part of a nutritional supplement given to him by a teammate.
- *August 23:* The French newspaper *L'Equipe* accuses Lance Armstrong of having illegally used EPO to help win the 1999 Tour de France. The paper analyzed six-year-old urine samples with a new test for EPO, but Armstrong vigorously denies he ever used any illegal drugs and claims that the supposed positive tests have no validity.
- *October 1:* Bill Romanowski, a recently retired NFL linebacker and part of the 1996 and 1997 Super Bowl Champion Denver Broncos, admits in a published book, *Romo, My Life on the Edge*, to have used THG from 2001 to 2003 (though he never tested positive for steroids).
- *November 15:* The MLB Players Association accepts a proposal from MLB commissioner Bud Selig to include amphetamines in drug tests of athletes, increase the number of tests administered over the year, and suspend players 50 games, 100 games, and permanently after, respectively, the first, second, and third positive test.
- *November 21:* The major professional wrestling organization, World Wrestling Entertainment (formerly the World Wrestling Federation), announces that it will begin requiring drug tests of its athletes.
- *November 24:* Dick Pound, the president of the World Anti-Doping Agency located in Montreal, states his belief that about a third of NHL players use performance-enhancing drugs. The NHL Players Association calls the comments incorrect and irresponsible. NHL officials also deny the league has a problem with steroid use.
- *December 13:* The Court of Arbitration for Sports (CAS) rules in support of a two-year suspension given by the U.S. Anti-Doping Agency to Tim Montgomery for use of banned substances. The suspension is based on information obtained from the BALCO investigation rather than a positive drug test.

Chronology

2006

- *January 15:* NHL drug testing formally begins.
- *January 19:* IOC President Jacques Rogge announces that the upcoming Turin Winter Olympics will increase the number of urine and blood samples taken from athletes for drug testing. In addition, authorities will perform other tests based on tips from undercover informants about drug use by athletes.
- *January 20:* NHL hockey player Bryan Berard fails a test required for international competition when his urine sample showed the presence of a steroid byproduct. Although suspended for two years from international competition, he has passed tests given by the NHL and can still play on his team, the Columbus Blue Jackets.
- *February 8:* IOC President Jacques Rogge expresses concern at the slow rate of acceptance of the World Anti-Doping Code and urges that all Olympic sports federations adopt the code. So far, only seven nations—Australia, New Zealand, Canada, Denmark, Sweden, Norway, and Monaco—have signed the doping code.
- *February 9:* Duke University announces a tough new steroid policy that will suspend athletes testing positive for steroids and other performance-enhancing drugs for one year and make them ineligible for sports competition after a second positive test. The change came after reports that players on the Duke baseball team used steroids. Athletes in all 16 varsity sports will now have to take unannounced tests.
- *February 24:* Tests given to 10 Austrian cross-country skiers after Italian authorities had raided the residence of the team turn out negative. The raid had been sparked by the appearance of Walter Mayer, an Austrian trainer who had been banned from the Turin Games after he allegedly had given blood-doping transfusions at the 2002 Salt Lake City Winter Games. Authorities found blood-doping equipment at the residence, which may be sufficient evidence even with the negative tests to sanction athletes.
- *March 13:* In an excerpt from a forthcoming book, *Game of Shadows*, published in *Sports Illustrated*, two reporters from the *San Francisco Chronicle* claim that baseball star Barry Bonds had used high doses of steroids and other performance-enhancing drugs since 1998. Relying on sources and records from the federal investigation of BALCO, the reporters say that Bonds took injections as well as pills, cream, and liquid taken orally. Further, Bonds was using the drugs in 2001 when he broke the home run record. Baseball commissioner Bud Selig said the league would look into the allegations.
- *March 30:* MLB commissioner Bud Selig announces an investigation of players accused of steroid use—Barry Bonds, Gary Sheffield, and

Jason Giambi. The investigation follows accusations that had recently been published about Bonds and will be led by former senator George Mitchell.

- *May 31:* A search warrant is issued for the house of Jason Grimsley, a pitcher for the Arizona Diamondbacks who admitted using steroids. Sources who have seen the full version of the search warrant claim that Grimsley has named several other famous ballplayers as having used steroids.
- *July 1:* The Tour de France bars four of the top finishers in the 2005 race, including the two favorites to win this year, Italian Ivan Basso and German Jan Ullrich, from competing. Their names and those of many other professional cyclists showed up in an investigation of a Madrid clinic suspected of assisting with blood doping.
- *July 17:* Dr. James Shortt, a South Carolina physician who illegally prescribed steroids and human growth human to NFL players on the Carolina Panthers, is sentenced to one year and one day in prison. However, Shortt can delay reporting to the prison while appealing the sentence.
- *July 27:* The Phonak cycling team confirms that American Floyd Landis, who just won the Tour de France, tested positive during the race for unusually high levels of testosterone. Formal action will await replication of the drug test using the second vial of the urine sample.
- *August 5:* Like the first sample, a second urine sample given by Tour de France winner Floyd Landis shows high levels of testosterone. Landis denies using steroids but his cycling team terminates his contract. After deliberation by the U.S. Anti-Doping Agency and an appeal, Landis faces likely suspension and loss of his tour championship.
- *August 23:* Professional Golf Association Commissioner Tim Finchem says that professional golf does not need drug testing. Golf associations in most other nations allow for testing, but U.S. golf officials do not see the kinds of problems faced by football and baseball that would justify similar policies in the United States.
- *August 23:* World record-holder in the 100-meter sprint Justin Gatlin agrees to an eight-year suspension for a second positive drug test (the first for a banned stimulate in 2002, the second for synthetic testosterone in 2006). In return for his cooperation, Gatlin avoided the lifetime ban usually applied to second offenders. He will be able to compete again at age 32.
- *September 7:* Gold-medal winner and sprinter Marion Jones is cleared of drug use and allowed to continue competing. After evidence of the blood-boosting drug EPO is found in one urine sample, a test of the second sample proves negative. Jones maintains that she has never taken performance-enhancing drugs, including EPO, and believes that the first test resulted from lab mistakes.

Chronology

- *September 16:* The World Anti-Doping Agency rejects a ban on hypoxic or hyperbaric chambers that some athletes use to simulate high-altitude conditions and increase red blood cells. Experts suggest that the chambers or tents can cause sickness and weaken the immune system. WADA decides to have the IOC Medical Commission further consider the health effects of the training device before taking any action against it.
- *September 21:* A judge sentences Mark Fainaru-Wada and Lance Williams, two *San Francisco Chronicle* writers, to 18 months in jail for not revealing the source of leaked grand jury testimony they used in *Game of Shadows*, their book on Barry Bonds, use of steroids in Major League Baseball, and the BALCO scandal. They are free while appealing the sentence but agree that, to protect the freedom of the press, they will not reveal their source.
- *October 3:* *Sports Illustrated* reports that Patrick Arnold, the chemist who created the designer steroid THG, has been subpoenaed by the grand jury investigating Barry Bonds and BALCO. Arnold has already been sentenced to three months in prison and three months on house arrest for his role in the BALCO scandal but now may be required to testify about the use by others of the drugs he created.
- *October 24:* Shawne Merriman, a linebacker and defensive end for the NFL San Diego Chargers, is suspended for four games after testing positive for steroids. The suspension follows those of two other NFL players, Atlanta Falcons guard Matt Lehr and Detroit Lions defensive tackle Shaun Rogers.
- *December 27:* In a 2-1 decision overturning three lower court decisions, the 9th U.S. Circuit Court of Appeals ruled that federal prosecutors can have access to 2004 drug test results of MLB players. By agreement with MLB, the players gave the samples under the condition of anonymity, but the ruling allows prosecutors to match results with names and use the findings in a grand jury investigation of steroid use by Barry Bonds and other players.

CHAPTER 4

BIOGRAPHICAL LISTING

The listing to follow contains brief biographic sketches of athletes, sports leaders, scientists, and politicians who have participated in important events and controversies involving drugs and sports.

Lyle Alzado, 15-year National Football League (NFL) player with the Cleveland Browns, Denver Broncos, and Oakland Raiders. He admitted taking steroids continuously during his career from 1969 to 1985, and, having become addicted, taking them during the years of his retirement. After being stricken with brain cancer and before dying in 1992 at age 43, he blamed the disease on his excessive use of steroids and human growth hormone (hGH).

Greg Anderson, personal trainer whose clients included baseball players Barry Bonds and Jason Giambi. As part of the BALCO investigation, he was convicted in 2005 for distributing steroids. Although he denied having provided steroids to Bonds, their association raised suspicions about Bonds's use of banned drugs.

Jacques Anquetil, French cyclist and five-time winner of the Tour de France. In 1967, he admitted that cyclists used stimulants but argued that fans wanted to see the faster racing that stimulants brought.

Lance Armstrong, seven-time U.S. Tour de France champion. In 2005, the French newspaper *L'Equipe* accused him of having used EPO to help win the 1999 race. Armstrong vigorously denied he ever used any illegal drugs and claimed that the supposed positive tests had no validity. The debate has continued to keep drug use by long-distance cyclists in the news.

Dr. Jamie Astaphan, former physician to Canadian track star Ben Johnson. According to investigators, he provided steroids to Johnson and other Olympic athletes (although he initially denied the charge). It may be that the steroids he gave to Johnson led to the positive test and disqualification at the 1988 Seoul Olympics.

Bobby Barnes, high school football coach in Buckeye, Arizona. After suspending 10 players from the team when he discovered their steroid use, he received praise for his action from politicians and sports leaders but also faced anger from school fans when the loss of the players led to a poor record.

A. A. Berthold, German professor and researcher. He demonstrated in 1849 that substances released from the testes into the blood brought about masculine sex characteristics. After surgically implanting testes into the abdomen of castrated roosters, he found that the combs stayed large and bright and correctly reasoned that the testes were responsible.

Gary Bettman, National Hockey League (NHL) commissioner. He has denied that many players in the league use performance-enhancing drugs. Given pressure from Congress, however, he negotiated a testing program with the NHL Players Association that began in January 2006.

Barry Bonds, record-setting baseball player on the San Francisco Giants. In 2001, he hit 73 home runs, eclipsing the recent record of 70 set by Mark McGwire in 1998. The increase in his weight and muscle that occurred around the same time as his home run record seemed consistent with steroid use, and his personal trainer was convicted in 2005 for illegal distribution of steroids. Bonds admitted in 2003 grand jury testimony to unintentionally using steroids called "the cream" and "the clear," but nothing more. Then in March 2006, an excerpt from a forthcoming book, *Game of Shadows,* claimed to have documented use of steroids and other performance-enhancing drugs by Bonds since 1998 and during the year he broke the home run record.

Jim Bouton, former Major League Baseball (MLB) pitcher and author of the 1970 best-selling book *Ball Four.* In the book, which detailed his 1969 baseball season, he described the use by players of greenies—a slang term for amphetamine pills or speed.

Charles Edouard Brown-Sequard, French scientist who claimed that substances from the testes improved physical and mental energy. In 1889, at age 72, he injected himself with extracts from the testicles of dogs and guinea pigs to see the effects on his well-being. Scientists today discount his claim that the extract improved his health, but he did lead others to examine the effects of hormones more scientifically.

Jim Bunning, former MLB ballplayer, current member of the Hall of Fame, and Republican senator from Kentucky. He has co-sponsored legislation requiring strict drug testing and consistent penalties for all the major professional sports—baseball, football, basketball, and hockey—that the Senate is currently considering.

Adolf Butenandt, Nobel Prize–winning German chemist. Along with another researcher (Yugoslav Leopold Ruzicka) working separately, he synthesized testosterone in the lab in 1935. The discovery allowed, after some chemical adjustments, the use of testosterone to treat men with inadequate testosterone and, ultimately, to improve athletic performance of men and women.

Ken Caminiti, former MLB player on the San Diego Padres and winner of the Most Valuable Player Award in 1996. Some years later, he admitted that steroids helped him win the award. After taking steroids for the first time at age 33, he immediately made remarkable strides in his performance, increasing his annual home runs from 26 to 40. He remained unapologetic over his use of the drug, saying that at least half of the players used steroids at the time. After retirement, he faced other drug problems and died in 2004 at age 41 from a drug overdose of opiates and cocaine.

Jose Canseco, former baseball player on the Oakland Athletics and several other teams. According to his 2005 book *Juiced*, he brought steroids to Major League Baseball in 1985 and to some of his Oakland teammates later in the 1980s. While a player, Canseco denied steroid use, but he later admitted that steroids improved his performance and accused other famous players of having used them as well. These charges led to congressional hearings about steroid use and to stronger policies against drugs in professional sports.

Tommy Chaikin, former college football player at the University of South Carolina. In a 1988 story in *Sports Illustrated*, he told of his steroid use and the psychological damage it caused. The story described his use of steroids, the use of steroids by about half his teammates, and his near suicide. The story helped make the public and politicians aware of the extent of steroid use in college sports.

Linford Christie, British runner and winner of the gold medal for the 100-meter race in the 1992 Barcelona Olympics. He tested positive for the steroid nandrolone in 1999 but after appealing the result was cleared of all charges. A disciplinary committee could not conclude beyond a reasonable doubt that the positive test actually came from using the steroid.

Rick Collins, lawyer, bodybuilder, and advocate of legalizing steroids for adults. Along with specializing in the defense of persons arrested for steroid possession, he has become a public voice for a more tolerant attitude toward steroid use, a choice that he believes adults should be free to make based on their own judgment. He worries more about the loss of freedom from steroid laws than the risk to health from responsible steroid use.

Victor Conte, founder of BALCO, a sports supplement company, who was convicted of illegally distributing steroids. He gave the designer steroid tetrahydrogestrinone (THG) to several famous Olympic athletes, baseball players, and football players. After a federal investigation and national publicity about his activities, he pled guilty to the distribution charges and was sentenced to four months in jail and four months house arrest.

Steve Courson, former player with the Pittsburgh Steelers and Tampa Bay Buccaneers. A steroid user during his career, he spoke after his retirement from football about the widespread use of the drug and the risk to health that it presented to players. He has testified before Congress, written a book, *False Glory* (1991) about his experiences, and called for more action to address the problem of steroids in sports. Courson died November 10, 2005, in a tree-cutting accident.

Antonio Davis, former National Basketball Association (NBA) player with the New York Knicks and president of the NBA Players Association. In testimony before Congress, he said that use of steroids and other performance-enhancing drugs is virtually nonexistent in the NBA but also that NBA players are committed to a strong testing program.

Paul de Kruif, U.S. writer and author of the 1945 book *The Male Hormone.* In summarizing studies that showed the growth of body size and muscle from synthetic testosterone, he publicized its benefits for health and athletic performance.

Rick DeMont, U.S. swimmer and gold medal winner at the 1972 Munich Olympics who tested positive for ephedrine. Although legitimately used to treat asthma, ephedrine has stimulating properties that led the International Olympic Committee (IOC) to ban its use and to revoke DeMont's gold medal. DeMont appealed the decision, arguing that he used the medicine for his asthma, but the IOC rejected the appeal.

Manfred Donike, German scientist and expert on performance-enhancing drug testing. He developed a new test for steroids that, when first tried at the 1980 Summer Moscow Olympics, screened for excessive testosterone levels. When adopted by the IOC in 1983, the test prompted athletes using steroids to change their usage pattern to avoid detection.

Bjorn Ekblom, Swedish professor at the Institute of Physiology and Performance in Stockholm. His research in the late 1960s and early 1970s found that blood doping, a process of transfusing blood before competition, could increase oxygen use by the body and improve performance. In principle, blood doping simulated the benefits of high altitude training, where lower levels of oxygen in the air help increase red blood cell concentration in the body.

Manfred Ewald, former East German minister of sport who led the country's highly successful training program of Olympic athletes. Under his leadership, young athletes were given steroids, often without their consent, to improve performance. Although lauded in the 1970s and 1980s for the success of East Germany in the Olympics, he was convicted in 2000 of contributing to the bodily harm of minors.

Donald Fehr, executive director of the MLB Players Association. Representing the players union, he initially resisted incorporating tough drug testing as he saw it as a threat to the privacy rights of the players. He recently has agreed, under pressure from Congress, to a more comprehensive policy and harsher punishments for violators.

Jessica Foschi, U.S. swimmer who tested positive for steroids in 1995. She claimed to have never used steroids and believed the positive test result came from an effort to sabotage her career. In response to a suit, the U. S. Swimming Federation accepted her arguments and lifted her ban from competition, but the international swimming governing body did not. Eventually, an international court of arbitration ruled in Foschi's favor.

Bill Fralic, former offensive lineman with the Atlanta Falcons. In 1989 testimony before the U.S. Senate, he said that steroid use was rampant in the NFL and urged lawmakers to take action on the problem.

Charlie Francis, Canadian trainer of sprinter Ben Johnson. He helped supply Johnson with steroids but was surprised by Johnson's positive test at the 1988 Seoul Olympics. Having scheduled steroid use to avoid positive tests at the time of competitions, Francis believed that the test must have come from a mistake or some kind of sabotage. After the scandal, he admitted giving steroids to many other Canadian athletes.

Justin Gatlin, American sprinter and gold-medal winner who shares the world record in the 100 meters. After testing positive in 2006 for steroids, his second drug offense, he agreed to an eight-year ban from racing.

Martina Fehrecke Gottschalt, East German swimmer forced to take steroids while training as a young girl. As part of the East German national swimming program, she attended a special boarding school where, along with intense training and special foods, she received 40 pills a day, among them a steroid manufactured in East Germany. Although she won several junior championships, due in part to steroids, she never became an Olympic champion but later ended up with liver ailments and other health problems.

Tyler Hamilton, U.S. cyclist who won a gold medal at the 2004 Athens Olympics. A few weeks after winning the medal, he tested positive for an illegal blood transfusion, which led to his suspension from racing for two years. He has denied blood doping and appealed the suspension.

Thomas Hicks, U.S. marathoner and first athlete documented to have used stimulants in the Olympic Games. In 1904, only eight years after the modern Olympics had started, he won the marathon but collapsed at the finish of the race. His handlers admitted giving him strychnine and brandy during the race to keep him going.

Manfred Hoeppner, former medical director of the East German Olympic program. He helped administer a program of training for young athletes that included steroid use. The program provided dozens of pills, including steroids, to athletes at state training schools. Along with Manfred Ewald, he was convicted in 2000 of contributing to the bodily harm of minors.

Hulk Hogan, professional wrestling star with the World Wresting Federation in the 1970s and 1980s. He has admitted to using steroids, which helped build his 6-foot 8-inch, 303-pound muscular physique.

Taylor Hooton, high school athlete who committed suicide after secretly using steroids. His father, Don, who believes famous athletes should take responsibility for the pro-drug influence they have on children, started a foundation to stop steroid use.

C. J. Hunter, U.S. shot put athlete banned from competition after flunking several drug tests. Married to and then divorced from Marion Jones, he accused his former wife of using performance-enhancing drugs to win her Olympic medals.

Knut Jensen, Danish cyclist. He collapsed, fractured his skull, and died during the road race at the 1960 Rome Summer Olympics. Tests revealed the presence of amphetamines in his blood.

Ben Johnson, Canadian sprinter and former world-recorder holder in the 100 meters. The world's fastest man at the time, he tested positive for steroids after winning a gold medal at the 1988 Summer Olympics in Seoul, Korea. Stripped of his medals and former records, Johnson admitted to having used steroids and human growth hormone for many years. The highly publicized scandal made worldwide headlines and acquainted fans with the use of steroids by athletes.

Marion Jones, U.S. runner who won five medals at the 2000 Sydney Olympics. She earned the informal titles of fastest woman and best woman athlete in the world after her Olympic performance. A few years later, however, steroid distributor Victor Conte said that he supplied her with human growth hormone and watched her inject it. Jones disputed the claim and sued Conte for defamation, but others said much the same, including her former husband C. J. Hunter. While competing in 2006, she tested positive for use of EPO but was cleared when the test of a second urine sample turned up negative.

Florence Griffith Joyner ("Flo Jo"), U.S. runner, winner of three gold medals at the 1988 Seoul Olympics, and former record holder in the women's 100-meter race. Her astonishing speed—her time in the Olympic trials of 10.49 seconds shattered the existing record of 10.76—led to suspicions that she used steroids. She was also accused of using human growth hormone. She consistently denied taking performance-enhancing drugs and never tested positive, but her unexpected death from an epileptic seizure in 1998 at the young age of 38 restarted the rumors about past steroid abuse.

Fred C. Koch, U.S. scientist at the University of Chicago. With Lemuel C. McGee he isolated a small amount of a male hormone from 40 pounds of bull testicles. When injected in small amounts, the substance returned the sex characteristics (such as the red comb) to castrated roosters and demonstrated the existence and influence of the male sex hormone.

Floyd Landis, American cyclist who in 2006 became the third American to win the Tour de France but failed a drug test during the race. Several days after the race, the Phonak cycle team announced that Landis had unusually high levels of testosterone in his urine sample. When analysis of the second urine sample showed the same, Landis was fired by Phonak (and subsequent tests proved the testosterone came from a synthetic source). The U.S. Anti-Doping Agency brought doping charges against Landis, who has denied the charges and appealed to have them dismissed.

Ernst Laquer, Dutch professor who gave the name testosterone to the male hormone. His discovery of the chemical structure of the hormone made it possible to synthesize testosterone in the lab.

Carl Lewis, U.S. athlete and winner of 10 Olympic medals. Although losing to Ben Johnson in the 100-meter race at the 1988 Seoul Olympics, he received the gold medal after Johnson tested positive for steroids. Lewis had implied earlier that Johnson used steroids to win his races.

Hans-Gunnar Liljenwall, Swedish competitor in the Olympic modern pentathlon. Testing positive for excessive alcohol at the 1968 Mexico City Olympics, he became the first Olympian disqualified for drug use.

Kerry Lynch, U.S. Nordic skier who won a silver medal at the 1987 World Championships. He lost the medal and was banned from competition for two years after admitting to blood doping.

Terry Madden, CEO of the U.S. Anti-Doping Agency. He has advocated comprehensive testing of U.S. athletes participating in the Olympics and strong punishments of those found to use performance-enhancing drugs. The agency had success at the 2004 Athens Olympics, where no U.S. athletes tested positive for banned substances.

Arnold Mandell, psychiatrist who served as team physician for the San Diego Chargers from 1972 to 1974. In *The Nightmare Season*, a book about his experiences with the football team, he described the use of amphetamines by players. He also interviewed 87 players on 11 NFL teams, finding that two-thirds used amphetamines occasionally and one-half used them regularly.

Walter Mayer, former coach of the Austrian Nordic team (a sport that involves cross-country skiing and ski jumping). After being banned in 2002 from participation in future Olympics because of allegations that he performed blood transfusions at the Salt Lake City Winter Games, he showed up at the Austrian team quarters at the 2006 Turin Olympics. Word of his presence led Italian authorities to raid the quarters in search of evidence of doping. Mayer escaped but later was captured after trying to crash through a police roadblock.

John McCain, Republican senator from Arizona. As a member of the Senate Committee on Commerce, he has harshly criticized the leaders of MLB for not doing enough to eliminate drugs from baseball, and he proposed legislation that would require all the major professional sports to follow tougher rules for drug testing and punishment.

Lemuel C. McGee, U.S. scientist at the University of Chicago. With Fred C. Koch he isolated a small amount of a male hormone from 40 pounds of bull testicles. When injected in small amounts, the substance returned the sex characteristics (such as the red comb) to castrated roosters and demonstrated the existence and influence of the male sex hormone.

Mark McGwire, former baseball player with the Oakland Athletics and St. Louis Cardinals who shattered the single-season record by hitting 70 home runs. His huge build, admitted use of a steroid-related supplement called androstenedione, and record-setting performance (the previous record of 61 by Roger Maris had been in place since 1961) raised suspicions that he used steroids. Although accused by fellow player Jose Canseco of taking steroids, McGwire has not admitted publicly to using the drug.

Tim Montgomery, U.S. runner who broke the 100-meter world record in 2002. His involvement in the BALCO scandal and admission to use of steroids and human growth hormone led to a two-year ban and loss of his record.

Dave Morrissette (Moose), former NHL player. As an enforcer (a player who intimidates the other team with fighting and physical play), he was one of the few NHL players to admit using steroids but says that other enforcers in the league did the same.

Chuck Noll, former coach of the NFL Pittsburgh Steelers. In testimony before Congress, he expressed concern about steroids but estimated that use of the drug was not as extensive as many claimed.

Rafael Palmeiro, player for the Texas Rangers, Baltimore Orioles, and other MLB teams. Accused by Jose Canseco of using steroids, he stated under oath before Congress that he never used the drug. Soon after, however, he tested positive for steroids and was suspended by MLB. He denied knowingly taking banned substances, claiming they must have come from a nutritional supplement given to him by a teammate. Although investigated for perjury, he did not face prosecution.

Drugs and Sports

Ken Patera, former U.S. weightlifting champion. In 1971, he became one of the first to publicly disclose his steroid use. After losing to his Russian competitor, Vasily Alexeev, in the previous year, he said that he expected to do better in the 1972 Munich Olympic Games through use of steroids.

Rowdy Roddy Piper, former professional wrestling star. He has admitted to using steroids during his career.

Dick Pound, president of the World Anti-Doping Agency located in Montreal. He created controversy after saying that about a third of NHL players used performance-enhancing drugs, a claim NHL players called wrong and irresponsible.

Fritz Pregl, Austrian scientist who researched the effects of testosterone. With Ockar Zoth he injected himself with the extract of bull testicles and then observed the consequences of the injections for the strength of his fingers during a series of exercise. A paper published in 1896 concluded that the extract increased muscular strength.

Tamara Press, Soviet athlete who won gold medals in the shot put and discus in the 1964 Tokyo Olympics. Known as the Flower of Leningrad, Press had a remarkably muscular and powerful physique for a woman and may have been an early user of steroids.

Harry "Butch" Reynolds, U.S. sprinter, medal winner in the 1988 Seoul Olympics, and former world-record holder in the 400 meters. In 1990, he was suspended for a positive steroid test. He contended in a suit that irregularities in the testing produced a false positive and that the procedure violated his constitutional rights. Although Reynolds won his appeal of the suspension in U.S. courts, international authorities blocked him from participating in the Olympics.

Jacques Rogge, Belgian orthopedic surgeon and president of the IOC since 2001. While president, he worked to make it increasingly difficult for athletes to use performance-enhancing drugs.

Bill Romanowski, recently retired NFL linebacker and player with the 1996 and 1997 Super Bowl Champion Denver Broncos. In a book published in 2005, *Romo, My Life on the Edge*, he admitted to having used the steroid THG from 2001 to 2003, though he never tested positive for performance-enhancing drugs.

Pete Rozelle, former NFL commissioner who set up the league's first anti-drug policy. In 1983, he sent a letter to all players reminding them of the NFL policy against abuse of legal prescription drugs, including steroids, and in 1986 he banned use of anabolic steroids and similar growth-enhancing substances. He followed the new policy with the first formal program of urine testing during 1987 and 1988 preseason training camps.

Leopold Ruzicka, Nobel Prize–winning Yugoslav chemist. Along with another researcher (Adolf Butenandt) working separately, he synthesized testosterone in the lab in 1935. With some chemical adjustments, testosterone could be used to treat men with inadequate testosterone and, ultimately, to improve athletic performance.

Dr. Allan J. Ryan, former president of the American College of Sports Medicine. In the 1970s, he disputed claims that anabolic steroids could improve performance and, in so doing, contributed to the loss of credibility of the medical field with athletes who used and benefited from steroids.

Alex Sanchez, first MLB player suspended for a positive steroid test. In 2005, while playing for the Tampa Bay Devil Rays, his positive test led to a 10-day suspension. He denied having ever taken steroids and blamed unknown ingredients in some over-the-counter drugs he bought.

Marty Schottenheimer, former coach of the NFL Cleveland Browns and current coach of the San Diego Chargers. In testimony before Congress, he expressed concern about steroids, but estimated that use of the drug was not as extensive as many claimed.

Arnold Schwarzenegger, seven-time winner of bodybuilding's most prestigious title, Mr. Olympia (1970–1975 and 1980), actor, world-famous movie star, and governor of California. He has admitted taking steroids as a bodybuilder before they became illegal but now recommends that bodybuilders not do the same.

Bud Selig, Major League Baseball commissioner. After facing criticism from Congress for not having a comprehensive drug policy in MLB, he worked in 2004 and 2005 with the players union to strengthen the testing procedures and the punishments for violations of drug policy.

Tommy Simpson, British cyclist who died during the 1967 Tour de France race. His death from complications related to amphetamine use, following that of cyclist Knut Jensen seven years earlier in the 1960 Rome Olympics, made known the life-threatening risks of drug use for athletes.

Mary Decker Slaney, runner who holds the American records in the 800 meters, 1,500 meters, 1 mile, 2,000 meters, and 3,000 meters. In 1996, she tested positive for steroid use but argued that menstruation or alcohol consumption could skew the steroid test among women and made her results invalid. Although experts disagreed, U.S.A. Track and Field lifted her suspension and dropped the doping charges.

Michelle Smith, Irish Olympic swimmer. The three gold medals and one bronze medal she won at the 1996 Atlanta Olympic Games raised suspicions of drug use. She had never placed better than 17th in previous Olympics, her discus-throwing husband had been suspended for failing a drug test, and she had a bulky physique. In 1998, an out-of-competition drug test found that her urine contained enough whiskey to kill a human, and she was suspended for four years for using a masking agent.

Onterrio Smith, former running back for the NFL Minnesota Vikings. In 2005, he was found during a routine airport check to be carrying a device called a whizzinator. Advertised as a way to pass drug tests, the device uses a plastic bladder to pass clean urine through a fake penis. He denied having used it for a NFL drug test.

Sammy Sosa, player on the MLB Chicago Cubs and Baltimore Orioles. In 1998, he followed close behind Mark McGwire by hitting 66 home runs. Although accused of using steroids, he has denied doing so under oath.

David Stern, commissioner of the National Basketball Association. Under pressure from Congress, he and representatives of the NBA Players Association agreed in 2005 to improve their program for drug testing and increase the penalties for violators.

Paul Tagliabue, National Football League commissioner. Building on existing policies of his predecessor, Pete Rozelle, he set up a comprehensive drug policy in the early 1990s that served as a model for other professional sports leagues.

William N. Taylor, U.S. physician and expert on anabolic steroids. In several books, he favored the medical use of testosterone and opposed steroids for performance enhancement. An early critic of the spread of steroids in sports, he has pushed for stronger laws and tougher punishments.

James Toney, heavyweight boxer who tested positive for steroids after defeating his opponent John Ruiz in a championship match. He blamed the positive test on medication for an injured shoulder but nonetheless lost his championship title, was banned for two years from competing for the title, and faced a suit from Ruiz.

Gene Upshaw, executive director of the NFL Players Association. Although initially opposed to drug testing of all players, he worked with the NFL to develop one of the most comprehensive and thorough policies in professional sports.

Frank D. Uryasz, former National Collegiate Athletic Association (NCAA) official in charge of drug education and testing. He has testified before Congress about the NCAA program and its efforts to eliminate drug use among student-athletes.

Lasse Viren, Finnish long-distance runner who won gold medals in the 5,000- and 10,000-meter races at the 1976 Montreal Olympic Games. During the Games, television announcers mentioned rumors that he used blood doping. Viren's denied the allegations, which stemmed from little more than his gold medal victories in two strenuous running events, but the story alerted others to the practice.

Robert Voy, U.S. physician who served as the chief medical officer of the U.S. Olympic Committee from 1984 to 1989. Believing the use of anabolic steroids and other performance-enhancing drugs to be commonplace among Olympic athletes, he criticized sports authorities for not doing more to stop the problem.

Tom Verducci, writer for *Sports Illustrated.* In dozens of stories in the past decade, he raised awareness of the use of steroids in baseball and drugs in sports more generally. He has criticized baseball players Mark McGwire and Barry Bonds for the steroid-aided records they have set. Given new drug-testing policies, however, he sees the future of baseball optimistically.

Willy Voet, former assistant to the Festina cycling team who helped distribute drugs to the team riders. In 1998, French custom officials discovered prescription drugs, narcotics, EPO, hGH, testosterone, and amphetamines in his car, which led to the disqualification of many riders in that year's Tour de France. The resulting scandal documented the widespread reliance on drugs by racers and led to changes in drug testing policy.

Charles E. Yesalis, professor at Penn State University and nationally recognized expert on steroids. He did early surveys on the use of steroids by youth, testified before Congress on the problems of steroids, and wrote numerous articles and books on the topic.

John Zigler, team physician for the U.S. weightlifting team during the 1950s. After discovering the successful use of steroids by the Soviet weightlifting team, he introduced with great success a new anabolic steroid product call Dianabol (manufactured by Ciba Pharmaceutical Company) to American weightlifters.

Oskar Zoth, Austrian scientist who researched the effects of testosterone. With Fritz Pregl he injected himself with the extract of bull testicles and then observed the consequences of the injections on the strength of his fingers during a series of exercise. A paper published in 1896 concluded that the extract increased muscular strength.

CHAPTER 5

GLOSSARY

Below are definitions of technical terms that general readers will likely encounter in researching drugs and sports.

amphetamine   A highly additive drug (also known as speed) that stimulates the brain and central nervous system to increase energy and alertness.

anabolic   The process of building complex tissues from simpler molecules, especially the building of muscle.

anabolic-androgenic steroid   A precise term for chemically synthesized testosterone that highlights both desirable anabolic properties that build muscle and less desirable androgenic properties that increase male sexual characteristics. It means the same as anabolic steroid and, in most contexts, the same as steroid.

anabolic steroid   A chemically modified, synthetic form of the male hormone testosterone that can be taken externally through pills, injections, gels, or patches and is used primarily to build muscle. It is also known as the gear, juice, roids.

androgenic   Relating to the development of male sex characteristics such as growth of dense body hair, deepening of the voice, increased acne from oil produced by glands, greater sexual interest, and intensified male personality characteristics such as aggression and competitiveness.

androstenedione (andro)   A steroid precursor that became a popular alternative to steroids until it was made illegal (except by prescription) in 2004.

anti-estrogen   A substance that blocks the effects of estrogen in the body (usually to prevent tumors) and is used by athletes to counter the side effects of steroids.

barbiturate   A drug that depresses the central nervous system and can help athletes in some sports by relaxing muscles and nerves.

beta-2 agonist   A drug that opens the bronchial airways and often helps build muscle (*agonist* refers to a drug that stimulates natural processes in the body and *beta-2* to a cell receptor).

Glossary

beta blocker   A drug that, by slowing the heart rate, lowering blood pressure, and reducing muscle contraction, can help athletes in sports such as rifle shooting or archery where nervousness can harm performance.

blood doping   A process of increasing the oxygen-carrying capacity of blood by giving blood transfusions and adding red blood cells before athletic events.

boldenone undecylenate   An injectable steroid with the trade name Equipoise that was first developed for use in animals but later adopted by bodybuilders.

clearance time   The period needed to wash evidence of illegal drug use out of the body and avoid a positive drug test. It determines how soon before competition athletes need to stop using banned drugs.

clenbuterol   A nonsteroid, beta-2 agonist normally prescribed to open the bronchial airways of asthma patients but also used to increase muscle mass and reduce fat.

cocaine   A highly addictive stimulant drug that brings temporary feelings of pleasure and has, on occasion, been used by athletes to improve performance.

controlled substance   A drug or chemical substance whose possession and distribution are controlled or restricted by law because they are addictive and prone to abuse.

corticosteroid   A hormone that suppresses the immune system and symptoms of inflammation. Unlike anabolic steroids, these types of steroids have a variety of legitimate medical uses that do not contribute to growth of muscle mass; like anabolic steroids, they are called steroids for short.

corticotrophin   A hormone normally secreted by the pituitary gland and sometimes taken in synthetic form to increase the natural production of steroids in the body and improve athletic performance.

cortisone   A synthetic corticosteroid used to reduce inflammation and mask injuries that may hamper athletic performance.

criminalization   Making a formerly legal behavior illegal through passage of legislation.

cycling   Taking steroids for a specific time interval (or cycle) such as six to 12 weeks, then stopping for the same time span, and repeating the process. It allows the body and its hormone system to recover from the high amounts of testosterone.

dehydroepiandrosterone (DHEA)   A steroid precursor that, because of its medical uses for treating fatigue and lupus, was not included as a controlled substance in the 2004 Anabolic Steroids Control Act.

Depot-Turinabol   An injectable steroid manufactured in East Germany and given to East German athletes in the 1970s and 1980s as part of a state-sponsored Olympic training program.

designer steroid A term for a steroid that differs just enough in chemical composition from known steroids to make it difficult to detect.

diuretic A drug used to release water from the body and, sometimes for athletes, to dilute urine in a way that makes it harder to find banned substances.

doping The use of chemicals and substances to artificially boost sports performance. The International Olympic Committee refers to doping in somewhat more detail as the use of any substance that is foreign to the body, taken in abnormal amounts, or taken by an abnormal route into the body with the sole purpose of unfairly enhancing performance in competition.

elephant epidermis A thickening and coarsening of the skin that can result from use of human growth hormone.

ephedrine A stimulant that affects the central nervous system by increasing alertness, dilating the bronchia, and speeding the heart rate. It helps treat asthma, suppress appetite among dieters, and improve performance among athletes.

epitestosterone A hormone that is produced by the body at about the same rate as testosterone and, when measured in urine, can help determine if athletes have excess testosterone from taking steroids.

ergogenic Having the property of increasing muscular capacity for work and enhancing performance.

erythropoietin (EPO) A hormone normally produced by the kidneys to stimulate the production of red blood cells in the bone marrow of the body but also used in synthetic form to boost red blood cells of athletes.

gene therapy The introduction of new genes into the body as a way to fix genes that do not work properly or to add new, beneficial genes.

glucocorticosteroid A corticosteroid used to reduce inflammation.

gonadotrophin A hormone normally secreted by the pituitary gland and sometimes used in synthetic form to improve athletic performance by increasing the natural production of steroids in the body.

gynecomastia The development of small breasts in men that often results from steroid use.

half-life The time it takes for a drug to drop to one-half of its original concentration in the blood.

hormone A chemical produced in one part of the body, released into the bloodstream, and used by other parts of the body to regulate its functions.

human growth hormone (hGH) A hormone produced by the pituitary gland to regulate growth but also used in synthetic form to help deficient children grow or to help athletes of normal or large size grow stronger. It has the advantage over steroids of being harder to detect with urine tests.

Glossary

hypoxic or hyperbaric chamber A tent used by some athletes to improve training by simulating high-altitude conditions and increasing red blood cells.

insulin A hormone produced by the pancreas to regulate the use of carbohydrates by the body and sometimes taken as an aid for sports performance.

metabolite The byproduct of breaking down or metabolizing substances in the body. Drug tests search for metabolites of banned substances in urine rather than the substances themselves.

methandrostenolone An anabolic steroid with the trade name Dianabol that was once the most popular steroid but is no longer manufactured in the United States.

nandrolone An injectable anabolic steroid with the trade name Deca-Durabolin that has been the most common source of positive tests, in part because it is relatively easy to detect. It may, however, also show in urine for reasons other than taking steroids (such as eating beef from cattle treated with steroids).

Novocain A local anesthetic often used in sports to improve performance by masking pain from injuries.

Oral-Turinabol A steroid manufactured in East Germany in the form of pink and blue pills and given with vitamins to young East German athletes in the 1970s and 1980s as part of a state-sponsored Olympic training program.

oxandrolone An anabolic steroid with the trade name Anavar that is known for increasing strength but not size and is popular among women because of its limited androgenic effects.

oxymetholone An anabolic steroid with the trade name Anadrol that is considered the strongest oral steroid available and results in androgenic effects that many find hard to tolerate.

pharmacogenomics The study of how genetic makeup affects the response to a particular drug and the process of using this knowledge to design more effective drugs with fewer side effects.

plateauing Reaching the point where users develop a tolerance to steroids such that they no longer seem to contribute to muscle development. The body may become so saturated with testosterone that cells no longer accept it.

prostate gland A gland in the male reproduction system located just below the bladder and surrounding the canal that empties the bladder. Some steroid products can enlarge the gland and block urination.

pseudoephedrine A variant of ephedrine found in over-the-counter cold medicine that can affect athletic performance.

pyramiding A process of beginning a cycle of steroid use with low doses, slowly building to a peak, and then slowly reducing steroid intake to zero before the off period. The slow buildup allows the body to adjust to the higher testosterone levels and the builddown allows the body to adjust to the decline.

'roid rage   Extreme anger that may be a side effect of steroids.

scheduled substance   A drug or chemical substance that, under the Controlled Substances Act, is included in one of the five schedules or classifications as dangerous, addictive, and illegal.

speedball   A mixture of heroin and cocaine used in the late 1800s to stimulate activity and prevent fatigue during long-distance bicycle races.

stacking   Taking multiple steroids at the same time so that the combination will build muscle better than one steroid alone.

stanozolol   An anabolic steroid with trade names of Winstrol and Stromba that comes in oral and injectable forms and is one of the most popular products used by athletes.

Stasi   The East German secret police of the Ministry for State Security. It had responsibility for a program to make steroids a regular part of training for East German athletes.

steroid   A family of substances that have a certain chemical structure. It most often refers to anabolic steroids used to increase muscle growth but also to corticosteroids or glucocorticosteroids used to relieve swelling and inflammation.

steroid (or testosterone) precursor   In its natural form, a substance in the body that aids in producing testosterone and, in its manufactured form, a supplement used to allow the body to produce more of its own testosterone.

strychnine   A stimulant taken in the past in small doses to improve athletic performance but also a deadly poison in large doses.

testes   The male reproductive organs or paired testicles that produce testosterone and sperm.

testosterone   A hormone that causes the development of male sex characteristics such as sperm production, the growth of facial and body hair, and the development of muscles, bone mass, and sex drive. Although present in small amounts in women, testosterone comes primarily from the testes and reaches much higher levels among males.

testosterone cypionate   An injectable steroid with trade names of Depo-Testosterone and Testacyp that has strong androgenic effects but is known to produce dramatic gains in size and strength.

testosterone enanthate   An injectable steroid similar to testosterone cypionate in its effects.

tetrahydrogestrinone (THG)   A designer steroid that became the source of a recent scandal about drugs in sports when it was found that several famous U.S. athletes used the product.

vasodilator   A drug that, by causing the blood vessels to expand, may improve athletic performance.

PART II

GUIDE TO FURTHER RESEARCH

CHAPTER 6

HOW TO RESEARCH DRUGS AND SPORTS

Although often thought of narrowly in terms of games, championships, records, winners, and losers, sports has much wider social significance. Athletic competition has become a central part of modern life and is affected by many of problems of wider society. Drug use in sports is a prime example. It raises issues beyond concerns of who wins and loses. It involves questions of medicine, science, social science, law, and policy and relates to a wide variety of amateur and professional sports. As a result, the subject of drugs and sports has generated a considerable amount of information—and controversy. Those new to the topic can become easily overwhelmed by all the available material. As an aid to doing research on drugs and sports, it helps to follow some general suggestions and some more specific advice about where to find useful sources and what Internet and print resources to consult. Those who research drugs and sports face several challenges.

First, writings on the topic span a variety of fields of study. Drugs and sports are related to the chemistry of drugs, the psychological motivations to use drugs, the social pressure to win, the medical and psychiatric harm of drugs, the laws against drug use, the rights of athletes, the testing policies of sports organizations, the ethics of competition, the history of sports, and the vulnerability of teens to drugs. Further, stories on drugs in sports involving new accusations, positive drug tests, and congressional legislation appear in the newspapers regularly. Few can master all the specialized fields of study and keep up with all the news on the topic.

Second, the literature on the topic sometimes reflects strong political and moral views that often make it hard to separate facts from beliefs. These views come into play, for example, in debates over the proper role of the government in restricting certain types of drugs or forcing sports leagues to follow certain testing policies. On one side, many view use of banned performance-enhancing drugs in sports as unfair and unethical and consider those who have won events, broken records, and achieved excellence by taking steroids as cheaters. They often back harsh punishment, rigorous testing, and government control, and they criticize sports organizations for not having done enough to stop drug use among their athletes. On the other side, drug use has over the years become so widespread that many athletes have concluded they must do the same if they are to compete. Some people believe that careful steroid use by adults under medical supervision differs little from other special surgeries such as improving vision or relying on computerized training equipment to improve performance. They are concerned that accusations and punishments for drug use have gone so far as to violate the rights of athletes. Use of drugs in sports, in their view, does not justify the harsh response common today. These differences in viewpoints can lead to widely varying interpretations of the facts and issues.

Third, studies of drugs and sports often cover technically difficult material. In some cases, the difficulties come from the terminology of drug chemistry. Many will be unfamiliar with scientific terms such as epitestosterone, corticosteroid, androgenic, and metabolite, with such drug names as methandrostenolone, stanozolol, nandrolone, and androstenedione, and with slang words such as stacking, pyramiding, and cycling. In other cases, difficult material comes from understanding the physical, medical, and psychological effects of performance-enhancing drugs. In still other cases, researchers face complex legal issues involving rights against unreasonable search and seizure, protection from false drug test results, or definitions of scheduled and controlled substances.

TIPS FOR RESEARCHING DRUGS AND SPORTS

How can researchers overcome these challenges? Here are some tips.

- **Define the topic and questions carefully.** Rather than researching drugs and sports, it is better to examine more focused, in-depth research topics. Examples might include the physical or psychological side effects of performance-enhancing drugs, the discovery and development of new performance-enhancing drugs, the drug-testing policy of a major professional sport, the attractions of drugs for athletes, the ability to hide drug use from tests, the case for legalization of steroids, and the extent of steroid use by teens. With so many choices available, making the research manageable requires care and precision in selecting topics. Doing so can help avoid being overwhelmed by the material and allow for an in-depth treatment of the selected topic.

- **Consider the underlying perspectives.** The annotated literature review in the next chapter includes a wide selection of readings that represent all perspectives. Relying on a variety of sources will help avoid bias from the values and beliefs that shape views on drugs and sports. Considering the background and potential biases of the authors can help separate opinions and emotion from facts and reason.

- **Evaluate sources.** In reviewing books and articles, check the date of publication to make sure the information is recent. Also check the qualifications of the author and the citation of sources to make sure the information is reliable and check the presentation of alternative views to make sure the information is fair. Books and articles often differ in their audience, with some more focused on popular audiences and some more focused on scholarly audiences. Both popular and scholarly materials are useful, but it helps to recognize how they differ in the depth of information, citation of sources, and recentness of publication. In reviewing Internet sources, even more care is needed. Nearly anyone can post documents, and there are often no checks on the reliability of the information that the documents contain. Evaluate the qualifications of the author, the legitimacy of the sponsoring organization, and the potential for bias.

- **Master the basic facts and terms.** It is hard to make sense of much of the material on drugs and sports without having some familiarity with common terminology in the area. Try to grasp the meaning of technical terms, common slang, and key principles. Careful and precise use of these terms and ideas lends authority to research.

- **Search for balance.** Since complex questions about drugs and sports seldom have simple answers, do not accept claims at face value. Rather, search for balanced presentations based on evidence—even if highly technical—and careful weighing of the alternatives. Despite their personal beliefs, researchers should seek to understand the diverse views offered in the area of drugs and sports and treat both sides of the debates fairly.

To review various types of research resources, the material to follow considers online resources, print resources, and resources related to law and legislation.

ONLINE RESOURCES

GENERAL SITES

Given its ease in providing information, the Internet offers a good place to begin research on drugs and sports. The World Wide Web contains a variety of research, reference, and opinion pieces on the topic that those with an Internet connection can easily access. One can find useful facts and perspectives on nearly any aspect of drugs and sports by patiently working through even a small portion of available web sites. Finding a suitable site then suggests links to others, which in turn lead in new directions. Innovative ideas and fresh information emerge in this process. Indeed, many web documents are updated or created anew to keep up with recent events and the latest information.

However, the extraordinary wealth of information that the Internet makes available to researchers can be overwhelming. For instance, a Google search for the term *steroids* results in 34 million hits—an extraordinary and daunting number. The advice to define narrow topics for research applies particularly to using the Internet. Otherwise, combing through all the web sites listed by searches can result in wasted effort. In addition, the information obtained does not always meet high standards of reliability and balance. Unlike books and articles, web documents often do not go through a process of review and editing before publications. In some cases, they offer little more than the opinions of strangers.

Users must take care with materials obtained from web sites. Take note of who sponsors the site. Is the organization reputable? Does the author have expertise? Does the web site aim for objectivity? Is it written well and based on careful thinking? Those web sites where one can answer "yes" to these questions will be the ones to rely on the most. With this qualification in mind, Internet research can proceed in several ways.

Popular and general search engines such as Google (http://www.google.com), Yahoo! (http://www.yahoo.com), Alta Vista (http://www.altavista.com), Excite (http://www.excite.com), Lycos (http://www.lycos.com), Ask (http://www.ask.com), MSN (http://www.msn.com), and many others can identify web sites that contain information on drugs and sports. Using these search engines effectively requires thoughtful selection of search terms and patient effort but can lead to unexpected and intriguing discoveries.

The web also includes directories or indexes on performance-enhancing drugs. In Yahoo!, a helpful directory of web sites, information, and organizations is easy to find. Go to the Yahoo! home page and do a directory search for *drugs in sports*. Another directory search for *drugs and medications* will provide links on steroids, human growth hormone, EPO, and many other performance-enhancing drugs. Google likewise has a directory with a broad list of topics. On the Google home page, click "more" and then "Directory"; then do a directory search for *drugs*, *sports*, *steroids*, or other terms. Alternatively, browse through the directory categories relating to sports, health, and drugs.

Other directories besides those of Yahoo! and Google are available as well. Of particular interest, About.com provides background information on anabolic steroids. Simply search for the term from the home page (http://www.about.com). Searching more broadly for *sports drugs* will turn up hundreds of web sites.

Web sites devoted to sports are also helpful sources of information. A search for stories on steroids at *Sports Illustrated*'s web site (http://www. SportsIllustrated.com) turns up nearly 1,000 citations, many more current than those found in other directories. A similar search of ESPN.com (http://www.ESPN.com) will likewise turn up a large number of stories.

ORGANIZATION SITES

Knowledge of key organizations—government, sports, and research—is crucial for researching drugs and sports. Chapter 8 lists a variety of such organizations, and consulting the home pages of a few can particularly help researchers.

Three key government agencies deal with issues involving drugs and sports: the National Institute on Drug Abuse (http://www.drugabuse.gov/ NIDAHome.html), the Drug Enforcement Administration (http://www. usdoj.gov/dea), and the White House Office of National Drug Control Policy (http://www.whitehousedrugpolicy.gov). These agencies focus mostly on drug use outside of sports, but a search within their web pages turns up much information on steroids and other performance-enhancing drugs. Organizations responsible for enforcing doping policies in sports also have web sites. These include the World Anti-Doping Agency (http://www. wada-ama.org/en), the U.S. Anti-Doping Agency (http://www.usantidoping. org), and the National Collegiate Athletic Association (http://www.ncaa. org/wps/portal). Medical organizations such as the American Academy of Sports Medicine (http://www.nasm.org) and sports organizations such as the International Olympic Committee (http://www.olympic.org) can likewise be good research sources.

SITES ON SPECIFIC DRUGS AND SPORTS TOPICS

Along with getting resources from broad—and perhaps overwhelming—general searches and from organizations with wide-ranging goals, it helps to begin by researching particular sites. Here are some recommended sites, organized by the major topics on drugs and sports.

Doping

One useful web site with links to recent news stories on doping is Drugs in Sport (http://www.drugsinsport.net). A government perspective can be found on a web site sponsored by the White House (http://www.white-housedrugpolicy.gov/prevent/sports/doping.html). It provides background information on doping and links to many other pages. The FindLaw web site lists many links to news stories and legal issues on doping (http://news.findlaw.com/legalnews/sports/drugs/index.html). These general pages on doping can then be reviewed before investigating more specific topics.

Medical and Scientific Aspects

Researchers might begin with a series of government documents on the dangers of steroid use found at http://www.steroidabuse.gov, sponsored by the National Institute on Drug Abuse. The web site has links to a variety of other sites that present the consensus view on the medical harm of steroids and that urge athletes to avoid drugs. The National Collegiate Athletic Association (NCAA) also has a web site on the effects of performance-enhancing drugs that aims to help athletes make responsible decisions (http://www.drugfreesport.com/choices/drugs/index.html).

Social and Policy Aspects

Web sites focusing on social and policy aspects of drug use in sports generally take a negative view. They offer advice to parents, coaches, and community members on how to stop youth from taking all types of illegal drugs. Examples of such sites come from the White House Office of National Drug Control Policy (http://www.usantidoping.org/athletes/cheating_health.html), the National Institute on Drug Abuse (http://www.drugabuse.gov/SteroidAlert/Steroidalert.html), and the Drug Enforcement Administration (http://www.deadiversion.usdoj.gov/pubs/brochures/steroids). However, one site takes the opposite view—that responsible use of steroids by adults should be legal and medically supervised. For this viewpoint, see the Legal Muscle web site of Rick Collins (http://www.legalmusclebooks.com).

Olympic Sports

The most instructive sites on Olympic sports come from the agencies that conduct testing. The World Anti-Doping Agency (http://www.wada-ama.org/en/index.ch2) and the U.S. Anti-Doping Agency (http://www.usantidoping.org) describe their organization and antidoping goals. These pages also have links to descriptions of testing procedures, statements on the goals of drug testing, and lists of banned substances.

Professional Sports

Web sites with testimony from recent congressional hearings on the use of drugs in sports can introduce researchers to current controversies. Many hearings address a different sport, such as baseball (http://reform.house.gov/GovReform/Hearings/EventSingle.aspx?EventID=23320), football (http://reform.house.gov/GovReform/Hearings/EventSingle.aspx?EventID=25679), and basketball (http://reform.house.gov/GovReform/Hearings/EventSingle.aspx?EventID=27415). The hearings include testimony from witnesses and politicians with a variety of views.

PRINT SOURCES

Despite the ease of obtaining a wealth of information from the Internet, books and print articles available from libraries and bookstores remain the primary source of information. Good books integrate material that is otherwise scattered, present information in a logical and understandable format, and allow for a comprehensive approach to the issues. Edited volumes present multiple perspectives on a topic but usually with a meaningful framework, while other books present a single but in-depth viewpoint—and both have advantages. Exploiting these advantages requires use of catalogues, indexes, bibliographies, and other guides.

BIBLIOGRAPHIC RESOURCES

Researchers will want to rely on a local city or university library, especially for print materials. To supplement these libraries, the Library of Congress catalogue offers a comprehensive bibliographic resource (http://catalog.loc.gov). To browse holdings by subject, click "Basic Search," then type in *steroids*, *doping*, or other specific terms and highlight "subject browse". The many listed subject headings will prove useful for further research. Alternatively, a keyword search of *drugs sports* returns a list of 9,976 references. The list can be narrowed by adding limits to search results.

Yahoo! contains a listing of catalogues for specific libraries (http://dir.Yahoo.com/Reference/Libraries). The web site allows users to browse through catalogues outside their local library and possibly discover new references. Each library will have its own search procedures but, to be efficient, stick to the general rule of searching for specific and narrow keywords.

Bookstore catalogues not only allow for searches of books currently in print on any variety of sports topics but also have another advantage. They often include summaries and reader reviews of books that can demonstrate their relevance and value. In some cases, it is possible to browse through an electronic version of parts of a book. At the same time, bookstore catalogues will not have as many out-of-print (though still valuable) books as libraries. Still, it helps to search electronic bookstores such as Amazon.com (http://www.amazon.com) and Barnes and Noble (http://www.barnesandnoble.com).

Most libraries have periodical indexes for searching for print articles. *OCLC First Search* contains an electronic version of *Reader's Guide Abstracts*, which lists articles in a large number of magazines. However, users need access to a subscribing library for this database. *InfoTrac* also compiles articles for general interest audiences and sometimes includes an abstract with citations, or abstracts with the full text. It likewise requires library privileges. *Ingenta Library Gateway* (http://www.ingenta.com) has more than 19 million citations from nearly 20,000 journals and allows searches for scholarly articles in the areas of medicine, science, and social science. Searching *Ingenta* is free, but delivery of an article requires a fee. Often, specific magazines, such as *Time* (http://www.time.com/time), have a web site that allows users to search for articles.

Libraries usually subscribe to catalogues of newspaper articles, a crucial source of information on current events. In addition, many newspapers maintain a web site with an archive of past articles. The *New York Times*, for example, allows searches of past articles (as well as the day's major stories) at http://www.nytimes.com. Most articles from the previous seven days are free, but accessing earlier or premium articles requires a fee. A search on drugs and sports will, as is typical, return too many stories to sort through, and narrower searches will work better. *The Washington Post* also provides a web site at http://www.washingtonpost.com, but likewise requires purchase of older articles. Yahoo! (at http://dir.yahoo.com/News_and_Media/Newspapers/) lists links to many newspapers that allow access via the web. Local libraries also have inhouse databases for finding newspaper articles.

SPECIFIC BOOKS AND ARTICLES ON DRUGS AND SPORTS

Along with general bibliographic resources for print materials and an annotated bibliography, it helps to have a few books and articles to get started. The appendices to this volume include a useful overview of scientific research on steroids, federal laws prohibiting most steroid use, and a crucial Supreme Court decision on drug testing. In addition to these documents, a list of highly recommended books and articles organized by the major topics of drugs and sports follows.

General

A few recent books provide good starting points for those researching drugs and sports. Charles E. Yesalis and Virginia S. Cowart, in *The Steroids Game: An Expert's Inside Look at Anabolic Steroid Use in Sports* (Champaign, Ill.: Human Kinetics, 1998), offer an excellent introduction to this common and often abused performance-enhancing drug. In *Pumped: Straight Facts for Athletes about Drugs, Supplements, and Training* (New York: W.W. Norton, 2000), Cynthia Kuhn, Scott Swartzwelder, and Wilkie Wilson have written a more technical but still helpful review of the evidence on the benefits and side effects of sports drugs. Many fine articles on drug use in sports have appeared over the years in *Sports Illustrated*. For a recent overview of the continuing problem, see "Steroids R Us" by Stephen Cannella *(Sports Illustrated*, vol. 102, no. 15, April 11, 2005, pp. 20–21). Although more dated, several articles on drugs and sports in an issue of *World Health* (July/August 1995, p. 9) consider the problem from an international perspective.

Scientific and Medical Aspects

Many of the books on the science and medicine of performance-enhancing drugs are too technical for most researchers. *Anabolic Steroids and Other Performance-Enhancing Drugs* (London: Taylor and Francis, 2003), by Pat Lenehan, is dense in the material it presents but still more accessible than most. An article based on an interview with a leading drug-testing scientist—"The Steroid Detective: Interview with D. Catlin" (*U.S. News & World Report*, vol. 137, no. 22, December 20, 2004, p. 19) by Kim Clark—discusses doping issues with a minimum of technical detail. An article on the scientific literature by John M. Tokish, Mininder S. Kocher, and Richard J. Hawkins, "Ergogenic Aids: A Review of Basic Science, Performance, Side Effects, and Status in Sports" (*American Journal of Sports Medicine*, vol. 32, no. 6, September 2004, pp. 1543–1553), reviews the evidence on the risks of performance-enhancing drugs.

Social and Policy Aspects

The many congressional hearings on steroids cover social and policy aspects of drugs and sports. The hearings not only present the views of senators and representatives but include testimony from a wide variety of experts. The U.S. Senate hearing on *Steroids in Amateur and Professional Sports—The Medical and Social Costs of Steroid Abuse* (Washington, D.C.: U.S. Government Printing Office, 1989) led to legislation making anabolic steroids a controlled substance. It contains testimony from athletes and experts on the dangers of steroids. A more recent hearing of the U.S. House of Representatives, *Anabolic Steroid Control Act of 2004* (Washington, D.C.: U.S. Government Printing Office, 2004), provides testimony on the dangers of steroid precursors and led to legislation making them controlled substances. An article that describes concerns about teen use of steroids and steroid-related drugs in *Newsweek* (Jerry Adler, "Toxic Strength: High School Athletes and Steroids" vol. 144, no. 25, December 20, 2004, pp. 44–50, 52) emphasizes the need for social programs to prevent such use. For another point of view, however, see Maxwell J. Mehlman's "What's Wrong with Using Drugs in Sports? Nothing" (*USA Today*, August 12, 2004, p. 13A).

Olympic Sports

A book on the background to the problems of drug use in Olympic sports comes from Dick Pound, the current president of the World Anti-Doping Agency, and his book *Inside the Olympics: A Behind-the-Scenes Look at the Politics, the Scandals, and the Glory of the Games* (Etobicoke, Canada: John Wiley and Sons Canada, 2004). For more recent material on doping at the 2004 Summer Olympics in Athens, see the article "Doping" by Charlie Gillis (*Maclean's*, vol. 117, no. 34, August 23, 2004, pp. 20–21, 23). For more recent material on doping at the 2006 Winter Olympics in Turin, see the article "Athletes Are Facing Increased Vigilance" by Lynn Zinser and John Eligon *New York Times*, February 12, 2006, sect. 8, p. 9). Otherwise, books and articles listed in Chapter 7 focus on specific scandals involving East German athletes, Ben Johnson, Marion Jones, and Chinese swimmers.

Professional Sports

News of steroid use by professional baseball players fills the sports pages these days. A recent book by Will Carroll, *Juiced: The Real Story of Baseball's Drug Problems* (Chicago: Ivan R. Dee, 2005), is a good source on this topic. An even more recent book has received substantial media attention for its accusations that Barry Bonds used banned drugs; *Game of Shadows: Barry Bonds, BALCO, and the Steroids Scandal that Rocked Professional Sports* (New York: Gotham Books, 2006) by Mark Fainaru-Wada and Lance Williams carefully documents the use of performance-enhancing drugs by Bonds and other athletes. For a summary of congressional testimony that had earlier publicized the problem of drug use in baseball, see the article "A Major League Mess" in *Newsweek* (vol. 145, no. 13, March 28, 2005, pp. 26–27) by Mark Starr and Eve Conant.

LEGAL RESEARCH

The search for federal laws on drugs and sports is relatively straightforward because only a few laws have been passed. The text of the most important ones—the 1970 Controlled Substances Act, the 1990 Anabolic Steroids Control Act, and the 2004 Anabolic Steroids Control Act—can be found through a web search. For more detail—and more complexity—a search of the U.S. Code will turn up a variety of specific laws. Go to the Cornell Law School web site (http://www4.law.cornell.edu/uscode), and click "Title 21 on Food and Drug" to search for laws on steroids, sports, and doping. It is harder to find information on state laws, but *Legal Muscle: Anabolics in America* (East Meadow, N.Y.: Legal Muscle Publishing, 2002) by Rick Collins summarizes the laws and penalties for steroid use and distribution in all 50 states.

Several court decisions directly address the issue of use of drugs in sports (see Chapter 2). The cases usually involve athletes protesting suspension for drug use. Information on the most publicized cases can be found through searches of newspapers *(New York Times)* and general search engines (Google, Yahoo!). To obtain written decisions for cases on drugs and sports, electronic law libraries such as Westlaw and Lexus-Nexus include court opinions (but require access through a subscribing library). Opinions of the Supreme Court can be obtained from the Legal Information Institute (http://www.law.cornell.edu).

CHAPTER 7

ANNOTATED BIBLIOGRAPHY

The following annotated bibliography on drugs and sports contains five sections:

- overviews
- scientific and medical aspects
- social and policy aspects
- Olympic sports
- professional sports

Within each of these sections, the citations are divided into subsections on books, articles, and web documents. The topics and citations include technical and nontechnical works, in-depth and short treatments, and research and opinion pieces.

OVERVIEWS

BOOKS

Aretha, David. *Steroids and Other Performance-Enhancing Drugs.* Berkeley, N.J.: Enslow Publishers, 2005. Like many other books on steroids written for junior high and high-school students, this one warns readers of the risks of health problems, violence, and addiction that come from steroid use. Although short, the book provides information on steroids that is direct and easy to understand.

Donohoe, Tom, and Neil Johnson. *Foul Play: Drug Abuse in Sports.* Oxford, UK: Blackwell, 1988. One of the first books to express concern about the spread of drugs in sports, this work demonstrates how little the problem has changed in more than 15 years. The authors, both scientists who nonetheless write clearly and for nonspecialists, give examples of misuse of drugs by athletes and describe how the spread of drugs has harmed sports competition.

Dudley, William, ed. *Drugs and Sports*. San Diego: Greenhaven Press, 2000. The essays in this short book are aimed at teens and present a fair but still largely negative and discouraging view of drugs in sports. Citing examples such as steroid use by East German swimmers and American baseball players, the essays discuss the pressures that lead athletes to use drugs and the difficulties of controlling the problem.

Fitzhugh, Karla. *Steroids*. Chicago: Heinemann Library, 2005. Part of a series for adolescents on drugs and drug abuse, this short book aims to help teens make intelligent decisions about steroids and understand the pressures that might lead them to try the drug. It also provides information on how steroids affect the body and the mind. To help make the material interesting, it supplements the technical information with case studies of users, counselors, and medical professionals.

Goldman, Bob, and Ronald Klatz. *Death in the Locker Room II: Drugs and Sports*. Chicago: Elite Sports Medicine Publications, 1992. The first edition of this book gave an early warning about the spread of drugs in sports and the harm of drugs for athletes. In this updated edition, Dr. Goldman, a world-champion strength athlete, tells the stories and provides photos of many athletes who became sick or sometimes died from, in his view, the misuse of steroids and other performance-enhancing drugs. The book, described as an exposé, aims to shock more than carefully review the evidence.

Kuhn, Cynthia, Scott Swartzwelder, and Wilkie Wilson. *Pumped: Straight Facts for Athletes about Drugs, Supplements, and Training*. New York: W. W. Norton, 2000. The authors, researchers in pharmacology at Duke University Medical School, provide clear and accessible scientific answers to questions about the benefits and safety of a wide variety of performance-enhancing drugs. Taking a skeptical attitude and relying on scientific information rather than on personal claims and anecdotes, they conclude that many of the drugs do not work as well as advocates claim. The book is aimed at athletes wanting to improve their performance but is a useful reference for others as well.

Levinson, David, and Karen Christensen, eds. *Encyclopedia of World Sport*. Great Barrington, Mass.: Berkshire Publishing, 2005. Along with listings for hundreds of sports, this encyclopedia contains several pages on drugs and drug testing. The pages offer an overview of the topic, covering key points about the history of the problem, the motivations for use of drugs by athletes, and current policies. The entry is clearly written and accessible.

Monroe, Judy. *Steroids, Sports, and Body Image: The Risks of Performance-Enhancing Drugs*. Berkeley, N.J.: Enslow, 2004. This book for young people warns of the "disastrous effects of steroids" and the steps that can be taken to avoid them. It offers tips on drug-free training that can help teens gain athletic success the healthy way. The attention to body image highlights the fact that many teens are attracted to steroids for the way it makes them look rather than for the way it helps them perform in sports.

Roleff, Tamara L., and James Haley, eds. *Performance-Enhancing Drugs*. San Diego: Greenhaven Press, 2002. Part of the At Issue series, this book presents competing viewpoints on the use of drugs in sports. The articles it includes present opinions of both sides of debates over testing, Olympic oversight, health effects, and performance benefits.

Rutstein, Jeff. *The Steroid Deceit: A Body to Die For*. Boston: Custom Fitness, 2005. The author, a trainer who abused steroids for three and a half years, now warns of the dangers of the drug to others, particularly teens. He talks about his own experiences with steroids—both the benefits in building the kind of body he wanted and the damage it did to his life. He also provides information on the dangers of steroids to the health and psychological well-being of users.

Taylor, William N. *Anabolic Steroids and the Athlete, 2nd Edition*. Jefferson, N.C.: McFarland, 2002. A comprehensive and understandable overview of steroid use in sports that covers history, policy, medical effects, and drug testing. The author expresses his strong opinions and sometimes overwhelms the reader with technical details but generally provides a wealth of useful information. This second edition updates the first edition written 20 years earlier but still reflects the theme that anabolic steroids should be used for medical uses and not to improve sports performance.

———. *Macho Medicine: A History of the Anabolic Steroid Epidemic*. Jefferson, N.C.: McFarland, 1991. Both an early advocate of the medical uses of steroids and an early critic of the performance-enhancing uses of steroids, Dr. Taylor wrote this book to warn others about what he called the steroid epidemic. The history covers the views of physicians and policy makers on the spread of steroids more than the views of athletes. For example, Taylor describes how many physicians and sports groups dismissed the value of steroids in the 1970s and the evidence that emerged in the 1980s to clearly establish the benefits of steroids for sports performance.

Todd, Terry, "A History of the Use of Anabolic Steroids in Sport," in Jack W. Berryman and Roberta J. Park, eds., *Sport and Exercise Science: Essays in the History of Sports Medicine*. Urbana: University of Illinois Press, 1992, pp. 319–350. Only one article in this edited volume addresses the issues of drugs in sports, but the article lists historical facts not easily found elsewhere. Terry Todd, a former weightlifter and now a professor, traces how primitive forms of drug use by athletes in the 19th century developed into the more sophisticated forms of doping in the 1980s.

Annotated Bibliography

Yesalis, Charles E., and Virginia S. Cowart. *The Steroids Game: An Expert's Inside Look at Anabolic Steroid Use in Sports.* Champaign, Ill.: Human Kinetics, 1998. Dr. Yesalis, a well-known professor and expert on steroids, collaborates with Cowart, a medical writer, to offer an accessible, informative, and accurate overview of steroid use in sports. The book discusses the benefits and harm of steroids, programs to prevent steroid use and deal with addiction, and methods used to test for steroids. To make the material of interest to teens as well as adults, the book supplements technical information with numerous stories about the use of steroids by athletes.

ARTICLES

Cannella, Stephen. "Steroids R Us." *Sports Illustrated*, vol. 102, no. 15, April 11, 2005, pp. 20–21. In reviewing reported instances of steroid use across a variety of sports, the author states, "It now seems that steroids, rather than the thrill of victory and the pain of defeat, are what unite the wide world of sports." The article also discusses the congressional hearings as well as the demands of politicians for sports leagues to do more to deal with the steroid problem.

Gambaccini, Peter. "The Unfair Advantage." *Sport*, vol. 83, October 1992, p. 18. As noted in this article, reliance on performance-enhancing drugs had not abated even four years after the scandal involving the use of steroids by Olympic runner Ben Johnson. The article discusses new concerns about use of human growth hormone to increase muscle size, an asthma drug called clenbuterol to reduce fat, and so-called break drugs to stop puberty (used by young female gymnasts).

Husch, Jerri. "Drugs and Sports." *World Health*, July/August 1995, p. 9. In a special issue on preventing drug abuse, the World Health Organization magazine includes an article on the growing problem of drugs used for sports performance. The article presents figures on the extent of the problem and describes possible prevention programs.

Noakes, Timothy D. "Tainted Glory—Doping and Athletic Performance." *New England Journal of Medicine*, vol. 351, no. 9, August 26, 2004, pp. 847–849. This article in a prestigious medical journal expresses its opposition to the use of performance-enhancing drugs by athletes. The author describes how the drugs have distorted the upper range of human athletic performance and threatened the moral integrity of modern sport. As would be expected in a medical journal, he also emphasizes the concern of physicians that the drugs create health risks for athletes.

Taylor, William N. "Super Athletes Made to Order: Anabolic Steroids and Synthetic Human Growth Hormone." *Psychology Today*, vol. 19, May 1985, pp. 62–66. This early article warns of the health dangers from use of anabolic steroids and human growth hormone to improve sports performance. It argues for making these drugs controlled substances. Such restrictions are needed to overcome the financial incentives and national prestige that come from superior athletic performance and make it hard for athletes to resist drug use.

WEB DOCUMENTS

"Doping." Office of National Drug Control Policy. Available online. URL: http://www.whitehousedrugpolicy.gov/prevent/sports/doping.html. Updated September 27, 2005. This web site sponsored by the White House drug control office defines doping as "the use of a substance or method that is potentially harmful to the athlete's health and/or is capable of enhancing performance. It also refers to the presence in an athlete's body of a prohibited substance or evidence of the use of a prohibited method." It lists the most common drugs used in doping and the health risks they may cause. Although short, the page offers an overview of the variety of drugs used by athletes.

"Doping (Sport)." Wikipedia, the Free Encyclopedia. Available online. URL: http://www.en.wikipedia.org/wiki/Doping_(sport). Accessed December 2006. This short introduction to the problem of sports doping describes the most common drugs used by athletes and the policies of sports organizations. It also provides a list of athletes found guilty of using drugs in Olympic Games and in baseball.

"Drugs in Sports News." Drugs in Sports. Available online. URL: http://www.drugsinsport.net. Accessed December 2006. Along with a listing of recent news stories on doping, this web site offers an archive of past stories and a list of other web-based resources. The page is sponsored by Welsh sports enthusiasts who are also experts on drug and alcohol misuse.

"FindLaw Drug Watch: Drug Use in Sports." FindLaw: Legal News and Commentary. Available online. URL: http://www.news.findlaw.com/legalnews/sports/drugs/index.html. Accessed December 2006. This legal information service compiles links to other web sites on drug policies of major sporting organizations, common performance-enhancing drugs, drug-testing laws, and preventing drug use. The page itself offers little information but is a handy link to information elsewhere.

"Full Coverage: Drugs in Sports." Yahoo! News. Available online. URL: http://www.news.yahoo.com/fc/Sports/Drugs_in_Sports;_ylt=A86.I0eiX_9DJRAAfAiQFs0F;_ylu=X3 oDMTA2ZGZwam4yBHNlYwNmYw—. Accessed December 2006. Yahoo! maintains a page with recent news stories, feature articles, and editorials on drugs in sports. By compiling stories from a variety of newspapers and sources, the web site allows researchers and sports fans to find the latest information quickly and easily. The stories focus more on news than analysis and background but can help keep researchers up to date.

"NIDA InfoFacts: Steroids (Anabolic-Androgenic)." National Institute on Drug Abuse. Available online. URL: http://www.drugabuse.gov/Infofacts/Steroids.html. Updated March 2005. This short and clearly written document describes the extent of steroid use by teens and the health hazards that may result. Largely aimed to discourage steroid use, it states, "Depression often is seen when the drugs are stopped and may contribute to dependence on anabolic steroids. Researchers report also that users may suffer from paranoid jealousy, extreme irritability, delusions, and impaired judgment stemming from feelings of invincibility."

"Research Report: Anabolic Steroid Abuse." National Institute on Drug Abuse. Available online. URL:http://www.drugabuse.gov/ResearchReports/Steroids/Anabolicsteroids.html. Updated September 2006. This clearly written and useful report summarizes the research on anabolic steroids in the form of questions and answers. The questions ask why do people take anabolic steroids, what are the health consequences of steroids, and are anabolic steroids addictive? Each question is answered in a few paragraphs. The page provides an excellent starting point for learning about the topic.

"Ten Drug Scandals." CBS News Online. Available online. URL: http://www.cbc.ca/sports/indepth/drugs/stories/top10.html. Posted January 19, 2003. This article ranks government-sponsored cheating by East German Olympic athletes as the number one drug scandal, Ben Johnson as number four, the Tour de France drug use as seven, and use of steroids by baseball players as number eight. For each of these and six others, the article includes several paragraphs describing the scandal and its importance. This helpful review covers early as well as more recent scandals.

Zaccardi, Nick. "Anabolic Steroids." Monterey Preventive Medical Clinic. Available online. URL: http://www.wellnessmd.com/anabolics.html. Updated February 25, 2004. A University of Massachusetts expert presents an introduction to steroids that provides more detail than most web sites but also is shorter and more accessible than most articles and books. Although the references are not easy to track, this page is a good place to start for those beginning research on the topic.

SCIENTIFIC AND MEDICAL ASPECTS

BOOKS

Bahrke, Michael S., and Charles E. Yesalis, eds. *Performance-Enhancing Substances in Sport and Exercise*. Champaign, Ill.: Human Kinetics, 2002.

Drugs and Sports

Comprehensive and technical, this edited volume presents the latest research on a variety of performance-enhancing drugs, including steroids, blood doping, narcotics, diet supplements, alcohol, marijuana, stimulants, and designer drugs. Readers may choose to skip over the details from chemistry, physiology, pharmacology, and medicine, and they should recognize that the scientists who evaluate claims about the benefits of drugs generally take a skeptical view. Otherwise, the information is current and useful, particularly the chapter on the history of doping in sports.

Carson-DeWitt, Rosalyn. *Encyclopedia of Drugs, Alcohol, and Addictive Behavior. 2nd Edition.* New York: Macmillan Reference, 2001. This four-volume encyclopedia contains entries on specific drugs, each with information on its effects and health risks. Entries on anabolic steroids, amphetamines, and other performance-enhancing drugs disclose little about their use in sports but give background information that can help explain the attraction of athletes to the drugs and the risks they face from taking them.

Ciola, Tom. *Steroids Kill: Will You Be the Next Victim.* Orlando, Fla.: Axion, 2004. The title highlights the theme of this book, which includes interviews with ex-steroid users as well as information about the dangerous, even deadly, side effects of steroids. It aims to scare potential users from trying the drug.

Daniels, Richard C. *The Anabolic Steroid Handbook.* Eastbourne, UK: Gardners Books, 2003. A reference guide to using steroids, this book advertises itself as an aid to building an awesome physique like that of a professional bodybuilder. Based on the theme that knowledge is a powerful tool, it describes a variety of steroid products, their proper dose and usage, and their side effects.

Icon Group International. *Anabolic Steroids—A Medical Dictionary, Bibliography, and Annotated Research Guide to Internet References.* San Diego: Icon Group International, 2003. This book, which can also be purchased in digital form, aims to help medical professionals, students, and members of the public conduct research on anabolic steroids. It provides definitions of key terms, references, and a guide to Internet sources.

Lenehan, Pat. *Anabolic Steroids and Other Performance-Enhancing Drugs.* London: Taylor and Francis, 2003. Although short in length and sometimes technical in wording, this book offers a helpful overview and introduction to steroid use. It provides a social history of the spread of steroids, a summary of the medical consequences of steroid use, and a review of some of the recent controversies and developments in drug testing. The book ends with a description of each of the most common steroid products.

Llewellyn, William. *Anabolics 2005.* Broadbeach, Australia: Body of Science, 2005. Called the authoritative source for information on steroids, this book contains more than 500 pages on 140 muscle-building products. The volume is the latest of a series aimed at bodybuilders and weightlifters who would like to use steroids. The author is outspoken—and controversial—in his advocacy of the safe use of steroids.

Miah, Andy. *Genetically Modified Athletes: Biomedical Ethics, Gene Doping and Sport.* New York: Routledge 2004. The use of genetic technology to improve sports performance raises ethical issues that, according to this book, the current approach to dealing with doping cannot handle. The book, aimed mostly at academics, examines this issue by questioning whether authorities should even try to protect sport from genetic modification. It addresses questions about the definition of cheating, the right to genetic privacy, the usefulness of terms such as doping, and the notions of personal autonomy and personhood in the context of advances in genetic technology.

Mottram, David R. *Drugs in Sport. 3rd Edition.* London: Routledge, 2003. A technical volume largely for scholars and scientists, this book is similar to Bahrke and Yesalis's *Performance-Enhancing Substances in Sport and Exercise.* Chapters review the most recent research, particularly in Britain and Europe, on the benefits and risks of performance-enhancing drugs. Readers can learn the most from the chapter summaries, which offer conclusions in less technical language than the rest of the chapters.

Naam, Ramez. *More than Human: Embracing the Promise of Biological Enhancement.* New York: Broadway Books, 2005. Although a broad study of the potential uses of biological technology to deal with problems of health, disability, and aging, this book also discusses how the technology affects sports. The author notes, for example, that EPO boosts the natural production of red blood cells in the body and that gene therapy can help the body improve itself naturally. The future will make it increasingly difficult to separate the use of external drugs by athletes from natural processes. In general, the book takes a positive view about the future application of biotechnology to sports.

Tamburrini, Claudio, and Torbjorn Tannsjo, eds. *Genetic Technology and Sport: Ethical Questions.* New York: Routledge, 2005. Experts from sports science, genetics, philosophy, ethics, and international sports administration consider how new genetic technology may affect sports and the ethical debates that surround the use of genetic technology to improve performance of healthy athletes rather than treat injury and disease.

Wadler, Gary I., and Brian Hainline, eds. *Drugs and the Athlete.* Philadelphia: F.A. Davis, 1989. Written for scientists and containing chapters on each of the major banned substances, this book is of most interest for how the understanding of drugs and sports has changed in the last several decades. Bahrke and Yesalis's *Performance-Enhancing Substances in Sports and Exercise* provides more current information, but this book shows how current knowledge has developed.

Yesalis, Charles E., ed. *Anabolic Steroids in Sport and Exercise. 2nd Edition.* Champaign, Ill.: Human Kinetics, 2000. Like the volume edited by Yesalis on performance-enhancing substances more generally, this edited volume on steroids offers a sometimes highly technical but still useful overview of the research on effects and side effects. Chapters cover numerous topics related to steroids: history, incidence of use, prevention, health effects, psychological effects, dependence, testing, legal issues, and women's issues. Even those uninterested in the scientific details can benefit from the introductory and concluding sections of the chapters.

ARTICLES

Alexander, Brian. "The Awful Truth about Drugs." *Outside*, vol. 30, no. 7, July 2005, pp. 101–108. Also available online. URL: http://outside.away. com/outside/features/200507/drugs-in-sports-1.html. Posted July 2005. Drug-testing expert Dr. Don Catlin, who runs the UCLA Olympic Analytic Laboratory, which analyzes the samples of athletes for drugs, is profiled in this article. Catlin is surprisingly pessimistic about the effectiveness of drug testing (despite his own role in identifying the designer drug THG and developing tests for its presence in the urine of athletes). He sees it as all too easy for athletes to stay ahead of the drug testers and argues for radical change in the current approach to stopping drug use. This article is an excellent overview of the difficult issues and debates involving drug testing.

Bahrke, M. S., C. E. Yesalis, and J. E. Wright. "Psychological and Behavioral Effects of Endogenous Testosterone and Anabolic-Androgenic Steroids: An Update." *Sports Medicine*, vol. 22, no. 6, December 1996, pp. 367–390. This review concludes that there is an association between psychological problems and steroid use. The authors suggest, however, that severe psychological problems are rare: "With estimates of over 1 million past or current users in the US, an extremely small percentage of individuals using anabolic-androgenic steroids appear to experience mental disturbances severe enough to result in clinical treatment and medical case reports."

Baum, Antonia. "Eating Disorders in the Male Athlete." *Sports Medicine*, vol. 36, no.1, 2006, pp. 1–6. Eating disorders exist among men, although less commonly than among women. As noted in this article, the problem has a link to steroids. Athletes who want to stay muscular yet thin or keep within weight limits of their sports sometimes take the risky step of combining steroids with extreme diets. The article gives advice to physicians, coaches, trainers, and family members about how to treat the problem.

Behar, Michael. "Will Genetics Destroy Sports?" *Discover*, vol. 25, no. 7, July 2004, pp. 40–45. Although the application of gene therapy to humans is years away, the technology has the potential to significantly improve the size and strength of muscles. As a result, the World Anti-Doping Agency has already banned the nontherapeutic use of genes, genetic materials, and cells to improve performance. This article discusses how advances in science affect sports and doping.

Birkeland, Kåre I., and Peter Hemmersbach. "The Future of Doping Control in Athletes: Issues Related to Blood Sampling." *Sports Medicine*, vol. 28, no. 1, 1999, p. 25. Although drug testing had relied only on urine samples for decades, new forms of testing using blood samples began in the 2000s. This article reviews the differences in the two types of tests, the benefits of using blood tests, and the ethical and legal issues raised by taking blood samples.

Boyce, Eric G. "Use and Effectiveness of Performance-Enhancing Substances." *Journal of Pharmacy Practice*, vol. 16, no. 1, 2003, pp. 22–36. This article provides an introduction for pharmacists to the use and effects of selected performance-enhancing drugs and supplements. With a better understanding of the drugs, pharmacists and other health-care professionals can help monitor use by the public and control illegal use by athletes.

Brehm, Mike. "Hair-Loss Drug Causes Goalie to Fail Test." *USA Today*, February 10, 2006, p. 8C. The World Anti-Doping Agency recently banned the use of a chemical called finasteride because it can mask the presence of steroids in urine. However, the anti-baldness drug Propecia contains finasteride. Jose Theodore, the former goalie of the NHL Montreal Canadians and currently with the Colorado Avalanche, failed a pre-Olympic drug test because of his longtime use of Propecia. The NHL approved the use of the drug as a medicine for therapeutic use, but Olympic authorities have not.

Bronson, Franklin H., and Curt M. Matherne. "Exposure to Anabolic-Androgenic Steroids Shortens Life Span of Male Mice." *Medicine and Science in Sports and Exercise*. vol. 29, no. 5, May 1997, pp. 615–619. Although exposing human subjects to the potential harm of excess steroids is unethical, some insights on the risks of the drug can come from studies of animals. In this study, 52 percent of mice given high doses of steroids died, 35 percent given low doses died, and 12 percent given no steroids died. The mice with steroids showed increased liver and kidney tumors and heart problems. The results from mice do not apply directly to humans, but the results suggest there are reasons to be concerned about the health effects of steroids.

Drugs and Sports

Campos, Daniel R., Mauricio Yonamine, and Regina L. de Moraes Moreau. "Marijuana as Doping in Sports." *Sports Medicine*, vol. 33, no. 6, 2003, pp. 395–399. This review of the literature on the effects of marijuana finds that it may reduce anxiety but otherwise does not have beneficial effects for sports performance. A high incidence of positive tests for the drug among athletes nonetheless suggests that many believe it will help improve their performance. The authors hope the findings about the limited benefits will discourage athletes from using of marijuana before competitions.

Carroll, Will. "The Creator." *Sports Illustrated*, vol. 102, no. 17, April 25, 2005, pp. 18–19. The author meets with a man (who does not give his name) reputed to have created the designer drug THG. The creator says that producing new designer drugs is not hard and will allow athletes to stay a step ahead of testers. The article gives some insight into the secret world of steroid development and the difficulty of eliminating drugs from sports. It also tells an interesting story of how the creator manages to meet with the author while keeping his identity secret.

Cazeneuve, Brian. "Risky Business: C. Clausen's Research on Supplements." *Sports Illustrated*, vol. 98, no. 14, April 7, 2003, p. 70. Olympic walker Curt Clausen uses dozens of legal nutritional supplements every day. He warns athletes, however, that they need to take special care to know what ingredients are included in their pills, powders, and drinks. Some products include banned ingredients that the labels do not list.

Clark, Kim. "The Steroid Detective: Interview with D. Catlin." *U.S. News and World Report*, vol. 137, no. 22, December 20, 2004, p. 19. Don Catlin heads a University of California Los Angeles drug lab that analyzes urine samples from professional athletes. He and his lab played a key role in discovering the chemical makeup of the designer steroid THG and developing a test for it. In this interview, Catlin discusses the BALCO scandal and the implications it will have for drug testing.

Diamanti-Kandarakis, Evanthia, Panagiotis A. Konstantinopoulos, Joanna Papailiou, Stylianos A. Kandarakis, Anastasios Andreopoulos, and Gerasimos P. Sykiotis. "Erythropoietin Abuse and Erythropoietin Gene Doping: Detection Strategies in the Genomic Era." *Sports Medicine*, vol. 35, no. 10, 2005, pp. 831–840. Although technical in nature, this article discusses an issue of special concern these days—the limitations of tests for EPO and the development of new forms of EPO that are even harder to detect. It then discusses possible new approaches to overcome existing test limitations.

Fox, Marisa. "Brave New Foods: Foods That Work Like Drugs." *Women's Sports and Fitness*, vol. 3, no. 6, June 2000, pp. 104–107. Suggesting that certain foods can provide an alternative to performance-enhancing drugs, this article describes some of these "functional foods" or superfoods and their benefits. A functional food is one that provides health benefits beyond basic nutrition, and the field of nutritional medicine suggests that many foods can help athletes perform better.

Grant, Eleanor. "Of Muscles and Mania: Steroid Induced Psychosis among Bodybuilders; Study by Harrison G. Pope Jr. and David L. Katz." *Psychology Today*, vol. 21, September 1987, p. 12. This article reports on the findings of a classic study that athletes and bodybuilders using steroids are prone to paranoia, hallucinations, delusions of grandeur, and violent tendencies. The findings come from interviews of steroid users, who sometimes describe hearing voices and often describe extreme mood swings. The symptoms appear to have started with steroid use and ended when steroids were discontinued. The findings have had considerable influence on the understanding of the risks of steroids.

Gruber, Amanda J., and Harrison G. Pope, Jr. "Psychiatric and Medical Effects of Anabolic-Androgenic Steroid Use in Women." *Psychotherapy and Psychosomatics*, vol. 69, no. 1, 2000, pp. 19–26. The authors gave psychiatric exams to 75 dedicated women athletes recruited from gyms in the Boston area. They found that 33 percent formerly or currently used steroids and other performance-enhancing drugs and that users showed more physical and psychological problems than non-users.

Hecht, Annabel. "Anabolic Steroids: Pumping Trouble." *FDA Consumer*, vol. 18, September 1984, pp. 12–15. An early statement from the FDA, a government agency in charge of ensuring the safety of food and drugs, describes the health risks of steroids. It claims, however, that studies have not demonstrated the ability of steroids to improve performance—studies since then have clearly demonstrated the benefits of steroids.

Jereski, Laura. "It Gives Athletes a Boost—Maybe Too Much: Erythropoietin." *Business Week*, December 11, 1989, p. 123. An early story about EPO, a drug that increases the body's production of oxygen-carrying red-blood cells, describes research on the drug's benefits and side effects. At the time of the article, tests did not exist to detect use of the drug, but they do now.

Johnson, Steven. "A Cut Above: Elective-Enhancement Surgery for Athletes." *Wired*, vol. 13, no. 3, March 2005, pp. 25–26. Noting that tests can now more easily catch drug users than in the past, the article suggests that athletes may turn to other ways to improve performance. For example, some types of elective surgeries can strengthen ligaments that allow pitchers to throw harder. With recovery time from surgery growing shorter, elective surgery may become a new form of performance enhancement in sports.

Jones, Chris. "Vicodins for Breakfast." *Esquire*, vol. 142, no. 4, October 2004, pp. 112–116. Vicodin is a painkiller that contains a form of codeine.

It is easy to take but become less effective over time and leads users to take increasingly large doses. This article tells about an anonymous NFL football player who took the painkiller to deal with the injuries during the season and the health risks he and other players face from overuse of the drug.

Kam, P. C. A., and M. Yarrow. "Anabolic Steroid Abuse: Physiological and Anaesthetic Considerations." *Anaesthesia*, vol. 60, no. 7, July 2005, pp. 685–692. This article describes possible health consequences of steroid use that might add special risk to those undergoing surgery. It suggests that anesthetists become familiar with these consequences, as steroid use might affect the health of their patients.

Keane, Helen. "Anabolic Steroids and Dependence." *Contemporary Drug Problems*, vol. 30, no. 3, fall 2003, pp. 541–562. The author argues that steroid users do not become dependent or addicted in the same way as users of other drugs. Unlike cocaine or heroin, the physiological source of dependence on steroids has not been identified by researchers, which makes the meaning of steroid dependence or addiction less clear.

Leder, Benjamin Z., Christopher Longcope, Don H. Catlin, Brian Ahrens, David A. Schoenfeld, and Joel S. Finkelstein. "Oral Androstenedione Administration and Serum Testosterone Concentrations in Young Men." *Journal of the American Medical Association*, vol. 283, no. 6, February 9, 2000, pp. 779–782. This article attempts to settle debates over whether the steroid precursor androstenedione has effects similar to steroids themselves. The study finds that taking high doses of the precursor increases testosterone and concludes that it does have steroidlike effects.

Liotard, Philippe. "Sport Medicine: to Heal or to Win?" *The UNESCO Courier*, vol. 53, no. 9, September 2000, p. 37. This article discusses the dilemma faced by sports physicians: How do they reconcile demands of society and patients for drugs that help performance with ethical considerations about fairness in sports? It offers advice to doctors on when and how to respond to requests of athletes for drugs and on how to decide if a request is medically legitimate. While most articles on drugs and sports focus on the athletes, this one focuses on physicians.

Matheson, Gordon O. "Steroids in Sports." *Physician and Sportsmedicine*, vol. 33, no. 5, May 2005, p. 6. The author argues that physicians should refuse to serve as team doctors when their position involves helping athletes use performance-enhancing drugs. Their duty is to prevent and treat health problems rather than to make healthy athletes perform better.

Maughan, R. J. "Contamination of Dietary Supplements and Positive Drug Tests in Sport." *Journal of Sports Sciences*, vol. 23, no. 9, 2005, pp. 883–889. Even legal nutritional supplements can include, through accidental or intentional contamination in manufacturing, substances banned by athletic organizations. Athletes are responsible for all banned substances in their body, even if they unknowingly take them with nutritional supplements. This article describes the risks athletes face in using such supplements.

Pärssinen, M., U. Kujala, E. Vartiainen, S. Sarna, and T. Seppälä. "Increased Premature Mortality of Competitive Powerlifters Suspected to Have Used Anabolic Agents." *International Journal of Sports Medicine*, vol. 21, 2000, pp. 225–227. In finding that powerlifters who used steroids died earlier than population controls, this study argues that stronger measures to stop steroid use will contribute to the long-term health of athletes.

Pear, Marcia J. "Steroid Roulette: Taking Male Hormones Is Risky Business for Women. Case of Cyclist C. Olavarri." *Women's Sports and Fitness*, vol. 14, October 1992, pp. 18–19. Along with the usual information on the medical and psychological harm of steroids, this article tells of the experience of one woman athlete who used steroids. According to cyclist Cindy Olavarri, the damage from steroid use ended her athletic career.

Pincock, Stephen. "Gene Doping." *Lancet*, vol. 366, Supplement, December 17, 2005, pp. S18–S19. The author discusses the response of the World Anti-Doping Agency to the potential use of gene doping or gene therapy to improving athletic performance. He describes the problems in detecting use of gene doping by athletes and the various approaches that authorities might try to overcome the problems. He also argues that gene doping, which could lead to serious health problems, unethically distorts scientific developments intended only to treat disease.

Pope, H. G., Jr., E. M. Kouri, and M. D. Hudson. "Effects of Supraphysiologic Doses of Testosterone on Mood and Aggression in Normal Men." *Archives of General Psychiatry*, vol. 57, no. 2, February 2000, pp, 133–140. This experiment observed the psychological effects of taking steroids among 56 volunteer men ages 20–50. The results showed little psychological change for about 84 percent of the subjects but increases in symptoms of mania and depression for the other 13 percent. The authors conclude that steroids can cause psychological harm but that the effects vary for individuals.

Rinaldi, Robin. "Pill Primer." *Runner's World*, vol. 40, no. 4, April 2005, pp. 52–53. Legal pain relievers that users can buy and take without a prescription get little attention in discussions of drugs and sports. However, this article notes that, along with the benefits they bring, pain relievers can cause problems for athletes. When used to reduce muscle discomfort or swelling, they can give runners (and other athletes) a false sense of security, leading them to train too strenuously and risk greater injury.

Sokolove, Michael. "The Lab Animal: Enhancing Athletic Performance through Drugs and Genetic Manipulation." *New York Times Magazine*,

January 18, 2004, pp. 28–33, 48, 54, 58. After briefly describing how science has aided sports performance in the past, this article discusses how advances in human genetics may do the same in the future—though in a completely new way. Given its special nature, gene therapy for sports is almost impossible to detect with current technology. Once again, science may change the nature of sports competition.

"Sports-Supplement Dangers." *Consumer Reports*, vol. 66, no. 6, June 2001, pp. 40–42. This report on sport supplements, including various types of steroid precursors, reviews the scientific evidence on their effectiveness and health consequences. It concludes that, despite the billions of dollars spent by Americans on the products, they produce only small changes in performance, while having the potential to upset the body's hormonal balance. The article states that more controls on the marketing and sales of these products are necessary.

Tokish, John M., Mininder S. Kocher, and Richard J. Hawkins. "Ergogenic Aids: A Review of Basic Science, Performance, Side Effects, and Status in Sports." *American Journal of Sports Medicine*, vol. 32, no. 6, September 2004, pp. 1543–1553. Sports physicians are urged in this article to become more familiar with the benefits and risks of performance-enhancing drugs. To help in this goal, the article reviews the evidence on the effects and side effects of steroids, human growth hormone, amphetamines, EPO, and a variety of supplements. It concludes that "an understanding of these products is essential for the sports medicine practitioner to provide sound, safe advice to the athlete."

Trenton, Adam J., and Glenn W. Currier. "Behavioural Manifestations of Anabolic Steroid Use." *CNS Drugs*, vol. 19, no. 7, 2005, pp. 571–595. This article by two psychiatrists reviews the literature on the adverse psychological impact of steroid use by athletes. It identifies how steroid use is linked to aggression, violence, mania, dependence, and sometime psychosis and suicide, and it offers suggestions on how to treat the symptoms and promote recovery.

Vogel, Gretchen. "Mighty Mice: Inspiration for Rogue Athletes?" *Science*, vol. 305, July 30, 2004, p. 633. This report on so-called super mice describes how a special gene given to mice can produce growth-factor proteins, build more muscles, allow for faster recovery from injury, and lead to longer life span. The article discusses possible future efforts to give humans similar genes. Along with creating a new form of doping that would not be detectable in the blood, the use of these genetic techniques raises serious ethical questions.

Walsh, Julie. "Caffeine Boost or Java Jive? Effects on Athletic Performance." *Women's Sports and Fitness*, vol. 17, September 1994, pp. 67–68. At one time banned during Olympic competition, high levels of caffeine may or may not help performance. This article reviews the conflicting evidence, suggesting that caffeine will affect individuals differently and that the choice to use it as a performance enhancer is a personal matter.

Wartik, Nancy. "Athletes on Prozac?" *American Health*, vol. 14, July/August 1995, p. 44. Although several athletes have improved their performance by taking the antidepressant Prozac, this article notes that the drug should be prescribed carefully and may in some cases impair rather than improve performance. On the plus side, Prozac may deal with depression that can slow training and motivation; on the minus side, athletes may mistake depression for tiredness from overtraining and rely on Prozac rather than changing their training regimen.

Weintraub, Arlene. "Can Drug-Busters Beat New Steroids?" *Business Week*, no. 3887, June 14, 2004, pp. 82–83. The main problem in battling efforts by some athletes to use new and undetectable drugs comes largely from funding. Athletes will readily pay for new ways to improve their performance through drugs because it helps them make more money. Funds for scientists to improve drug testing have not kept pace with the financial incentives for new methods of doping. The article concludes that without greater funding, drug cheats will maintain the upper hand in the struggle over testing in sports.

Wolff, Alexander. "A Bitter Pill: Death of S. Bechler Highlights Need for Federal Government to Come to Terms with Ephedra." *Sports Illustrated*, vol. 98, no. 9, March 3, 2003, p. 21. After Orioles pitcher Steve Bechler died during spring training, the medical examiner found the presence of the herb ephedra in Bechler's body. The article reports that many other fatalities have been linked to ephedra, an herbal substance contained in some over-the-counter nutritional supplements. Despite the risks of ephedra to athletes and others, the FDA reports that it does not yet have enough evidence of ephedra's dangers to ban the nutritional substance.

Yonamine, Mauricio, Paula Rodrigues Garcia, and Regina Lúcia de Moraes Moreau. "Non-Intentional Doping in Sports." *Sports Medicine*, vol. 34, no. 11, 2004, pp. 697–704. Drug tests are not able to distinguish drugs taken intentionally to improve performance from drugs taken inadvertently or accidentally absorbed. For example, unintentionally breathing in second-hand marijuana smoke or taking unlisted ingredients in nutritional supplements can lead to drug violations. This article reviews scientific research to determine when claims that positive tests did not result from intentional drug taking might hold true.

Zorpette, Glenn. "Andro Angst: Should the U.S. Regulate Over-the-Counter Supplements?" *Scientific American*, vol. 279, no. 6, December 1998, p. 22. The use of the steroid precursor androstenedione by baseball star Mark McGwire led the author to review the scientific evidence on the benefit and harm of this and other nutritional supplements. He interviews several scientists who believe that steroid precursors act like anabolic steroids and, like steroids, should require prescriptions. Many others came to share this view, and steroid precursors became controlled substances in 2004.

WEB DOCUMENTS

"All in the Mind?" Steering for Steroids. Available online. URL: http://www.whyfiles.org/090doping_sport/5.html. Accessed December 2006. Part of a series of articles on drugs and cycling, this piece on "roid rage" quotes psychiatrist Harrison Pope, who says he has been "involved in a dozen murder cases where someone went on steroids and killed somebody without a history of violence or crime beforehand." Scientific studies have not been able to replicate the psychological harm of steroids found in the real world, however. The problem is that athletes take three to four times the steroids dose as researchers could ethically give in an experiment. The article therefore focuses on real-world cases of steroid-related aggression.

"Anabolic Steroid Abuse." National Institute on Drug Abuse. Available online. URL: http://www.steroidabuse.gov. Accessed December 2006. The National Institute of Drug Abuse (NIDA) has campaigned to warn the public (and teens in particular) about the dangers of steroids. This NIDA web site includes a press release about the extent of the problem, a short video of teens discussing media influences and the attraction to steroids, and several publications. The page makes it clear that the federal agency views steroids as a problem comparable to problems of recreation drug use.

"A Testing Time for Athletics." BBC Sport. Available online. URL: http://www.news.bbc.co.uk/sport1/hi/athletics/841641.stm. Posted July 25, 2000. During the late 1990s, a surprising number of elite Olympic athletes tested positive for the steroid nandrolone. This article suggests that the positive test results could have come from sources other than intentional injection of nandrolone to enhance performance (which most athletes know is almost certain to result in a positive test). Instead, the test results could have come from an unlisted ingredient in pills or food.

"Chemical Warfare: The Dangers of Anabolic Steroids." Natural Strength. Available online. URL: http://www.naturalstrength.com/steroids/default.asp. Accessed December 2006. Sponsored by Bob Whelan, a bodybuilder devoted to drug-free strength training, this page has links to dozens of articles on the risks of anabolic steroids and the benefits of natural strength training. The articles range from opinion pieces to news stories, all with an antisteroid orientation.

"Common Terms Used in the Bodybuilding Community and in the Medical Field." Steroid Information. Available online. URL: http://www.steroidinformation.com/bodybuildingterms.htm. Accessed February 2006. Terms such as anabolic, androgen, gear, cycle, and diuretics are defined on this page. Also included are links to pages on the history of steroids, medical uses of steroids, side effects, and obtaining steroids. The page, although sponsored by a company that sells steroid-related products, provides information from the perspective of users.

DeFrancesco, Laura. "The Faking of Champions." Nature Biotechnology. Available online. URL: http://www.nature.com/news/2004/040823/full/nbt0904-1069.html. Posted August 2004. This article discusses research on the so-called Schwarzenegger mice that have added significant muscle mass after a special gene has been inserted into their cells. This gene therapy research suggests the potential for human athletes to use gene doping to improve their performance.

"Drugs in Sports." Choices in Sports. Available online. URL: http://www.drugfreesport.com/choices/drugs/index.html. Accessed December 2006. Sponsored by the NCAA and aimed at college athletes, this web site provides information on performance-enhancing drugs, drug testing, and making responsible decisions. For each of the drugs it describes, the web site explains why someone would want to use it, what effects it has, how it is used for therapeutic (rather than performance) purposes, and what adverse reactions are associated with it. The page also includes information on nutritional supplements and sports nutrition.

Fahey, Thomas D. "Anabolic-Androgenic Steroids: Mechanism of Action and Effects on Performance." Encyclopedia of Sports Medicine and Science. Available online. URL: http://www.sportsci.org/encyc/anabster/anabster.html. Posted March 7, 1998. More than most other web documents, this one gives information on the biochemical response of cells to steroids. It also describes the psychological and physical harm of steroids.

"FDA Statement on THG." U.S. Food and Drug Administration. Available online. URL: http://www.fda.gov/bbs/topics/NEWS/2003/NEW00967.html. Posted October 28, 2003. After publicity about the newly developed designer steroid tetrahydrogestrinone (THG), the FDA determined that it is an illegal drug, is closely related to other steroids, and cannot be prescribed or sold without first going through a rigorous review by the FDA.

Kuipers, Harm. "Anabolic Steroids: Side Effects." Encyclopedia of Sports Medicine and Science. Available online. URL: http://www.sportsci.org/encyc/anabstereff/anabstereff.html. Posted March 7, 1998. This entry describes the side effects of steroids for liver function, the male reproduction system, the female reproduction system, the cardiovascular system, and personality. It notes that the severity of side effects depends on the drug, dosage, and duration of use but otherwise points to many sources of harm from steroids.

"Modafinil: THG's Partner in Crime?" CBS Sports Online. Available online. URL: http://www.cbc.ca/sports/indepth/drugs/stories/modafinil_faq.html. Posted January 19, 2003. Modafinil is a prescription drug used to help people who suffer from the sleep disorder narcolepsy to stay awake during the day, but athletes also use it to increase alertness. Of special interest, the drug may help mask the use of the designer steroid THG. This story tells more about the drug and lists the athletes, usually competitors in track and field, who have tested positive for it.

Quinn, Elizabeth. "Androstenedione." About.com. Available online. URL: http://www.sportsmedicine.about.com/cs/drugs_doping/a/aa042199a.htm. Posted April 1999. An article on the steroid precursor nicknamed "andro" highlights the similarities it has with steroids. It notes, however, that the drug is not considered a controlled substance, but this has since been changed by Congress in 2004.

"Steroids: Play Safe, Play Fair." American Academy of Pediatrics. Available online. URL: http://www.aap.org/family/steroids.htm. Accessed December 2006. This web site from an association of medical professionals makes a special point about the effects of steroids on growth of middle- and high-school athletes. It states that "anabolic steroids, even in small doses, have been shown to stop growth too soon." The academy also notes that supplements such as "andro" pose risks to teens.

"Steroids Threaten Health of Athletes and Integrity of Sports Performance: American College of Sports Medicine Calls for Increased Vigilance in Identifying and Eradicating Steroid Use." American College of Sports Medicine. Available online. URL: http://www.acsm.org/publications/newsreleases2003/steroids102403.htm. Posted October 23, 2003. The world's largest sports medicine and exercise science organization has 20,000 members. In this press release, the organization calls the health risks of steroids severe and condemns the development of newly designed steroids that make it hard to detect them in standard drug tests.

"Street Terms: Drugs and the Drug Trade. Drug Type: Steroids." Drug Facts, Office of National Drug Control Policy. Available online. URL: http://www.whitehousedrugpolicy.gov/streetterms/ByType.asp?intTypeID=46. Updated April 6, 2005. This page lists the commonly used names of steroids (including slang terms) and offers a brief definition of each.

"The Dope on Banned Drugs." Drugs and Sports: CBC Sports Online Indepth. Available online. URL: http://www.cbc.ca/sports/indepth/drugs/glossary/dictionary.html. Accessed December 2006. For each of 16 performance-enhancing drugs, this short drug dictionary describes the clinical uses, benefits for athletes, reason for banning, sports most associated with its use, and athletes who have tested positive.

"WADA Gene Doping Symposium Reaches Conclusions and Recommendations." World Anti-Doping Agency. Available online. http://www.wada-ama.org/en/newsarticle.ch2?articleId=3115229. Posted December 5, 2005. Scientists at this recent symposium discussed ways to develop tests for gene doping and prevent the use of genetic methods by athletes to improve their performance unfairly. This press release summarizes the conclusions of the meetings and the plans of WADA to deal with gene doping.

SOCIAL AND POLICY ASPECTS

BOOKS

Collins, Rick. *Legal Muscle: Anabolics in America.* East Meadow, N.Y.: Legal Muscle, 2002. Written by a bodybuilder and lawyer who specialized in defending athletes arrested for steroid possession and distribution, Collins's book differs from nearly all others on drug use in sports. Arguing that steroids are safe when used responsibly by adults, he calls for legalization of the drug. The book makes the case for these claims but more so than other books discusses legal issues. It describes the existing laws, the legal risks to steroid users, and the efforts used by law-enforcement personnel to catch steroid users. Taking an unpopular stance, this is a unique and interesting book.

Hoberman, John, and Verner Moller, eds. *Doping and Public Policy.* Odense: University Press of Southern Denmark, 2005. The articles in this volume consider doping from the perspective of those trying to develop a consistent set of policies worldwide. They cover topics such as antidoping campaigns, European policies, and strategies to prevent drug use.

———. *Testosterone Dreams: Rejuvenation, Aphrodisia, Doping.* Berkeley: University of California Press, 2005. This history of synthetic testosterone since its discovery in 1935 argues that the drug has had more influence on culture than many think. Steroids have encouraged popular hopes that medicine can make people feel younger, healthier, and happier. The author views such claims (or fantasies) skeptically, but he sees the future as leading to increased rather than decreased use of steroid-related drugs. With the growth of marketing by pharmaceutical companies to enhance well being and the desire for self-improvement in sports and elsewhere in society, new uses of testosterone products will emerge and present new dangers to society.

Houlihan, Barrie. *Dying to Win: Doping in Sport and the Development of Anti-Doping Policy.* Strasbourg: Council of Europe, 1999. This book offers a history of drug use in sports and antidoping policy with special attention to Europe. Although a bit dated, it provides useful background material on the spread of drugs in international sports and the efforts of sports authorities to control the spread.

Jendrick, Nathan. *Dunks, Doubles, Doping: How Steroids are Killing American Athletics.* Guilford, Conn.: Lyons Press, 2006. The author, an athlete and journalist, interviews Olympic athletes, professional bodybuilders, and physicians about the attraction to steroids and the risks they present. It gives special attention to the social and economic forces that generate this attraction and to the failure of sports organizations to take the steps necessary to stop drug use. Of special interest is the material on famous athletes who have been caught using steroids and what happened to their careers afterward.

Johnston, Lloyd D., Patrick M. O'Malley, Jerald G. Bachman, and John E. Schulenberg. *Monitoring the Future National Results on Adolescent Drug Use: Overview of Key Findings 2004.* Bethesda, Md.: National Institute on Drug Abuse, 2005. Also available online. URL: http://www.monitoringthefuture. org/pubs/monographs/overview2004.pdf. Accessed December 2006. This survey of high-school students has asked questions since 1975 about use of all types of drug use and has included questions on steroids since 1991. The trends presented in this volume show rising steroid use in the last 15 years among seniors, but a more recent decline for 8th and 10th graders.

McCloskey, John, and Julian Bales. *When Winning Costs Too Much: Steroids, Supplements, and Scandal in Today's Sports.* Lanham, Md.: Taylor Trade, 2005. This recently published book does not offer arguments and ideas that differ much from many other antisteroid books. It does include, however, a wealth of examples, stories, and incidents of drug use by athletes that have been culled from newspapers, magazines, and books. The writing style tends toward long lists of drug use by athletes and the risks of steroids, but the coverage of current issues is comprehensive.

O'Leary, John, ed. *Drugs and Doping in Sport: Socio-Legal Perspectives.* London: Cavendish, 2000. The essays in this volume address a growing field in legal studies—sports law. The authors of the essays are academics, legal practitioners, and administrators with interests in issues such as personal liberties, drug testing, and public policy. However, the book focuses on British rather than American law.

Schneider, Angela, Fan Hong, and Robert Butcher, eds. *Doping in Sport: Global Ethical Issues.* New York: Routledge, 2006. More so than other books on genetic technology and sports, this one gives special attention to how different cultures, societies, political systems, countries, and continents view the ethics of doping. Given that nations as well as individual athletes compete at the Olympics, the different ways that nations approach the problem has implications for the fairness of sports competition in the future.

U.S. House of Representatives. *Abuse of Steroids in Amateur and Professional Athletes, Hearing before the Subcommittee on Crime of the Committee on the Judiciary, House of of Representatives, One Hundred First Congress, Second Session.* Washington, D.C.: U.S. Government Printing Office, 1990. This hearing gives special attention to the threat of addiction to steroids among young people and includes an article on the topic in the appendices. It also discusses the risks of human growth hormone for young athletes.

————. *Anabolic Steroid Control Act of 2004, Hearing before the Subcommittee on Crime, Terrorism, and Homeland Security of the Committee on the Judiciary, House of Representatives, One Hundred Eighth Congress, Second Session,* Washington, D.C.: U.S. Government Printing Office, 2004. Witnesses from the Drug Enforcement Agency and U.S. Anti-Doping Agency make the case for adding steroid precursors to the list of controlled substances (which since 1990 has included steroids). Letters from the Major League Baseball Players Association and the American Medical Association supplement the testimony in support of the change.

————. *Anabolic Steroid Restriction Act of 1990, Hearing before the Subcommittee on Crime of the Committee on the Judiciary, House of Representatives, One Hundred First Congress, First Session.* Washington, D.C.: U.S. Government Printing Office, 1989. The House hearing that helped lead to the (renamed) Anabolic Steroid Control Act of 1990 had fewer celebrities than the Senate hearings on the act. It instead focused on the use of steroids by teens and on the easy ways they could obtain the drug. The witnesses include a law enforcement official, a scientist and expert on steroid use, a high school principal, and Olympic athlete Carl Lewis.

U.S. Senate. *Steroids in Amateur and Professional Sports—The Medical and Social Costs of Steroid Abuse, Hearing before the Committee on the Judiciary, United States Senate, One Hundred First Congress, First Session.* Washington, D.C.: U.S. Government Printing Office, 1989. The Senate hearings that helped produce the Anabolic Steroid Control Act of 1990 included more than a dozen famous players, coaches, and league sports officials as witnesses. Focusing on college and professional football, the witnesses generally agreed on the dangers of drug use in sports and the threat of steroids to teens. Their views shed light on the extent of the problem during the 1980s, a time when steroids had spread widely in sports such as American football and other sports.

Waddington, Ivan. *Sports, Health and Drugs: A Critical Sociological Perspective.* London: Taylor and Francis, 2000. Although academic in nature and filled with such terms as *critical theory, ideology,* and *medicalization,* this book offers more than most on the social background of drug use in sports. The author argues that increased reliance of athletes on drugs stems from a more general and growing reliance of the public on drugs and medicine for well-being and from the increased importance given to winning. Along with these ideas, the book provides information on the history and current circumstances of drug use in sports.

ARTICLES

Adler, Jerry. "Toxic Strength: High School Athletes and Steroids." *Newsweek*, vol. 144, no. 25, December 20, 2004, pp. 44–50, 52. This cover story highlights the special and frightening risks that face high school steroid users. It notes that more than 300,000 students in 8th through 12th grade use steroids, and about one-third of them are girls. Along with presenting facts on health risks, it also tells of high school athletes taking steroids who later committed suicide.

Angier, Natalie. "Drugs, Sports, Body Image and G.I. Joe." *New York Times*, December 22, 1998, p. F1. Also available online. URL: http://www.bebeyond.com/LearnEnglish/BeAD/Readings/SteroidsGIJoe.html. Posted December 22, 1998. This article cites the work of Dr. Harrison G. Pope, Jr., a Massachusetts psychiatrist, on the changing shape of G.I. Joe action figures. According to this psychiatrist their increasing, even grotesque muscularity might contribute to the attraction among teens to use steroids. As Dr. Pope states, "Steroids made it possible for men to look as big as supermen, and now we see that standard reflected in our toys for the very young."

Bird, Edward J., and Gert G. Wagner. "Sport as a Common Property Resource: A Solution to the Dilemmas of Doping." *The Journal of Conflict Resolution*, vol. 41, no. 6, December 1997, pp. 749–766. The authors are critical of the reliance on a centralized bureaucracy to test for drugs. They believe that such a system gives responsibility for drug enforcement to an outside organization that athletes distrust and resent. Instead, athletes themselves should take responsibility to develop norms against unfair drug use and informally enforce the norms among themselves.

Chaikin, Tommy. "The Nightmare of Steroids: Personal Story of a South Carolina Football Player." *Sports Illustrated*, vol. 69, October 24, 1988, pp. 82–88. This gripping and sad story of how excess use of steroids by a college football player nearly led to suicide gives a personal view of the psychological effects of this drug. Chaikin's experience does not seem typical of steroid users but illustrates the risks that some will face.

Colvin, Geoffrey. "We Hate Big Pharma—But We Sure Love Drugs." *Fortune*, vol. 150, no. 13, December 27, 2004, p. 56. This discussion of the pharmaceutical industry in the United States notes that, despite the controversy over the profits of the big companies and the high cost of drugs, Americans are highly attracted to the idea that pills can make life better. One indication of the more general demand for drugs shows in the acceptance of steroids by sports athletes. Yet, steroid use may not seem so unusual given that nonathletes are using prescription drugs more than ever before.

Donovan, R. J., G. Egger, V. Kapernick, and J. Mendoza. "A Conceptual Framework for Achieving Performance Enhancing Drug Compliance in Sport." *Sports Medicine*, vol. 32, no. 4, 2002, pp. 269–284. Noting that the only approach to eliminate drug use among athletes has been testing and punishment, this article considers how to change the beliefs and attitudes of athletes so they are less attracted to drugs (and in so doing reduce the dependence on testing). It considers how personality, perceptions of risk and benefits of drug use, and the influence of peers, morality, and legitimacy all affect the choice to use drugs. It then draws implications for how programs can modify these characteristics to reduce attraction to performance-enhancing drugs.

Eitle, David, R. Jay Turner, and Tamela McNulty Eitle. "The Deterrence Hypothesis Reexamined: Sports Participation and Substance Use among Young Adults." *Journal of Drug Issues*, vol. 33, no. 1, winter 2003, pp. 193–221. This study follows a sample of preteens to young adulthood, finding that those who participate in sports are just as likely to use drugs as those who do not participate. The deterrence hypothesis, which suggests that sports help teens avoid drugs, receives little support.

Erdely, Sabrina Rubin. "Juicers in Blue." *Men's Health*, vol. 20, no. 8, October 2005, pp. 168–170, 172–173, 210. Steroid use has become increasingly common among police as well as athletes. Some police officers believe that lifting weights and taking steroids has become necessary to deal with large and aggressive criminals. Others worry that steroid use will lead to unnecessary violence by police. This article discusses the nature of the problem and the efforts of police departments to deal with it. Although not directly related to sports competition, steroid use by police officers reflects the widespread attraction to performance-enhancing drugs.

Gladwell, Malcolm. "Drugstore Athlete." *The New Yorker*, vol. 77, no. 26, September 10, 2001, pp. 52–59. This article discusses debates about the immorality of drug use in sports. It notes that testing cannot by itself prevent drug use and in fact may both wrongly identify some athletes as drug users and fail to identify other athletes who do use drugs.

Hampton, Tracy. "Researchers Address Use of Performance-Enhancing Drugs in Nonelite Athletes." *JAMA*, vol. 295, no. 6, February 8, 2006, pp. 607–608. This article in the journal of the American Medical Association discusses research on the use of performance-enhancing drugs by young people and reviews what physicians can do to help deal with the problem.

Hewitt, Bill. "Juiced Up: Steroid Use by Teen Boys and Young Men." *People*, vol. 61, no. 21, May 31, 2004, pp. 92–93, 95–96. This article focuses on the spread of steroids from high school athletes to other teens who hope the drug will make their bodies more attractive. The article also gives statistics on steroid use by high school students and reviews the health risks to teens from the practice.

Hoberman, John M. "Listening to Steroids." *The Wilson Quarterly*, vol. 19, winter 1995, pp. 35–44. This history of drug use in sports suggests that, given the strong attraction of athletes to anything that will help their performance, preventing drug use in sports will remain difficult. The article further provides many examples of how the performance-enhancing and therapeutic components of drugs overlap. Because of this overlap, the difference between the two components will become increasingly blurred and make prevention even more difficult.

———. "Sports Physicians and the Doping Crisis in Elite Sport." *Clinical Journal of Sport Medicine*, vol. 12, no. 4, July 2002, pp. 203–208. Although organized medicine has opposed sports doping, individual physicians have helped athletes use performance-enhancing drugs for more than a century. This article considers the arguments used by a minority of physicians to justify illegal doping activities and concludes that physicians have played a significant, though largely unacknowledged role in the doping of elite athletes.

Houlihan, Barrie. "Anti-Doping Policy in Sport: The Politics of International Policy Coordination." *Public Administration*, vol. 77, no. 2, 1999, pp. 311–335. Although testing was once left to the individual federations that govern each sport, pressure has grown to coordinate doping policy across sports and across nations. This article traces the development of a coordinated policy and the establishment in 1999 of the World Anti-Doping Agency.

Kowalski, Kathiann M. "Drug Testing: Proving You're Clean." *Current Health* 2, vol. 23, November 1996, pp. 19–21. This article discusses the trend toward drug testing of high school athletes and employers. It reviews the arguments for and against the testing, but notes that the Supreme Court has ruled on the issue. The ruling found that the importance of deterring drug use in schools overrides concerns about invasion of privacy.

Maennig, Wolfgang. "On the Economics of Doping and Corruption in International Sports." *Journal of Sports Economics*, vol. 3, no. 1, 2002, pp. 61–89. An economist suggests that an effective way to reduce use of drugs in sports competition is to set financial penalties for violation at a sufficiently high level to make potential costs higher than the benefits.

Mehlman, Maxwell J. "What's Wrong with Using Drugs in Sports? Nothing." *USA Today* August 12, 2004, p. 13A. Also available online. URL: http://www.usatoday.com/news/opinion/editorials/2004-08-11-mehlman_x.htm. Posted August 11, 2004. Dr. Mehlman, a professor of law and bioethics at Case Western Reserve University in Cleveland, Ohio, takes a controversial stand in this opinion piece. He argues that athletes commonly risk injury from sports, and performance-enhancing drugs do little to increase that risk. Otherwise, there is nothing inherently wrong with using safe drugs. Drugs give athletes advantages just like better equipment and training methods, and it is unnecessary to ban or even jail athletes who use them.

Miller, Kathleen E., Grace M. Barnes, and Donald F. Sabo. "Anabolic-Androgenic Steroid Use and Other Adolescent Problem Behaviors: Rethinking the Male Athlete Assumption." *Sociological Perspectives*, vol. 45, no. 4, winter 2002, pp. 467–489. The male athlete assumption refers to the idea that young men use steroids primarily or only as a way to better their sports performance. In fact, the study finds that steroid use among high school students is associated with several other problem behaviors such as use of tobacco, excess drinking, fighting, suicide attempts, sexual risk, reckless driving, and extreme weight loss. These behaviors have little to do with sports. Steroid use among high school students thus takes the form of a health-compromising behavior rather than an athletic supplement.

Mitten, Matthew J. "Is Drug Testing of Athletes Necessary?" *USA Today (Periodical)*, vol. 134, November 2005, pp. 60–62. Mitten suggests an alternative approach to having sports leagues test their athletes. Instead, the federal government should take greater responsibility for prosecuting those who illegally distribute the drugs to athletes. In addition, athletes caught buying or using drugs should face fines and jail time rather than suspension. By penalizing athletes more harshly for drug use, such actions would send a strong antidrug message to young athletes.

Mooney, Chris. "Teen Herbicide." *Mother Jones*, vol. 28, no. 3, May/June 2003, pp. 18–22. The problem of teen use of nutritional supplements is discussed, with attention given to steroid precursors and their use to improve sports performance. The article describes the 1994 Dietary Supplement Health and Education Act, which contributed to the growth of the nutritional supplement industry and allowed companies to market products without a proven safety record. As a result, the overuse of the supplements by teens has become particularly worrisome.

Drugs and Sports

"Muscleheaded: Congressional Hearings on Steroid Use in Baseball." *National Review*, vol. 57, no. 6, April 11, 2005, pp. 16–17. Although opposed to drug use by athletes, this article criticizes the congressional hearings on steroids in sports as the worst kind of showboating. It argues that Congress can do little with legislation to stop the problem but has acted more for publicity value than policy goals.

Ostler, Scott. "Ban Drug Testing for Life." *Sport*, vol. 84, June 1993, p. 8. The author notes that drug testing is ineffective in stopping athletes from using drugs and is sometimes unfair in wrongly showing positive tests for clean athletes. He argues that, unless improvements are possible, drug testing should end. However, arguments like these have had little influence—testing has become more rather than less common and important since publication of the article.

Perry, Dayn. "Pumped-Up Hysteria: Minimal Effects of Steroid Use by Professional Athletes." *Reason*, vol. 34, no. 8, January 2003, pp. 32–39. This spirited criticism of antisteroid laws makes the case that the drug is not all that dangerous and did not have all that much to do with new baseball hitting records. Rather, the concern comes from exaggerated claims of politicians and others focused on moral issues. Reflecting the libertarian philosophy of the magazine, the author believes that steroids and many other drugs should remain legal and that the decisions about their use should be left to individual athletes.

Poole, Isaiah J. "Panel Finds No Reason to Charge Palmeiro With Perjury for Steroids Testimony." *CQ Weekly*, vol. 63, no. 44, November 14, 2005, pp. 3075–3076. After being accused of using steroids, baseball star Rafael Palmeiro went before Congress and testified that he had never used them. Soon after, however, Palmeiro underwent a mandatory drug test that showed presence of a steroid. Congress considered charging him with perjury but, as reported in this article, decided not to. It might have been hard to prove that Palmeiro, who claimed he came by the steroids unintentionally from a vitamin supplement given to him by a teammate, had ever taken steroids before his testimony.

Rosellini, Lynn. "Mom v. Steroids." *Readers Digest*, Janary 2006, pp. 141–145. After discovering anabolic steroids and needles in her son's room, Lori Lewis led an effort to stop steroid use by other students in the local high school. This article tells of her battle with the school coach and principal but ultimate success in alerting her town in Texas of the problem. Eventually, her campaign led to a random drug test program in the school district.

Scelfo, Julie, and Dirk Johnson. "Texas, Football and Juice." *Newsweek*, vol. 145, no. 10, March 7, 2005, pp. 46–47. This story about the injection of steroids by nine players on a Texas high school football team illustrates the spread and continuing use of steroids by teens. Some accused the coaches and administrators of ignoring the problem, even after a concerned parent warned them of its existence. High school football is very popular in Texas, but use of steroids by players can harm the reputation of the sport.

Stilger, Vincent G., and Charles E. Yesalis. "Anabolic-Androgenic Steroid Use among High School Football Players." *Journal of Community Health*, vol. 24, no. 2, April 1999, pp. 131–145. The findings reported in this study show that 6.6 percent of Indiana high school football players were current or former users of steroids and almost half said they could get steroids if they wanted. The study concludes that combating the use of steroids will require coaches and trainers to do more to educate players about the health risks.

Telander, Rick, and Merrell Noden. "The Death of an Athlete: High School Steroid User B. Ramirez of Ashtabula, Ohio." *Sports Illustrated*, vol. 70, February 20, 1989, pp. 68–72. This story reports on the first death of an athlete officially linked to steroid use. Benji Ramirez, a high school football player, died of a heart attack at age 17 during a team practice. The coroner claimed that the death resulted from an enlarged heart that was likely associated with the use of steroids by Ramirez.

Toufexis, Anastasia. "Shortcut to the Rambo Look: Use by Teenage Boys." *Time*, vol. 133, January 30, 1989, p. 78. Articles like this one appeared in the late 1980s to warn about the spread of steroids among teens. It cites figures that 6.6 percent of high school seniors, as many as 500,000 nationwide, have used steroids and describes the physical and mental health risks faced by teen users.

Walsh, Kenneth T. "'Steroids Don't Pay Off': Interview with A. Schwarzenegger." *U.S. News and World Report*, vol. 112, June 1, 1992, p. 63. Chair of the President's Council on Physical Fitness and Sports at the time, the former bodybuilder talks about his own steroid use, the temptation athletes face to use the drug, and ways to reduce steroid use in sports. Schwarzenegger believed he had to take steroids to keep up with other bodybuilders who used the drug but now believes that steroids should be eliminated from sports.

Wichstrom, Lars, and Willy Pedersen. "Use of Anabolic-Androgenic Steroids in Adolescence: Winning, Looking Good or Being Bad?" *Journal of Studies on Alcohol*, vol. 62, no. 1, January 2001, pp. 5–13. This study of Norwegian young people, ages 15–22, examined three motives for steroid use: enhancing sports performance, improving body image and appearance, and dealing with eating disorders. The results show that steroid use is associated with use of other drugs, involvement in power sports, and eating problems. The authors conclude that steroid use is another form of problem behavior rather than simply a means of sports enhancement among otherwise conforming youth.

Winner, Langdon. "The Era of the Enhanced Athlete." *Technology Review*, vol. 92, February/March 1989, p. 22. A discussion of ethical issues raised by performance enhancing drugs makes two points. One, the public criticizes steroids and similar drugs but not the use of painkillers, anti-inflammation drugs, and specialized diets to improve performance. Two, one way to make for fair competition is to have separate sports organizations and competitions, one for those not using drugs and one for those using drugs (special drug-free competitions now exist for powerlifters and bodybuilders).

Zachary, G. Pascal. "Steroids for Everyone!" *Wired*, vol. 12, no. 4, April 2004, pp. 97–98. The author makes the case that athletes should be allowed to use steroids. He claims that few differences exist between doping and other performance enhancements such as use of nutritional supplements, scientific training, and high-tech medicine. All depend on advances in technology that, when used safely, can help athletes improve and make sports more exciting.

WEB DOCUMENTS

"Athletes." NCAA: Choices in Sports. Available online. URL: http://www. drugfreesport.com/choices/athletes/index.html. Accessed December 2006. Along with its web site on Drugs in Sports, the NCAA has developed this web site to educate college athletes about the social and psychological aspects of drug use. The page, which focuses on recreational as well as performance-enhancing drugs, has sections on substances and the law, substances and ethics, substances and mental training, substances and getting help, and substances and individual responsibility.

"ATLAS: Athletes Training and Learning to Avoid Steroids." Division of Health Promotion and Sports Medicine, Oregon Health and Science University. Available online. URL: http://www.ohsu.edu/hpsm/atlas. html. Updated May 18, 2005. The ATLAS program has been lauded for its success in reducing steroid use among teen athletes. The program has received awards from the Center for Substance Abuse Prevention, Safe and Drug Free Schools, and *Sports Illustrated* (whose award comes with $1 million in funds and publicity). The program uses peer discussions to educate teen athletes about the risks of steroids. A related program call ATHENA (Athletes Targeting Healthy Exercise and Nutrition Alternative) does much the same for recreational drugs and alcohol.

"Coaches Playbook against Drugs." Office of Juvenile Justice and Delinquency Prevention. Available online. URL: http://www.ojjdp.ncjrs.org/

pubs/coachesplaybook. Accessed December 2006. Coaches obviously play an important role in preventing teen athletes from using drugs but often underestimate the extent of the problem among their players. This web site gives advice to coaches on the messages and activities that will discourage steroid use and provides a pledge form that students and coaches can use to make a written commitment to stay free of steroids.

Collins, Rick. "Anabolic Steroids and the Athlete: The Legal Issues." MESO-Rx: Anabolic-Androgenic Steroid Education. Available online. URL: http://www.mesomorphosis.com/articles/collins/anabolic-steroids-and-the-law.htm. Accessed December 2006. An attorney who specializes in defending steroid users reviews the state and federal laws and describes the typical experiences of those arrested for using steroids.

———. "Steroids and Sports: A Provocative Interview with Norm Fost, M.D." Steroid Law.com. Available online. URL: http://www.steroidlaw. com/steroid-law-45.html. Accessed December 2006. Dr. Fost, a pediatrician and ethicist at the University of Wisconsin, suggests in this interview that claims about the harm of steroids for heath and the immorality of steroid use are exaggerated by the media. Although he believes athletes should follow the rules of sports, he also believes that using steroids differs little from other efforts of athletes to gain a competitive advantage. To make competition fair, he suggests that all athletes should have equal and safe access to steroids.

"Drugs and Sports." Office of the National Drug Control Policy. Available online. URL: http://www.ondcp.gov/prevent/sports/index.html. Accessed December 2006. As part of the Executive Office of the President, the Office of the National Drug Control Policy sets policies, priorities, and objectives for fighting drugs more generally but also addresses the problem of drug use in sports. Its web site on drugs and sports offers facts on drug use by athletes and ways for coaches and educators to help reduce drug use among young people.

"Drug-Testing Program." National Collegiate Athletic Association. Available online. URL: http://www1.ncaa.org/membership/ed_outreach/health-safety/drug_testing/index.html. Accessed December 2006. Designed primarily for college athletes, this NCAA web site lists the substances it bans and describes the drug-testing program it has in place. Along with testing athletes at championship events, the NCAA also has an out-of-competition testing program for all sports. This page tells student-athletes what to expect during a test and describes the appeals process. The page also gives drug-testing statistics for 2002–04.

"Eradicating Steroid Use, Part IV: Examining the Use of Steroids by Young Women to Enhance Athletic Performance and Body Image." House Committee on Government Reform: Hearings. Available online.

URL: http://www.reform.house.gov/GovReform/Hearings/EventSingle. aspx?EventID=28694. Posted June 15, 2005. The last in a series of four, this hearing shifts the focus from professional sports to youth, particularly the growing use of steroids by young women. Testimony comes from two women athletes who describe their use of steroids and from experts on the harm to health of steroid use by young people. The use of steroids by young women to reduce body fat, which is often associated with eating disorders, gets special attention in the testimony.

"NIDA Community Drug Alert Bulletin—Anabolic Steroids." National Institute on Drug Abuse. Available online. URL: http://www.drugabuse. gov/SteroidAlert/Steroidalert.html. Posted April 17, 2000. Directed at citizens who want to do more to stop drug use in their communities, this short document defines anabolic steroids, the extent of use by teens, the way anabolic steroids are taken, and the health hazards of anabolic steroids. Most useful are several suggestions on how to discourage youth from taking steroids. For example, parents and coaches should not falsely deny the benefits of steroids but should present a balanced and credible picture that highlights risks along with benefits.

"President George W. Bush's State of the Union Remarks on Reducing Drug Use." News and Public Affairs, Office of National Drug Control Policy. Available online. URL: http://www.whitehousedrugpolicy.gov/news/ press04/012104.html. Posted January 21, 2004. In his January 2004 State of the Union address, President George W. Bush devotes several paragraphs to the problem of steroid use by professional athletes and the need to take action. These remarks appear on this page. To help bring about changes in drug regulations in professional sports, he said, "So tonight I call on team owners, union representatives, coaches, and players to take the lead, to send the right signal, to get tough, and to get rid of steroids now."

Saletan, William. "The Beam in Your Eye: If Steroids Are Cheating, Why Isn't Lasik." Slate. Available online. URL: http://www.slate.com/id/ 2116858. Posted April 18, 2005. The author responds to the controversy over steroids by arguing that drugs have some similarities to the widely accepted use of surgery and glasses to improve vision among athletes. Both are forms of performance enhancement. Saletan argues that steroids, like most medical procedures, are safe when used correctly and that critics of steroids are hypocritical.

"SATURN: Student Athlete Testing Using Random Notification." Division of Health Promotion and Sports Medicine, Oregon Health and Science University. Available online. URL: http://www.ohsu.edu/hpsm/saturn. html. Updated May 18, 2005. Funded by the National Institute on Drug Abuse, the SATURN program is attempting to determine if random tests of school athletes are effective in reducing substance abuse. The tests are given in schools without advance warning and look for the presence of performance-enhancing drugs, recreational drugs, and alcohol. Students must give a requested urine sample if they want to participate in sports. If the results of the program prove effective, it would encourage schools outside the initial study to participate in the program.

"Sports." The Cheating Culture. Available online. URL: http://www. cheatingculture.com/drugsinsports.htm. Accessed December 2006. *The Cheating Culture: Why More Americans Are Doing Wrong to Get Ahead*, author David Callahan argues that cheating has increased in American society because of increased competition in the marketplace. This web site extends the argument to cheating in sports. It provides links to news stories and background information on drug use in sports and has special sections on cheating in baseball, football, cycling, and Olympic sports.

"Steroid Abuse." Drug Enforcement Administration, Office of Diversion Control. Available online. URL: http://www.deadiversion.usdoj.gov/pubs/ brochures/steroids. Accessed December 2006. The Drug Enforcement Administration, the federal agency in charge of drug control, has responsibility for enforcement of antisteroid laws. As part of its enforcement campaign, the agency offers several short papers on the dangers of steroid use. One of the papers on this web site, "Steroid Abuse by Law Enforcement Personnel," discusses how abuse goes beyond sports to affect other professions where physical fitness and strength can be important.

"Steroid Abuse by School Age Children." Drug Enforcement Administration, Office of Diversion Control. Available online. URL: http://www. deadiversion.usdoj.gov/pubs/brochures/steroids/children/children.pdf. Posted March 2004. This guide for parents and school officials explains why children might come to misuse steroids and how counseling and education can help prevent use of the drug. The guide provides background information on steroids, their use, and their effects that can help those unfamiliar with the drug understand the attraction it has for teens and recognize symptoms of its use. Although in the form of a short booklet, it packs a lot of information into its eight pages.

"Tips for Parents." Parents: The Anti-Drug. Available online. URL: http:// www.theantidrug.com/get_involved/sports_tips_for_parents.asp. Accessed December 2006. The National Youth Anti-Drug Media Campaign sponsors a web site to help parents understand, prevent, and identify drug use by their children. The page gives special attention to performance-enhancing drugs. Tips include setting rules, getting to know teammates and friends, and teaching refusal skills.

Williams, Charles L. "Are We Really Shocked by Drugs in Sports?" Black Athlete Sports Network: Track and Field. Available oneline. URL: http:// www.blackathlete.com/Track&Field/051904.shtml. Posted May 19, 2004.

The author argues that the attraction to drugs in sports stems from tendencies in larger society to overuse and become addicted to food, alcohol, and drugs. He suggests that "If drug use in sports is to be eliminated the motivation(s) for taking them will have to be addressed. This means the contemporary values placed upon fame, glory, and money need to be reexamined and altered. Drug usage in society will have to be eliminated as well."

OLYMPIC SPORTS

BOOKS

Commission of Inquiry into the Use of Drugs and Banned Practices Intended to Increase Athletic Performance. Ottawa, Canada: Minister of Supply and Services Canada, 1990. Those wanting to know more about the background of the Ben Johnson steroid-use scandal can find a wealth of detail in this volume (known as the Dubin report, after commissioner Charles L. Dubin). It discusses use of performance-enhancing drugs by Canadian athletes more generally and makes recommendations for handling the problem. There is more detail here than most readers will need, and the volume is of interest mostly for historical reasons. Yet, it is a clear summary of how government officials viewed the problem of drugs in sports at the end of the 1980s.

Francis, Charlie, with Jeff Coplon. *Speed Trap: Inside the Biggest Scandal in Olympic History.* New York: St. Martin's Press, 1990. Ben Johnson's Canadian trainer writes about Johnson's career, use of steroids, and success as a runner. The last chapters contain a description of the discovery of Johnson's steroid use in a urine sample taken after his victory at the 1998 Seoul Summer Olympics.

Pound, Richard W. *Inside the Olympics: A Behind-the-Scenes Look at the Politics, the Scandals, and the Glory of the Games.* Etobicoke, Canada: John Wiley and Sons Canada, 2004. A former Olympic swimmer, long-time member of the International Olympic Committee and now president of the World Anti-Doping Agency, Pound says that the Olympic ideal "has been tainted by scandals, greed, and corruption—from bribery, to doping, cheating, politics, and exploitation." He considers doping scandals the greatest threat to Olympic sports today and gives much attention to them in the book.

Ungerleider, Steven. *Faust's Gold: Inside the East German Doping Machine.* New York: Thomas Dunn Books, 2001. This readable book draws on materials from the trials of former East German coaches, doctors, and sports officials who provided drugs to the country's Olympic athletes.

The stories of the former athletes, now adults but only teens when forced to use steroids as part of the East German Olympic team, are both sad and interesting. The book tells of the details of the drug use and the health problems that have resulted among many of the former athletes.

Voy, Robert, with Kirk D. Deeter. *Drugs, Sport, and Politics.* Champaign, Ill.: Leisure Press, 1991. Dr. Voy served as the chief medical officer of the U.S. Olympic Committee from 1984 to 1989. During that time, he became disenchanted with the widespread use of drugs by athletes and with the lack of more rigorous testing and harsher punishments. In this book, he describes the extent of the problem during the 1980s and the failure of officials to clean up the problem. He believes that officials have focused more on winning than the health of the athletes. One chapter on testing, for example, has the subtitle "Cover-ups, Lies, and Manipulation—All for the Sake of Gold."

Wallechinsky, David. *The Complete Book of the Summer Olympics: Athens 2004 Edition.* Wilmington, Del.: Sport Media, 2004. Filled with facts, records, statistics, and lists of participants, this book also tells of some of the drug scandals and doping disqualifications that have occurred over the years.

Wilson, Wayne, and Edward Derse, eds. *Doping in Elite Sport: The Politics of Drugs in the Olympic Movement.* Champaign, Ill.: Human Kinetics, 2001. This book focuses more on the role of Olympic officials in setting drug policies than with the athletes. Among the many topics covered are the failures of testing to eliminate drug use and the role of politics in preventing more rigorous testing and drug control. The book also presents a wealth of information on the history, national differences, and ethics of drug testing policy in Olympic sports.

ARTICLES

"Bans Void Records of Sprinters Montgomery and Gaines." *Jet*, vol. 109, no. 2, January 16, 2006, p. 51. The ban of sprinters Tim Montgomery and Chryste Gains did not come from positive drug tests but from evidence collected during the BALCO investigation. As reported in the article, the two athletes have to sit out to June 2007 and give up previous race victories and medals. The ability to ban athletes without positive tests has extended the ways authorities can investigate and punish drug use.

Begley, Sharon, and Martha Brant. "The Real Scandal: Drugs." *Newsweek*, vol. 133, no. 7, February 15, 1999, pp. 48–54. In discussing the widespread use of performance-enhancing drugs by Olympic athletes, this article calls the problem the greatest threat to international sports. It helpfully provides a list of athletes caught doping and the drugs most often used by athletes.

Burfoot, Amby, and Bob Wischnia. "From Dream to Nightmare: Testimony by Track Coach C. Francis during Canadian Government Inquiry into Steroid Use by B. Johnson." *Runner's World*, vol. 24, June 1989, p. 12. In reviewing the testimony of Charlie Francis, this article describes the eight-year program of steroid use of Ben Johnson. As Johnson's trainer, Francis encouraged use of steroids and guided Johnson so that he would not test positive at events. Francis said, however, that he never recommended use of stanozolol, the steroid for which Johnson tested positive at the 1988 Olympics.

Cain, Joy Duckett. "FloJo, Diva of the Dash." *Essence*, vol. 29, no. 8, December 1998, p. 174. This obituary of Florence Griffith Joyner reviews her accomplishments as an Olympic track star—her world record in the 100 meters set in 1988 still stood at the time of her death—and her life after she retired from competition in 1989. It also reviews accusations that Joyner used performance-enhancing drugs but notes that she never tested positive.

Clark, Kim. "The Gold-Medal Diet: Training for Sydney Olympics." *U.S. News and World Report*, vol. 129, no. 13, October 2, 2000, pp. 56–58. Sports with weight classifications such as judo, wrestling, weightlifting, and boxing require athletes to undergo special training before the Olympic Games. The training involves efforts to stay fit while also losing weight to stay below the maximum for their class. This article describes the training methods, which sometimes involve use of drugs to lose weight and diuretics to release water, and the risks of dehydration and starvation that come with the methods.

Cowley, Geoffrey, and Martha Brant. "Doped to Perfection: Olympics." *Newsweek*, vol. 128, July 22, 1996, p. 31. As part of a special issue on the 1996 Summer Olympics in Atlanta, this story discusses concerns about the use of drugs and the views of some experts that drug use had become epidemic among Olympic athletes. It also discusses the $3 million testing program and the 400-person staff to carry out the testing.

Craig, Simon. "Riding High: Alleged Drug Use by Cyclist A. Linton during 1886 Race from Paris to Bordeaux." *History Today*, vol. 50, no. 7, July 2000, pp. 18–19. This interesting article reviews one of the first possible cases of death from drug use in sports competition. Some believe that Arthur Linton's death in 1886 came from massive amounts of drugs taken during the bicycle race that same year. Doping was common in the sport at the time, but the author finds that Linton's symptoms were consistent with typhoid fever and cannot conclude that drugs caused the death.

"A Day of Reckoning: B. Johnson Admits He Took Steroids." *Maclean's*, vol. 102, June 26, 1989, pp. 32–33. Some time after testing positive for steroid use at the 1988 Olympics, sprinter Ben Johnson admitted using steroids.

This article reports his testimony under oath, his long history of taking performance-enhancing drugs, and his dishonesty in previously denying steroid use. It also describes how Johnson managed to avoid, in all but one crucial instance, testing positive.

Dickman, Steven. "East Germany: Science in the Disservice of the State: Secret Steroid Drug Program." *Science*, vol. 254, October 4, 1991, pp. 26–27. This article gives special attention to the unethical actions of scientists who help in the state-sponsored doping program of East Germany. It notes that scientists knew of the health risks of giving the drugs to young athletes but helped anyway.

Fisher, Ian, and Juliet Macur. "Drug Tests Are Clean, But Case Is Hardly Over." *New York Times*, February 24, 2006, p. D2. This article reports on the single most important drug-related event at the 2006 Turin Winter Olympic Games—the police raid on the residence of Austrian cross-country skiing and biathlete team members. The raid came from a tip that an Austrian trainer banned from the games for previous doping offenses was present at the residence. Ten skiers underwent drug tests after the raid and all turned out negative, but the presence of possible doping materials such as syringes and a bag of blood have led to further investigation.

Fraser, Albert D. "Doping Control from a Global and National Perspective." *Therapeutic Drug Monitoring*, vol. 26, no. 2, April 2004, pp. 171–174. This article offers a brief history of doping in sports and the creation of the World Anti-Doping Agency (WADA) as a way to set common doping control standards across nations. It also discusses the challenges faced by WADA in getting nations, sports organizations, and athletes across the world to accept the benefits of drug-free sports competition.

Galbraith, Jeff. "Dazed and Confused: Olympic Controversy Surrounding Snowboarder R. Rebagliati's Alleged Use of Marijuana." *Time*, vol. 151, February 23, 1998, pp. 78–79. Canadian snowboarder Ross Rebagliati tested positive for marijuana at the 1998 Winter Olympics in Nagano, Japan, and the International Olympic Committee stripped him of his medal. Rebagliati claimed the positive test came from inhaling second-hand marijuana smoke at a party. The Court of Arbitration for Sport overturned the IOC's decision, however, because the snowboarding governing body had never specifically banned marijuana use.

Gillis, Charlie. "Doping." *Maclean's*, vol. 117, no. 34, August 23, 2004, pp. 20–21, 23. Several track athletes found to have used banned drugs in past events performed poorly in the Athens Olympics when, apparently, they did not use the drugs. As discussed in this article, Tim Montgomery had earlier set a world record time of 9.78 in the 100 meters but in Athens posted a dismal time of 10.13 seconds. The article discusses the poor performance of several other famous track athletes whose athletic skills have deteriorated remarkably once free from drugs.

———. "Levelling the Field." *Maclean's*, vol. 117, no. 3, January 19, 2004, pp. 40–43. This article offers a Canadian perspective on the BALCO drug scandal and American track and field athletes more generally. It notes that international athletes had for many years privately accused U. S. athletes of gaining a competitive advantage by using drugs. Many now hope that the discovery of use of the designer steroid THG by some U.S. athletes will lead the U.S. Anti-Doping Agency to do more to make sure the nation's Olympic athletes are clean.

Healy, Tim, and David Hsieh. "Diving into Drugs: Chinese Women Swimmers and Other Athletes." *World Press Review*, vol. 45, no. 4, April 1998, p. 42–43. An inspection of the luggage of a Chinese woman swimmer traveling to Australia for the World Swimming Championships found enough human growth hormone for the 23-person Chinese swim team. Urine tests at the event also led to disqualification of four Chinese swimmers for use of banned substances. This article discusses other incidents that have led many to accuse China of sponsoring drug use by its Olympic athletes.

Hirsch, George A. "A Good Man for a Clean Sport: Frank Shorter Takes the Lead in the Fight Against Drugs." *Runner's World*, vol. 36, no. 6, June 2001, p. 10. Frank Shorter, gold-medal winner in the marathon at the 1972 Olympics, was appointed in 2000 as the chair of the U.S. Anti-Doping Agency, which became responsible for all Olympic drug testing in the same year. Shorter's illustrious career, drug-free reputation, and advocacy of clean sports should, according to the article, help convince athletes of the importance of drug testing and help eliminate drugs from Olympic competition.

———. "Keep the Olympic Dream Alive: Revelations of East German Doping Program Resulting in Marathon Gold Medal for W. Cierpinski." *Runner's World*, vol. 34, no. 2, February 1999, p. 10. It appears from papers released during the investigation of the East German Olympic doping program that the winner of the 1976 and 1980 gold medals in the marathon, Waldemar Cierpinski, may have illegally used drugs. The author of the article argues that, if conclusive proof is found, the International Olympic Committee should strip Cierpinski of his medals. American Frank Shorter, who came in second in the 1976 marathon, would then get the gold medal.

Jackson, Steven J. "Exorcizing the Ghost: Donovan Bailey, Ben Johnson and the Politics of Canadian Identity." *Media, Culture and Society*, vol. 26, no. 1, January 2004, pp. 121–141. According to this article, the scandal over use of steroids by Ben Johnson at the 1988 Olympics affected the feelings of Canadians about their country. It raised issues of race and national identity that continue to shape the views of Canadians about other athletes such as Canadian sprinter Donovan Bailey.

Kennedy, Donald. "Here Come the Olympics." *Science*, vol. 305, July 30, 2004, p. 573. An editorial in this prestigious scientific journal makes the point that science has contributed in important ways to sports and the Olympics. The 2004 events in Athens rely, for example, on new technologies and materials in pole vaulting, cycling, and yachting but also on technology for drug testing. The editorial concludes that sports in the future will come to depend even more on scientific advances in drug testing.

Kettmann, Steve. "Girlz II Men: East Germany's Steroid Enhanced Female Olympians." *The New Republic*, vol. 223, no. 1, July 3, 2000, pp. 17–18. This report on the trial of Manfred Ewald and Manfred Hoppner notes that the two defendants have been accused by 142 female plaintiffs of giving steroids to girls as young as 11. The article describes the accomplishments of East German athletes and the unethical, even illegal measures taken to reach those accomplishments. It also describes some of the current health problems experienced by the women athletes that appear to stem from taking steroids at a young age.

Kuehls, Dave. "Back on Track: Interview with B. Reynolds." *Runner's World*, vol. 28, June 1993, pp. 86–87. Butch Reynolds, U.S. record holder in the 400 meters, was suspended by the International Amateur Athletic Federation (IAAF) for two years because of a positive test for drugs after one race. He says the test was botched and sued the IAAF to overturn the suspension. This interview presents Reynolds's views on drug testing and the IAAF.

Layden, Tim. "Don't Stop Now: Drug Testing for Olympic Athletes." *Sports Illustrated*, vol. 100, no. 22, May 31, 2004, p. 55. The author lauds the new zero-tolerance drug policy announced by USA Track and Field but calls for the agency to strictly enforce the long-overdue policy change. Involvement of track and field athletes in the BALCO scandal have tainted the accomplishments of Olympic sprinters in the past, and much needs to be done to make sure the teams sent to the Olympics are clean.

———. "Slow Motion: Sprinter M. Jones." *Sports Illustrated*, vol. 102, no. 26, June 27, 2005, pp. 80–81. The article describes the struggles of Marion Jones to regain the form that led her to set 12 of the best 20 times ever recorded for the women's 100 meters. At the same time, she has struggled to regain her reputation, which suffered from accusations by her former husband and others that she used performance-enhancing drugs.

———. "The Start of Something Big: M. Jones Victorious; C. J. Hunter Tests Positive for Drugs." *Sports Illustrated*, vol. 93, no. 13, October 2, 2000, pp. 40–50. This report on the 2000 Sydney Olympics highlights two related cases of success and failure. U.S. sprinter Marion Jones won the women's 100-meter race by a huge margin and would go on to win several other medals. Soon after, her husband, shot putter C. J. Hunter, tested positive for steroids. Although Jones did not test positive for drugs, her remarkable performance and close relationship with a known drug user raised suspicions about her own possible drug use.

Longman, Jere. "East Germany's Doping Chief, Manfred Ewald, is Dead at 76." *New York Times*, October 23, 2002, p. A21. This obituary traces the success Ewald had in building East German Olympic teams—in part through giving steroids to the nation's athletes—and the disgrace that came later. After the reunification of East and West Germany, revelations of his role in the doping regime in East Germany eventually led to his prosecution and conviction. He died of a lung infection soon after.

Maimon, Alan. "Doping's Sad Toll: One Athlete's Tale from East Germany." *New York Times*, February 6, 2000, sec. 1, p. 1. As a young girl, Martina Fehrecke Gottschalt unknowingly was given steroids while training in the East German youth sports program. This article tells of her experiences in the program and later involvement in the trial of those responsible for the program. She has, like other women given steroids while training as teens, experienced health problems and born a child with birth defects.

Panek, Richard. "Tarnished Gold: Use of Steroids by East German Swimmers during the 1976 Olympics." *Women's Sports and Fitness*, vol. 2, no. 4, May/June, 1999, pp. 124–127. Adding to the many sources of information on the East German steroid scandal, this article focuses on one sport, female swimming, and one event, the 1976 Olympics. In that year, the East German women's swim team so dominated the competition that the athletes faced accusations—later proved true—of using steroids to win their medals and set records. Of interest, the article reports the reactions of U.S. swimmers to their defeat and the possible cheating.

Phillips, Andrew. "The Olympic Drug Cloud." *Maclean's*, vol. 113, no. 41, October 9, 2000, pp. 52–53. The 2000 Summer Olympics in Sydney, Australia, began with new and more earnest efforts by the International Olympic Committee to stop use of drugs by athletes. This article discusses the changes in attitudes of Olympic leaders and corporate sponsors that led to the efforts and the added tests that will make it harder for athletes to use banned drugs. The games still faced controversy over drug use but represented a turning point in enforcement efforts.

Pierce, Charles. "Ten Years Later, He Can Laugh about It: Lifetime Ban of Runner B. Johnson for Performance Enhancing Drug Use." *Esquire*, vol. 131, no. 2, February 1999, p. 50. This sympathetic portrait of Ben Johnson comes 10 years after he was caught using steroids in the 1988 Olympics and six years after he was banned from competition for life when testing positive a second time for drugs. The author finds Johnson participating in an event on Prince Edward Island that involves a race with a car and two horses. He sees Johnson as treated as a drug villain when in fact the use of drugs was widespread and Johnson did little more than what many other athletes did.

Plymire, Darcy C. "Too Much, Too Fast, Too Soon: Chinese Women Runners, Accusations of Steroid Use, and the Politics of American Track and Field." *Sociology of Sport Journal*, vol. 16, no. 2, 1999, pp. 155–173. An analysis of the newspaper and magazine reports on the success of women runners from the People's Republic of China during 1993— a year of unprecedented success for the nation—finds evidence of discrimination. The author argues that the accusations made by writers about drug use were never proven and reflect biased perceptions that Western track and field groups have of Asian nations.

Rosellini, Lynn. "The Molecules of Sport: East German Athletes' Use of Steroids." *U.S. News and World Report*, vol. 112, February 17, 1992, pp. 56–57. An early report tells of the discovery of documents from the former East Germany, now united as part of Germany, on sports doping. According to the documents, physicians and scientists experimented with athletes to find the most effective and least detectable doses of various steroids. Physicians and scientists seemed to ignore the harmful side effects of the drugs in their pursuit of victory at the Olympics. Indeed, the article notes that at least four East German gold-medal winners in the 1988 Olympics, the last one East Germany participated in as a separate country, used steroids.

Smith, Gary. "Gotta Catch 'Em All: G. Trout Will Test for EPO and Other Drugs at Sydney Olympics." *Sports Illustrated*, vol. 93, no. 11, September 18, 2000, pp. 84–96. Authorities introduced a new test at the Sydney Olympics to detect EPO, a drug used to increase the red blood cell count of athletes in endurance sports. This article describes the development of the new test, the expensive equipment used to implement it, and the goal to eliminate use of EPO in the games. Scientists attempted to use new methods to get results in 24 hours when other tests usually take two weeks.

Srebnitsky, Aleksei. "Fallen Stars: Soviet Athletes." *The Unesco Courier*, vol. 45, December 1992, pp. 34–36. As part of an issue on the importance of sports in the former Soviet Union, this article describes how the state encouraged some athletes to take performance-enhancing drugs but did little to help the athletes after they retired and, in some cases, faced health problems because of their former drug use.

Drugs and Sports

Sullivan, Robert. "Breaking the Olympic Habit: Drugs." *Time*, vol. 156, no. 5, July 31, 2000, p. 51. This article on the need for unannounced, out-of-competition testing of Olympic athletes suggests that the lack of such testing comes from the weak leadership of International Olympic Committee President Juan Antonio Samaranch. According to the author, Samaranch's ambivalent attitude toward testing during his long tenure limited the success of the antidoping program and allowed athletes to figure out ways around the program. However, his replacement, Jacques Rogge, would begin a new effort to improve testing procedures.

"Was She Doped or Just Duped?" *Newsweek*, vol. 126, November 27, 1995, p. 78. This story about 15-year-old Jessica Foschi, who tested positive for steroid use after a swimming event, highlights the difficulties sometimes created by drug testing. Foschi claims she never used steroids, passed a lie-detector test, and believes her test sample was sabotaged. Even so, it took many years for her to be cleared of the charges.

Whitten, Phillip. "Strong-Arm Tactic: China's Female Athletes Break Sports Records with Aid of Drugs." *The New Republic*, vol. 217, November 17, 1997, p. 10. This article reports on the record-breaking performances of Chinese athletes in events ranging from weightlifting to swimming at the China national games. Observers see the remarkable performances as the result of a state-sponsored, national doping effort, akin to the one that occurred in East Germany during the 1970s and 1980s. The author is highly critical of the alleged doping, arguing that the violation of sports rules shows Chinese disregard for international norms.

Wickens, Barbara. "A Deepening Scandal: Physician J. Astaphan Testifies on Steroid Use by B. Johnson." *Maclean's*, vol. 102, June 5, 1989, pp. 49–50. The investigation of Ben Johnson's use of steroids by Canadian authorities discovered that his physician, Dr. Jamie Astaphan, had given steroids to Johnson and 13 other Canadian athletes. As reported in this article, Astaphan had denied giving steroids, but he changed his story to say that he gave steroids to help those who would otherwise have taken the drug without medical supervision.

"World Champion Sprinter Admits to Drug Use; Banned from Olympics." *Jet*, vol. 105, no. 23, June 7, 2004, pp. 47–48. This portrait of U.S. world-champion sprinter Kelli White tells of the discovery in 2003 that she used a banned stimulant. She further faced punishment when it was also found that she had used the designer steroid THG distributed by BALCO. She was banned from competition for two years as a result.

Zinser, Lynn. "With Drug-Tainted Past, Few Track Records Fall." *New York Times*, August 29, 2004, pp. 1, 16. This article notes that few track records were broken at the 2004 Athens Summer Olympics, and many world records are more than 10 years old. The poor performance contrasts with the stronger performance in the past when use of steroids and other drugs were more common. Suspicions remain that track athletes still use drugs, but it appears likely that they used them more in the past.

Zinser, Lynn, and John Eligon. "Athletes Are Facing Increased Vigilance." *New York Times*, February 12, 2006, sect. 8, p. 9. The increased efforts at the 2006 Turin Winter Olympics to discover drug use by athletes are described. Much attention has gone into developing tests to discover use of EPO, a substance that increases oxygen-carrying red blood cells and improves performance in endurance events.

WEB DOCUMENTS

"About WADA." World Anti-Doping Agency. Available online. URL: http://www.wada-ama.org/en/index.ch2. Accessed December 2006. The "About WADA" menu on this site covers topics on the history, mission, composition, and finances of this international organization devoted to stopping drug use in sports. Richard W. Pound, the chairman of WADA, offers a message on the page that highlights the value of drug-free sports and the progress made toward that goal by his agency.

"Annual Report." U.S. Anti-Doping Agency. Available online. URL: http://www.usantidoping.org/files/active/resources/press_releases/2004%20USADA%20Annual%20Report.pdf. Posted 2005. The 2005 report describes the history, mission, and leadership of the organization and then reviews the progress it has made in antidoping research and education. Of most importance is the section on testing and results management, which gives statistics on the number of in-competition, out-of-competition (no advance notice), and in-camp tests done from 2001–04.

"Anti-Doping Centre, Torino 2006." Olympic Games. Available online. URL: http://www.olympic.org/uk/games/torino2006/antidoping/index_uk.asp. Accessed December 2006. The web site for the 2006 Turin Winter Olympic Games lists the seven steps of the antidoping control procedure (beginning with notification and ending with communication of the disciplinary commission to the athlete) and provides a link to the IOC Medical and Scientific Director (Dr. Patrick Schamasch). With its strong antidoping stance, the IOC presents other information on the harm of performance-enhancing drugs and its battle to stop their use by athletes.

"Anti-Doping Rules Applicable to the XX Olympic Winter Games in Turin 2006." International Olympic Committee. Available online. URL: http://www.multimedia.olympic.org/pdf/en_report_1018.pdf. Posted November 11, 2005. This 35-page document describes in some detail the antidoping rules and procedures for the most recent Olympic Games. It reads like a legal document, in large part because the punishments often end up in arbitration or court, but athletes, trainers, coaches, and medical advisers must become familiar with the rules and procedures. The detail on testing and punishment can help researchers understand what athletes and the IOC face in dealing with doping.

Associated Press. "Doping Cases at the Athens Games: Numerous Medals Stripped Due to Drug Violations." MSNBC. Available online. URL: http://www.msnbc.msn.com/id/5859017. Posted August 29, 2004. This article lists the name and offense of each of the athletes who violated drug policies at the most recent Summer Olympic Games. Most of the athletes came from former Communist nations of Eastern Europe.

"Athlete Tools." U.S. Anti-Doping Agency. Available online. URL: http://www.usantidoping.org/athletes. Accessed December 2006. The U.S. agency with responsibility for testing and educating athletes about drug use provides links to its policies, a description of its testing procedures, and other information to help U.S. athletes participating in Olympic sports.

"Court of Arbitration for Sport." Court of Arbitration for Sport (CAS). Available online. URL: http://www.tas-cas.org. Accessed December 2006. Most disputes over drug tests and punishments now go to the CAS, an agency created to resolve sports disputes under a single authority rather than sending cases to the legal systems of more than 200 nations. This web site describes the CAS, its history, and its procedures.

"Drug Reference Online." U.S. Anti-Doping Agency. Available online. URL: http://www.usantidoping.org/dro/. Accessed December 2006. This page allows athletes to search for specific drugs to determine if they are banned from their sport and to obtain information on the drug, its effects, and its side effects.

"The Enforcer." CBS News Online. Available online. URL: http://www.cbc.ca/sports/indepth/drugs/stories/qa_dickpound.html. Posted January 19, 2003. In this article and interview, the head of the World Anti-Doping Agency, Dick Pound, talks about the efforts of his organization to eradicate drug use in sports by having the governing sports organizations adopt the code of his agency. Pound comments on efforts to detect new designer steroids, ways to do better testing and more strongly enforce punishments, and changes in drug policies of professional sports.

"Ensuring Fair Game." National Center for Drug Free Sport. Available online. URL: http://www.drugfreesport.com/index.asp. Accessed December 2006. This organization runs the drug-testing program for the National Collegiate Athletic Association and contracts with other organizations for drug testing. Its web site gives recent news on drug testing programs and background information on the organization and its services. Besides drug testing, it helps sports organizations develop drug policies and education programs.

Annotated Bibliography

"Factsheet: The Fight against Doping and Promotion of Athletes' Health." International Olympic Committee. Available online. URL: http://www.multimedia.olympic.org/pdf/en_report_838.pdf. Updated December 2005. This five-page document reviews the efforts taken by the International Olympic Committee to prevent drug use during the athletic events they sponsor. Of special interest, it lists the number of tests and the number of positive results for each of the Olympic Games since 1968. Partly because of better testing, the most recent games show the highest number of positive results.

Layden, Tim, and Don Yaeger. "Playing Favorites? An Ex-USOC Official Says Some Athletes Were Allowed to Bend the Drug Rules." SI.com. Available online. URL: http://www.sportsillustrated.cnn.com/si_online/scorecard/news/2003/04/15/sc. Posted April 15, 2003. This short article summarizes a scandal in drug enforcement by American sports agencies. Dr. Wade Exum, the director of drug control administration of the U.S. Olympic Committee from 1991 to 2000 claims that the committee allowed many famous athletes who tested positive for drugs to go unpunished and participate in Olympic events. The USOC disputes the claims but has since 2000 turned over testing to an independent organization, the U.S. Anti-Doping Agency. The change should help avoid the appearance that desire to win influences drug testing.

"The Medical Commission." International Olympic Committee. Available online. URL: http://www.olympic.org/uk/organisation/commissions/medical/index_uk.asp. Accessed December 2006. The IOC Medical Commission was created in 1967 to deal with the growing use of performance-enhancing drugs by Olympic athletes and now aims to protect the health of athletes and promote fairness in competition. It serves as the IOC representative to the World Anti-Doping Agency, which has responsibility for testing. Along with its efforts to fight doping, the commission provides general medical information to athletes.

"Prohibited List." World Anti-Doping Agency. Available online. URL: http://www.wada-ama.org/en/prohibitedlist.ch2#. Accessed December 2006. This page describes the history and development of the list of substances prohibited in sporting events by the International Olympic Committee and other sporting organizations. It also allows downloading of the 11-page list. Although the list contains a large number of drugs with unfamiliar names, the categories and headings used to organize the list highlight the kinds of substances that most sporting organizations outlaw.

"Staying Clean: The Fight Against Doping." IAAF: International Association of Athletic Federations. Available online. URL: http://www.iaaf.org/antidoping/index.html. Accessed December 2006. The IAAF opposes use of performance-enhancing drugs by athletes and supports rigorous testing programs. To help reach its goals, the organization offers a web site with information for athletes on testing rules and regulations, guidelines, statistics, and education. The web site also has links to anti-doping news.

"World Anti-Doping Code." World Anti-Doping Agency. Available online. URL: http://www.wada-ama.org/en/dynamic.ch2?pageCategory.id=250. Accessed December 2006. Those wanting to see the details of the anti-doping code can find the full 44-page document here. They can also find information on the background, legal aspects, and models of best practices for using the code.

PROFESSIONAL SPORTS

BOOKS

Bryant, Howard, *Juicing the Game: Drugs, Power, and the Fight for the Soul of Major League Baseball*. New York: Plume, 2006. The sports columnist for the *Boston Herald* accuses managers and owners of ignoring the problem of steroid use in baseball, all because the boom in home run hitting brought fans to the stadiums. He criticizes the commissioner for not taking action against drugs and the players union for opposing every effort to test players, and concludes that the spread of drugs in baseball has soiled the game's integrity. Offering more than criticism, the book also tells the story of how baseball changed in the last decade and the personalities that influenced its direction.

Canseco, Jose. *Juiced: Wild Times, Rampant 'Roids, Smash Hits, and How Baseball Got Big*. New York: HarperCollins, 2005. Former ballplayer Jose Canseco has had enormous influence on his sport. He was likely the first successful player to use steroids (beginning in the mid-1980s) and in this book became the first to describe the use of steroids by other players. His admissions and accusations led to congressional hearings on steroid use in Major League Baseball and to new antidrug policies. Although self-serving and highly personal, the book presents a revealing portrait of drugs in baseball.

Carroll, Will, with William L. Carroll. *Juiced: The Real Story of Baseball's Drug Problems*. Chicago: Ivan R. Dee, 2005. This in-depth treatment of drug use in baseball presents a nuanced approach to the problem, one that does more to report on the complex issues than take sides in the debates. The author, a baseball writer who interviewed a variety of sources, provides facts and explanations as well as stories on teen users, drug developers, drug testers, and advocates of steroid use. He writes clearly, explaining some complex topics, and gives helpful background on the nature of performance-enhancing drugs.

Courson, Steve, and Lee R. Schreiber. *False Glory: Steelers and Steroids: The Steve Courson Story.* Stamford, Conn.: Longmeadow Press, 1991. After using steroids while a star player on the Pittsburgh Steelers football team, Courson became an outspoken opponent of drugs in sports. In this book, he tells of discovering late in his football career that he suffered from heart problems—the result of his steroid use. He was one of the first to admit publicly to using steroids and to criticize the league and its players for letting drug use get out of hand. The NFL has taken steps to deal with the problem, but this early statement provides a picture of the NFL when steroid use was most common.

Coyle, Daniel. *Lance Armstrong's War: One Man's Battle against Fate, Fame, Love, Death, Scandal, and a Few Other Rivals on the Road to the Tour de France.* New York: HarperCollins, 2005. This highly praised book follows Armstrong as he trained for and won the 2004 Tour de France. It highlights not only Armstrong's amazing talent but also his remarkable desire to win. Although mostly a portrait of a fascinating person and athlete, the book addresses questions about Armstrong's use of performance-enhancing drugs.

Fainaru-Wada, Mark, and Lance Williams. *Game of Shadows: Barry Bonds, BALCO, and the Steroids Scandal that Rocked Professional Sports.* New York: Gotham Books, 2006. The two reporters for the *San Francisco Chronicle* who broke the story about BALCO tell the full story in this book. It gives special attention to baseball player Barry Bonds and his association with BALCO, claiming among other things that he had since 1998 used several types of steroids and human growth hormone. The information comes from records kept by BALCO, court papers, and documents written by federal investigators. Excerpts from the book that appeared in *Sports Illustrated* before publication received much attention and led Major League Baseball to begin an investigation of past steroid use.

Fotheringham, William. *Put Me Back on My Bike: In Search of Tom Simpson.* London: Yellow Jersey, 2003. Tommy Simpson may be most remembered today as a victim of drug use in sports. His death from heart failure during the 1967 Tour de France was brought on by hot weather, dehydration, and use of alcohol and amphetamines. This book tells the story of his accomplishments, athletic talent, desire for success, and ability to overcome—at least until his death—the obstacles of racing. Simpson has become something of a tragic legend, with fans still visiting the site where he crashed his bike and died.

Klein, Alan M. *Little Big Men: Bodybuilding Subculture and Gender Construction.* Albany: State University of New York Press, 1993. The use of steroids and other drugs has played an important part in the bodybuilding subculture, and this academic study gives attention to the drug issue in its research on the culture of bodybuilders. The discussion of drugs represents only one part of the larger study, but understanding the views, controversies, and experiences of bodybuilders gives some insight into the attraction to performance-enhancing drugs.

Light, Jonathan Fraser. *The Cultural Encyclopedia of Baseball. 2nd Edition.* Jefferson, N.C.: McFarland, 2005. The entry on "Drug Use and Abuse" covers both performance-enhancing drugs and recreational drugs. It reviews instances of known drug abuse, including amphetamine use by the 1985 Pittsburgh Pirates, the BALCO scandal, and disclosures about Jose Canseco and Mark McGwire, and it then describes efforts to test for drugs. The entry also includes quotes from players, owners, and sportswriters on the topic.

Lowe, Maria R. *Women of Steel: Female Bodybuilders and the Struggle for Self-Definition.* New York: New York University Press, 1998. In describing how female bodybuilders try to come to terms with the apparent contradiction between norms of feminine beauty and their desire for huge muscles, this sociological study discusses the use of steroids by women and bodybuilders more generally. The world of female bodybuilding is interesting and amazing, as are the stories and pictures of the women studied in this research.

Monaghan, Lee F. *Bodybuilding, Drugs, and Risk.* London: Routledge, 2001. To understand how bodybuilders justify the use of steroids, this study interviews amateur athletes in Great Britain. The bodybuilders recognize that drug use has given their sport a negative image but believe they know how to properly manage the risks of steroids while enjoying the benefits of an improved physique. In discussing these issues, the book also gives background information on the kinds of drugs used by bodybuilders.

Romanowski, Bill. *Romo: My Life on the Edge—Living Dreams and Slaying Dragons.* New York: William Morrow, 2005. One review called this autobiography odd because it is 70 percent apothecary. Former National Football League player Romanowski tells of the wide variety of drugs he used—including THG, ephedrine, and amphetamine-like diet drugs—and their characteristics. The book also tells of his part in the BALCO steroid scandal. Romanowski attributes his drug use to his effort over 16 years of professional football to excel in a difficult and demanding sport.

Schmidt, Mike, and Glen Waggoner. *Clearing the Bases: Juiced Players, Monster Salaries, Sham Records, and a Hall of Famer's Search for the Soul of Baseball.* New York: HarperCollins, 2006. Mike Schmidt, the former player for the Philadelphia Phillies who was inducted into the Hall of Fame in 1995, writes about how the game has changed—mostly for the worse—since he played. The problems go beyond use of steroids and drugs to include inflated statistics, uncaring owners, excessive salaries, and unapproachable players. Once a star player himself, Schmidt's criticisms carry special weight, and he uses his experience to identify the changes needed in baseball to restore the respect it once had.

Voet, Willy. *Breaking the Chain: Drugs and Cycling—The True Story*. Translated by William Fotheringham. London: Yellow Jersey, 2002. The former trainer and drug supplier for the Festina bicycle racing team was caught carrying a large supply of drugs to the 1998 Tour de France. Having admitted to helping team members use drugs, Voet ended up serving 16 months in jail, and his team ended up being removed from the race. The story tells in considerable detail all the drug use that goes on in cycling and calls for efforts to clean up the sport.

Woodland, Les. *The Crooked Path to Victory: Drugs and Cheating in Professional Bicycle Racing*. San Francisco: Cycle Publishing, 2003. An avid bicyclist and sports journalist, the author provides a history of cheating in cycling and shows that the sport has attracted more than its share of cheaters. It traces the cheating in six-day races that occurred more than 100 years ago through the high-tech cheating common today.

———. *The Unknown Tour de France: The Many Faces of the World's Greatest Bicycle Race*. San Francisco: Van de Plas, 2000. Along with offering a history of the Tour de France, portraits of cycling's most famous stars, and many stories about what happens behind the scenes, this book tells of the drug scandals that have harmed the image of professional cycling. Although for devoted rather than casual fans of the sport, the book has information of use to researchers wanting to know about use of drugs by cyclists.

ARTICLES

Alzado, Lyle. "I'm Sick and I'm Scared." *Sports Illustrated*, vol. 75, July 8, 1991, pp. 20–24. Former star football player Lyle Alzado tells of his use of steroids and other drugs during his career and even after his retirement. When diagnosed with brain lymphoma, which would soon kill him, Alzado blamed the disease on his drug use. The article received much attention: Although it cannot be proven that his drug use caused the cancer, his death is often used to illustrate the risk of steroids.

Antonen, Mel. "Players Stay Positive after the Positive." *USA Today*, January 24, 2006, p. 11c. A review of the performance of Major League Baseball players banned for steroid use finds mixed results after they became eligible to return. Several performed well after the suspension and are still sought after by teams, while a few others have been let go and have had trouble remaining in the league. The article interviews many of the suspended players to find out more about their experiences and views on drug use.

Bloom, Barry. "Born a Rebel." *Sport,* vol. 88, August 1997, pp. 20–22. This portrait of NFL quarterback and star of the Green Bay Packers, Brett Favre, discusses his past addiction to prescription painkillers. As illustrated by Favre, the painful injuries sustained in football increase the potential for abuse of prescription drugs.

Bodley, Hal. "Amphetamine Testing a Real Positive." *USA Today* November 16, 2005, p. 5C. Also available online. URL: http://www.usatoday.com/sports/baseball/columnist/bodley/2005-11-15-bodley-amphetmines_x.htm. Posted November 15, 2005. After ignoring amphetamine use in its drug-testing procedures, Major League Baseball and its players agreed to begin testing for the drug in 2006. The punishments are not as harsh as for steroids, but the author of the article lauds the change, arguing that amphetamine use has been widespread for decades and policies need to do more to stop the practice.

Brewer, Benjamin D. "Commercialization in Professional Cycling 1950–2001: Institutional Transformations and the Rationalization of Doping." *Sociology of Sport Journal,* vol. 19, no. 3, 2002, pp. 276-301. This article reviews the widespread and highly organized use of drugs in professional cycling. It argues that increasing commercialization of the sport and dependence on sponsors for financial support increased the demands on riders to do well and in turn led them to use performance-enhancing drugs. The article also emphasizes how doping in cycling has become highly rational, efficient, and modern.

Callahan, Gerry. "Andro Justice for All: M. McGwire's Home Run Record May Be Clouded Due to His Use of Androstenedione." *Sports Illustrated,* vol. 90, no. 8, February 22, 1999, p. 27. The discovery that baseball star Mark McGwire used the steroid precursor androstenedione (which was legal at the time) created controversy about the legitimacy of his home run record. The article also discusses research by Harvard scientists on the risks of taking andro. However, much more serious charges of using illegal steroids by McGwire came several years later and made the use of andro seem minor.

Curry, Lewis A., and Daniel F. Wagman. "Qualitative Description of the Prevalence and Use of Anabolic Androgenic Steroids by United States Powerlifters." *Perceptual and Motor Skills,* vol. 88, no. 1, February 1999, pp. 224–233. In a survey of 15 members of the U.S powerlifting team, 10 said they used steroids and five said they were able to pass doping tests despite their steroid use. The results demonstrate the differences between the high levels of reported drug use by athletes and the low levels discovered through testing.

Deacon, James. "The Tour de Shame." *Maclean's,* vol. 111, no. 32, August 10, 1998, p. 43. This report on the discovery of widespread drug use by racing teams in the 1998 Tour de France describes the teams and participants that, because of accusations of drug use, had to withdraw or voluntarily left the race.

Demak, Richard, and Jerry Kirshenbaum. "The NFL Fails Its Drug Test." *Sports Illustrated*, vol. 71, July 10, 1989, pp. 38–41. Highly critical of the National Football League testing policy during the 1980s, this article expresses many concerns that would lead the league to toughen its policy. It notes that, although drug testing in football was considered one of the best in professional sports at the time, several shortcomings made it ineffective and inconsistent.

Dohrmann, George. "BALCO Blows Up: Steroid Scandal." *Sports Illustrated*, vol. 101, no. 23, December 13, 2004, pp. 50–51, 53–54. This article reports on the involvement of Major League Baseball stars Barry Bonds and Jason Giambi in the BALCO steroid scandal. According to grand jury testimony both players gave, they used designer steroids supplied to them by BALCO (although Bonds said he did not realize the product he was given contained steroids). The article provides a clear summary of the events and issues in the controversy.

Drake, Geoff. "Bad Medicine: Cyclists Using EPO to Enhance Performance." *Bicycling*, vol. 38, June 1997, pp. 24ff. This article describes the widespread use during the 1990s of EPO, a drug that increases the production of oxygen-rich blood cells and increases performance in endurance sports such as cycling. It cites one source who claims that use of EPO is so common that cyclists do not even consider it cheating anymore. The discovery of a test for EPO in years to come will reduce use of the drug, but this article describes the problems it has presented to cycling.

Fainaru-Wada, Mark, and Lance Williams. "The Truth about Barry Bonds and Steroids." *Sports Illustrated*, vol. 104, no. 11, March 13, 2006, pp. 38–53. The excerpt from the authors' book, *Game of Shadows*, presents a powerful and well-documented case against Bonds. It gives details on how Bonds decided to use steroids, made contact with a supplier, changed his body, and broke new hitting records.

Gilbert, Bil. "Athletes in a Turned-On World," *Sports Illustrated*, vol. 30, no. 25, June 23, 1969, pp. 65–72. The first part of a three part exposé, this article describes the use of drugs by athletes in the 1960s—a period when drugs first started to spread through sports. Of more historical than factual interest, the article shows how athletes have been attracted to performance-enhancing drugs for some time.

Gillis, Charlie. "Spilling the Juice." *Maclean's*, vol. 118, no. 13, March 28, 2005, pp. 45–46. As described in this article, Canadian legislators have expressed concerns about drug use in professional sports (much like their U.S. counterparts). Canadian legislators have threatened to force sports leagues in their country to strengthen antidoping rules if the leagues do not do so on their own.

"Grappling with the Law: Promoter V. McMahon Charged with Providing Anabolic Steroids to Wrestlers." *Forbes*, vol. 152, December 20, 1993, p. 14. This article discusses concerns about steroid use in professional wrestling. The story relates charges by a U.S. attorney in Brooklyn, New York, that the head of the World Wrestling Federation, Vince McMahon, distributed steroids to his wrestlers. The details of the charges are less important than the evidence that professional wrestlers depend on steroids to look muscular in the ring.

Hall, Michael. "Lance Armstrong: L. Armstrong Being Accused of Doping." *Texas Monthly*, vol. 29, no. 7, July 2001, pp. 70–55, 127–133. Accusations of drug use have followed Lance Armstrong since at least his first Tour de France victory in 1999. This portrait of Armstrong, his battle against testicular cancer, and his early Tour de France victories takes the position that his outstanding performance rather than actual evidence of drug use has led some to make unfounded charges.

"Hockey's Little Helpers: Sudafed Use by NHL players." *Sports Illustrated*, vol. 88, February 2, 1998, pp. 74–76. Two trainers for National Hockey League teams estimate that 20 percent of players take Sudafed before games. The over-the-counter cold medicine contains a mild stimulant called pseudoephedrine that gives players a buzz and, some believe, helps their performance. The article poses concerns that taking Sudafed before hockey games at the Winter Olympics will lead to positive tests and a new drug scandal. Although no positive tests occurred, the use of Sudafed by players raised questions about the lack of a NHL drug policy.

Hyman, Mark. "Steroid Scandal? Pass the Peanuts." *Business Week*, no. 3913, December 20, 2004, p. 44. Many predicted that the steroid scandal in Major League Baseball would anger fans enough to keep them from going to the ballpark, but this article about the business of baseball claims the sport has stayed as popular as ever. Attendance at games has gone up, and interest in watching games with Barry Bonds has been particularly high, despite beliefs that he has relied on steroids to improve his performance.

Jenkins, Chris. "Players Admit Steroids Changed Baseball." *USA Today*, March 16, 2005, p. 1A. Also available online. URL: http://www.usatoday.com/sports/baseball/2005-03-15-steroids-mlb-cover_x.htm. Posted March 15, 2005. Of the many news stories generated by the congressional hearings and growing steroid scandals, this one offers more detail and background than most. It discusses the extent of steroid use in baseball, the reaction to accusations of steroid use made by Jose Canseco, and debates over the validity of recent record-breaking performances. It also interviews many past and current players about the problem of steroids.

Annotated Bibliography

Kingsbury, Alex. "Throwing Some Heat: Congress Scolds Baseball about Steroid Use." *U.S. News and World Report*, vol. 138, no. 11, March 28, 2005, p. 41. Reporting on the congressional hearing about use of steroids in baseball, this article goes beyond the usual reports of drug use by star players to focus more broadly on Major League Baseball policies. It reviews criticisms that the league should have done more to prevent or deal with the drug problem and highlights some of the legislative proposals made by congressional representatives to handle the problem.

Lindsey, Joe, and Bill Strickland. "Lance Stands Alone for Now." *Bicycling*, vol. 45, no. 9, October 2004, p. 52. In discussing Lance Armstrong's record six victories in the Tour de France (now seven victories), the article argues that science, equipment, and training now allow athletes to compete at elite levels for longer periods of time and older ages than in the past. The article notes that use of performance-enhancing drugs may also play in extending sports careers (although it does not suggest that Lance Armstrong has done so).

Mantell, Matthew E. "What is the UCI? International Cycling Union." *Bicycling*, vol. 30, June 1989, p. 64. The Union Cycliste Internationale (UCI), or International Cycling Union supervises the Tour de France and other top cycling events. This article criticizes the UCI for ineffective drug tests and lax punishment of violators. It notes that few positive tests had occurred among cyclists, despite beliefs among those knowledgeable of the sport that drug use is widespread. The problems described in the article would last for at least another decade.

McGrath, Ben. "Dr. Juice: J. Canseco." *The New Yorker*, vol. 81, no. 3, March 7, 2005, pp. 28–30. The author discusses the controversy over Jose Canseco's claims, made in his book *Juiced*, that many Major League Baseball players used steroids. Despite some claims that the accusations are false, the book and Canseco himself have received much attention.

Murphy, Austin. "J'Accuse!" *Sports Illustrated*, vol. 103, no. 9, September 5, 2005, pp. 22–23. This article describes the controversy over claims made by a French magazine that it had evidence proving Lance Armstrong used a banned drug to help him win the 1999 Tour de France. It also describes why the evidence does not meet the standard needed by the World Anti-Doping Agency for a positive test. For example, a positive test requires evidence in two urine samples (the French magazine had access to only one sample) and for the athlete to be present during the test of the second sample (Armstrong was not offered this opportunity).

Nack, William. "The Muscle Murders." *Sports Illustrated*, vol. 88, no. 20, May 18, 1998, pp. 96–100. Interviews in this article with several bodybuilders now in jail for murder suggest a link between steroid use and violence. The stories of the convicted athletes are sad and gripping and make a strong case for the risks of excessive steroid use.

Reilly, Rick. "Gutless Wonders: Baseball and Steroids." *Sports Illustrated,* vol. 103, no. 6, August 15, 2005, p. 124. This short editorial is highly critical not only of the use of steroids by baseball players and other professional athletes but also of their unwillingness to admit their dishonesty. Players who said they did not know the creams, supplements, medicines, and pills they took contained steroids are not only cheating to better their performance but also lying about it. At the very least, they should, according to Reilly, own up to their actions.

Schmitt, Gary. "No Hall, No Way." *Weekly Standard,* vol. 10, no. 45, August 15–22, 2005, p. 4. The discovery that Rafael Palmeiro used steroids leads the author to question the legitimacy of his baseball records. Even without drugs, Palmeiro was a good baseball player, but the drugs appeared to help him become an extraordinary star and reach some rarely attained batting statistics. Perhaps the best way to punish him and others who used steroids is, the author argues, to ban them from entrance into the Baseball Hall of Fame.

Shapin, Steven. "Cleanup Hitters: Review Article." *The New Yorker,* vol. 81, no. 9, April 18, 2005, pp. 191–192, 194. This review of three books relating to the steroid controversy in baseball questions Jose Canseco's claim that using steroids is no big deal. It cites sources ranging from President George W. Bush's State of the Union Address to documents from the National Institute on Drug Abuse to help make the case against steroids. The review also discusses the abuse of drugs in other sports and describes two other books that raise philosophical issues about the ethics and future of drug use.

Sokolove, Michael. "Souped-Up Slugger." *New York Times Magazine,* December 26, 2004, p. 44. This profile of former baseball star Ken Caminiti, who died recently from a drug overdose, discusses his use of steroids while a player and public confession to having used them. While many others players used steroids, few were so open about it, and none have gone on to have addiction problems as Caminiti did.

Starr, Mark, and Eve Conant. "A Major League Mess." *Newsweek,* vol. 145, no. 13, March 28, 2005, pp. 26–27. In reviewing the congressional testimony of baseball stars, this article gives special attention to retired superstar Mark McGwire. Calling him "sullen, resentful, and occasionally combative," the authors suggest that his testimony will harm his chances to reach the Baseball Hall of Fame in 2007, his first year of eligibility.

Stevens, Stuart. "Drug Test." *Outside* vol. 28, no. 11, November 2003, pp. 58–137. Also available online. URL: http://www.outside.away.com/outside/bodywork/200311/200311_drug_test_1.html. Posted November

2003. The author, an amateur cyclist, reports on an experiment in which he takes performance-enhancing drugs to see if they really help. He finds that the program of taking human growth hormone, EPO, and steroids did indeed increase his strength and endurance but also decides in the end that the risks and side effects of taking the drugs outweigh the benefits.

Swartz, Jon. "High Death Rate Lingers Behind Fun Façade of Pro Wrestling." *USA Today*, March 12, 2004, p. 1C. Also available online. URL: http://www.usatoday.com/sports/2004-03-12-pro-wrestling_x.htm. Posted March 12, 2004. The investigation of early deaths among professional wrestlers raises questions about whether the use of steroids and other drugs in the sport poses health risks to the wrestlers. Many deaths resulted from heart problems that could have been caused by changes to the heart muscle associated with steroids, and the stories of the wrestlers who died are tragic and revealing.

Swift, E. M. "Drug Pedaling: W. Voet Admits Providing Drugs for Festina Cycling Team." *Sports Illustrated*, vol. 91, no. 1, July 5, 1999, pp. 60–65. This story tells of the arrest of Voet for possession of illegal drugs and his admission of using the drugs for his cycling team during the Tour de France. It also discusses how the widespread use of drugs in long-distance cycling has tarnished the sport. Since the event, Voet has described a long history of doping in the sport in the book *Breaking the Chain* and in his admissions to prosecutors.

Verducci, Tom. "Getting Amped." *Sports Illustrated*, vol. 96, no. 23, June 3, 2002, pp. 38–39. Although steroid use gets most of the attention, baseball has had problems for many decades with use of illegal amphetamines by players. This article describes the extent of the use. With some estimates reaching 90 percent of players, amphetamine use has become so common that players have a name, "playing naked," for not using stimulants.

———. "The Injury Toll: Baseball Injuries and Steroids." *Sports Illustrated*, vol. 96, no. 23, June 3, 2002, p. 44. As a result of the over-muscled bodies of many baseball players likely brought on by steroid use, Major League Baseball has observed an increase in injuries. Further, players take longer to recover from the injuries they sustain. The article presents the statistics behind these claims and quotes experts who believe that players today carry more muscle than their frames can support.

———. "Juice and Truth." *Sports Illustrated*, vol. 102, no. 8, February 21, 2005, pp. 40–41. This review of Jose Canseco's tell-all book about steroid use in Major League Baseball, *Juiced*, considers the denials and counterclaims made in response to the book. The author concludes that Canseco may have exaggerated some claims and lacked evidence for others but appears to have captured much of the truth about steroids in baseball.

———. "Totally Juiced: Baseball and Steroids." *Sports Illustrated*, vol. 96, no. 23, June 3, 2002, pp. 34–40, 42, 44, 46, 48. This cover story describes the spread of steroids in baseball and the problems it presents for players who want to compete without drugs. It presents a strong and early case for a better drug and testing policy in Major League Baseball.

Weeks, Janet. "The First Lady of the Ring." *TV Guide*, vol. 47, no. 25, June 19–25, 1999, pp. 14–16. Female wrestling star Sable sued her employer, the World Wrestling Federation, for sexual harassment, unsafe working conditions, and steroid abuse. In this interview, Sable talks about the use of steroids and other drugs in professional wrestling.

Yaeger, Don. "Rx for Trouble: B. Romanowski and Drugs." *Sports Illustrated*, vol. 93, no. 7, August 21, 2000, p. 28. After his retirement from professional football, Bill Romanowski admitted in an autobiography to the use of steroids, but this article documents his other forms of drug use. As reported in the article, he was indicted in 2000 for fraudulently obtaining large amounts of phentermine, a prescription drug used for dieting. In large amounts, the drug mimics the effects of stimulants, and Romanowski apparently used the prescription drug during football games.

WEB DOCUMENTS

"Amphetamines in Baseball: Baseball's Dirty Little Secret." HBO: Costas Now. Available online. URL: http://www.hbo.com/costasnow/episode/episode.01.story.html. Posted May 13, 2005. Interviews with former and current ballplayers as part of a HBO television show highlight how widespread the use of stimulants has become in Major League Baseball. One former player estimates that 85 percent of players used the drug. The story notes that negotiations between baseball owners and players over drug testing had not discussed the issue of testing for amphetamines—the focus was limited to steroids. This and other articles about the problem of amphetamine use helped change that attitude and include amphetamines in new testing procedures.

"The BALCO Investigation." SFGate.com. Available online. URL: http://www.sfgate.com/balco. Accessed December 2006. Links to reports from the *San Francisco Chronicle* on the BALCO scandal are listed here in reverse chronological order. A review gives a detailed history of how the investigation began, unfolded, and ended, and seeing all the stories and athletes involved in the scandal highlights its importance. The reports also give special attention to the use of steroids by Barry Bonds of the San Francisco Giants baseball team.

"BALCO Investigation Timeline." USA Today Online. Available online. URL: http://www.usatoday.com/sports/balco-timeline.htm. Updated June

22, 2006. This time line begins with the founding of BALCO (Bay Area Laboratory Company) by Victor Conte in 1984, covers the efforts of federal investigators to prosecute company owners and employees, and ends with the sentencing of Conte to four months in prison in October 2005. The many athletes listed in the time line as users of BALCO drugs illustrate the attraction to what they thought were undetectable ways to gain a competitive advantage.

"Baseball's Steroid Hearings." NPR. Available online. URL: http://www. npr.org/templates/story/story.php?storyId=4540278. Accessed December 2006. National Public Radio has posted the nine stories it aired in March 2005 on the congressional hearings on use of steroids in baseball, and the web site allows one to hear the stories. Listening to the voices of those testifying and the comments of others about the hearings adds to information that is gained by reading the stories.

"Baseball Steroids Timeline." Sporting News.com. Available online. URL: http://www.sportingnews.com/yourturn/viewtopic.php?t=35463. Posted November 15, 2005. This time line of recent events begins on May 28, 2002, with the *Sports Illustrated* article in which former baseball player Ken Caminiti admitted that he used steroids to help win the 1996 Most Valuable Player Award. It reviews disclosures of steroid use by Jose Canseco, Barry Bonds, and others; the congressional hearings on steroid use; and the efforts of baseball team owners and players to fashion a program of testing and punishment that would satisfy Congressional critics.

"Chronology of the 1998 Tour de France Drug Scandal." CNN Sports Illustrated, CNNSI.com. Available online. URL: http://www.sportsillustrated. cnn.com/cycling/1998/tourdefrance/news/1998/08/02/drug_chronology/. Posted September 22, 1998. This detailed listing provides a near daily account of the events leading to the discovery of widespread use of drugs by cyclists in the 1998 Tour de France.

"Designer Drugs." Drugs and Sports, ESPN.com. Available online. URL: http://www.espn.go.com/special/s/drugsandsports. Posted October 18, 2005. This article is the last of an eight-part series that examines use of steroids, amphetamines, and recreational drugs in sports. This article, which lists the links to the earlier articles on other drugs, describes the nature of designer drugs and discusses the dangers to athletes.

"Doping in Cycling." Total Bike. Available online. URL: http://www.totalbike. com/October1999/drug_use.html. Accessed December 2006. A short introduction and history of use of performance-enhancing drugs in cycling and other sports, this document offers the following antidrug conclusion: "As the rewards of athletic glory are so high, there will be those willing to risk everything to gain them. To gain a more competitive edge, nothing works better than proper training, proper rest, good nutrition, correct technique, and good coaching."

"Drugs and Sports." Online NewsHour, PBS Online. Available online. URL: http://www.pbs.org/newshour/bb/sports/july-dec03/drugs_11-17. html#. Posted November 14, 2003. The text of a segment from the PBS show *NewsHour with Jim Lehrer* includes an interview with *Sports Illustrated* writer Tom Verducci about use of steroids in Major League Baseball. The writer discussed anonymous tests done by the league of all players and the finding reported in 2003 that 5 to 7 percent tested positive.

"Hearing on Steroids Legislation." U.S. Senate Committee on Commerce, Science, and Transportation. Available online. URL: http://www.commerce.senate.gov/hearings/witnesslist.cfm?id=1619. Posted September 28, 2005. Senators John McCain and Jim Bunning had introduced legislation to mandate federal testing standards for four major professional sports—baseball, football, basketball, and hockey. Representatives from the leagues and players associations for each sport provide testimony in this hearing, largely to defend their testing policy and oppose a federal law that would apply the same standard to each sport.

"MLB, MLBPA Announce New Drug Agreement." MLB.com. Available online. URL: http://mlb.mlb.com/NASApp/mlb/news/press_releases/press_release.jsp?ymd=20051115&content_id=1268552&vkey=pr_mlb&fext=.jsp&c_id=mlb. Posted November 15, 2005. After considerable prodding and threats from Congress, Major League Baseball and the Major League Baseball Players Association agreed on a tougher drug-testing and punishment policy for the 2006 season than they had in the past. This press release summarizes the key components of the policy: All players will be subject to at least two random, unannounced tests during the season, a year-round testing program will be expanded, and punishments will be increased. Those testing positive for steroids face penalties that start with suspension for 50 games; those testing positive for amphetamines first face mandatory evaluation and follow-up testing and then penalties that start with suspension for 25 games.

"National Football League Policy and Program for Substance Abuse 2005." National Football League and National Football League Players Association. Available online. URL: http://www.nflpa.org/PDFs/Shared/Drug_Policy_2005.pdf. Updated May 15, 2005. Considered to have one of the best substance-abuse policies in professional sports, the National Football League gives the details of its policy in this 33-page document. It describes the testing procedures players must undergo and the punishments faced by players for use of banned drugs. The policy is comprehensive in its inclusion of recreational drugs and alcohol as well as performance-enhancing drugs and in its careful attention to administering the policy, maintaining confidentiality, and allowing for appeals.

"Performance-Enhancing Substances Program." NHLPA.com: The Official Home of the National Hockey League Players' Association. Available online. URL: http://www.nhlpa.com/PerformanceEnhancing/index. asp. Posted February 23, 2006. The new policy of the National Hockey League summarized on this page allows for two "no-notice" urine tests during the period from training camp to the end of the season. Use of substances on the banned list of the World Anti-Doping Agency results in a 20-game suspension for the first offense, a 60-game suspension for the second offense, and permanent ban for the third offense.

"Restoring Faith in America's Pastime: Evaluating Major League Baseball's Efforts to Eradicate Steroid Use." House Committee on Government Reform: Hearings. Available online. URL: http://www.reform.house.gov/ GovReform/Hearings/EventSingle.aspx?EventID=23320. Posted March 17, 2005. This hearing, one of the most publicized in the history of the U.S. House of Representatives, included several famous baseball stars accused of using steroids: Jose Canseco, Sammy Sosa, Mark McGwire, and Rafael Palmeiro. It also heard testimony from medical experts on the dangers of steroids and from representatives of Major League Baseball and the players association. All the testimony is available on this page and makes for fascinating reading. This hearing led to public disgust with steroid use and eventually to a stronger policy for testing and punishing drug violations.

"'Roids on the Radar." CNN Sports Illustrated, CNNSI.com. Available online. URL: http://www.sportsillustrated.cnn.com/more/boxing/2002/ lewis_tyson/news/2002/06/03/fish_steroids/. Posted June 3, 2002. One of the few articles on steroids in boxing argues that no one knows the extent of use of the drug but many suspect it is spreading. The article suggests that more testing is needed to prevent growth of the problem and determine its current extent.

"Special Report: Drug Policy in Baseball. Event Timeline." MLB.com. Available online. URL: http://mlb.mlb.com/NASApp/mlb/mlb/news/ drug_policy.jsp?content=timeline. Accessed December 2006. Detailed and thorough, this timeline from Major League Baseball presents the events that produced pressure for a new policy and the struggles to find a policy that satisfied owners, players, and Congress. It gives special attention to the events in 2005, when players were first suspended for testing positive for steroids and owners and players finally reached agreement on a strict testing policy and severe punishments.

Stern, David, and Billy Hunter. "CBA Agreement Announced." National Basketball Association. Available online. URL: http://www.nba.com/news/ cba_trans_050621.html. Posted June 21, 2005. The NBA commissioner and the executive director of the National Basketball Players Association discuss the new collective bargaining agreement (CBA) and answer questions from the press about the agreement. Basketball has not experienced the problems with use of performance-enhancing drugs as have football and baseball, but the new policy indicates their commitment to more rigorous testing. A new component of the agreement allows for both random and announced drug testing during the season—a toughening of past policies that both Stern and Hunter hope will forestall efforts in Congress to impose its own drug testing procedures on professional sports.

"Steroid Use in Professional and Amateur Sports." U.S. Senate Committee on Commerce, Science, and Transportation. Available online. URL: http://www.commerce.senate.gov/hearings/witnesslist.cfm?id=1100. Posted March 10, 2004. This Senate hearing preceded the more famous 2005 House hearing (in which baseball players appeared). The goal of the hearing was to determine if existing policies effectively deterred athletes from using steroids. Despite defense of current policies from several witnesses (whose statements appear on this web site), committee members expressed concerns. Donald Fehr, executive director of the Major League Baseball Players Association, came under particularly hard questioning for opposing added drug testing of players.

"Steroid Use in Sports, Part II: Examining the National Football League's Policy on Anabolic Steroids and Related Substances." House Committee on Government Reform: Hearings. Available online. URL: http://www.reform.house.gov/GovReform/Hearings/EventSingle.aspx?EventID=25679. Posted April 27, 2005. Following its highly publicized hearing on steroid use in baseball, the House Committee on Government Reform heard testimony from representatives of the National Football League. In contrast to baseball, football had an effective testing procedure in place, and the commissioner and executive director of the players association describe the policy. In addition, coaches and medical experts involved in youth football describe their efforts to prevent teens from using steroids. And perhaps most interesting, a former player on the Pittsburgh Steelers, Steve Courson, talks about his own past use of steroids and the use of the drug by other players.

"Steroid Use in Sports, Part III: Examining the National Basketball Association's Steroid Testing Program." House Committee on Government Reform: Hearings. Available online. URL: http://www.reform.house.gov/GovReform/Hearings/EventSingle.aspx?EventID=27415. Posted May 19, 2005. Despite claims that steroids bring few benefits to basketball players and are rarely used in the National Basketball Association, congressional representatives were highly critical of the weak testing policy of the league. Testimony from the league commissioner, executive director of the players association, a trainer from the Houston Rockets, and one player minimized the seriousness of the problem and defended the existing policy. Even so, the criticisms faced by the league in this hearing and afterward would lead to a new and stronger testing and punishment policy.

CHAPTER 8

ORGANIZATIONS AND AGENCIES

The organizations and agencies listed here fall into five categories:

- federal government
- medical and scientific
- social and policy groups
- Olympics
- professional sports

For each organization, the listings include the web site address and e-mail. Many organizations do not list their e-mail address but some instead include a web-based form for submitting questions and comments via e-mail. In these cases, it is noted that e-mail is available via a web form. The listings also include phone numbers (when available), postal addresses, and brief descriptions.

FEDERAL GOVERNMENT

Drug Enforcement Agency (DEA)
URL: http://www.usdoj.gov/dea
E-mail: web form
Phone: (202) 307-7977
2401 Jefferson Davis Highway
Alexandria, VA 22301
Enforces controlled substance laws in the United States and supports programs to reduce the availability and use of illicit drugs, including performance-enhancing drugs.

Food and Drug Administration (FDA)
URL: http://www.fda.gov
E-mail: web form
Phone: (888) 463-6332
5600 Fishers Lane
Rockville, MD 20857
Promotes public health by reviewing clinical research and regulating food and medical products to ensure they are safe. Its goals have come to include regulating the use of nutri-

tional supplements that claim performance benefits for athletes.

National Institute on Drug Abuse (NIDA)
URL: http://www.nida.nih.gov
E-mail: information@nida.nih.gov
Phone: (301) 443-1124
6001 Executive Boulevard
Room 5213
Bethesda, MD 20892-9561
The agency's mission is to use science to understand and reduce abuse of and addiction to drugs, including performance-enhancing drugs.

National Institutes of Health (NIH)
URL: http://www.nih.gov
E-mail: nihinfo@od.nih.gov
Phone: (301) 496-4000
900 Rockville Pike
Bethesda, MD 20892
Supports scientific research and the application of knowledge to extend healthy life and reduce the burdens of illness and disability. It is the umbrella organization for the National Institute on Drug Abuse.

Office of National Drug Control Policy (ONDCP)
URL: http://www.
whitehousedrugpolicy.gov
E-mail: web form
Phone: (800) 666-3332
P.O. Box 6000
Rockville, MD 20849-6000
As part of the executive office of the president, it establishes policies, priorities, and objectives for the nation's drug control program.

Substance Abuse and Mental Health Services Administration (SAMHSA)
URL: http://www.samhsa.gov
Phone: (240) 276-2000
1 Choke Cherry Road
Rockville, MD 20857
Provides resources to individuals and communities on substance abuse prevention and treatment.

U.S. Department of Health and Human Services (HHS)
URL: http://www.hhs.gov
E-mail: web form
Phone: (877) 696-6775
200 Independence Avenue, SW
Washington, DC 20201
The major government agency for protecting the health of Americans and providing essential services. Through its agencies, the Food and Drug Administration, the Centers for Disease Control and Prevention, and the National Institutes of Health, it deals with many aspects of drug use for athletic performance.

U.S. Department of Homeland Security (DHS)
URL: http://www.dhs.gov/
dhspublic
E-mail: web form
Phone: (202) 282-8000
Washington, DC 20528
A new agency established after the September 11, 2001, attacks. Among its many roles, it has responsibility for intercepting drugs smuggled into the United States, including illegal performance-enhancing drugs that can be purchased legally in Mexico and other countries.

U.S. Department of Justice (USDOJ)
URL: http://www.usdoj.gov
E-mail: AskDOJ@usdoj.gov
Phone: (202) 514-2000
950 Pennsylvania Avenue, NW
Washington, DC 20530-0001
Prosecutes those who violate federal laws by using or distributing steroids; it played a major role in the BALCO investigation and prosecution.

U.S. House of Representatives Committee on Government Reform
URL: http://reform.house.gov
Phone: (202) 225-5074
2157 Rayburn House Office Building
Washington, DC 20515

The sponsor of a set of hearings on drug use in sports, including one on use of steroids by Major League Baseball stars.

U.S. Senate Committee on Commerce, Science, and Transportation
URL: http://commerce.senate.gov
Phone: (202) 224-5115
508 Dirksen Senate Office Building
Washington, DC 20510-6125
Has sponsored several hearings on drug use in sports and considered legislation to deal with the problem. The proposed legislation would set a single drug testing and punishment standard for the four major professional sports leagues.

MEDICAL AND SCIENTIFIC

American College of Sports Medicine (ACSM)
URL: http://www.acsm.org
E-mail: web form
Phone: (317) 637-9200
401 West Michigan Street
Indianapolis, IN 46202-3233
Members focus on the diagnosis, treatment, and prevention of injuries and on the advancement of exercise science. It opposes the use of steroids for sports performance.

American Medical Association (AMA)
URL: http://www.ama-assn.org

E-mail: web form
Phone: (800) 621-8335
515 North State Street
Chicago, IL 60610
Unites physicians nationwide to work on the most important professional and public health issues and has made recommendations for steroid-control laws.

Association of Professional Team Physicians (PTP)
URL: http://straws.com/ptp.htm
Phone: (203) 406-2900
200 First Stamford Place

2nd Floor
Stamford, CT 06902
Physicians from a variety of teams and leagues in this association deal with issues of drug use in preventing and treating sports injuries.

Institute for Preventative Sports Medicine (IPSM)
URL: http://www.ipsm.org
E-mail: info@ipsm.org
Phone: (734) 572-4577
P.O. Box 7032
Ann Arbor, MI 48107
A research organization devoted to preventing sports injuries and speeding rehabilitation.

Monitoring the Future (MTF)
URL: http://www.
   monitoringthefuture.org
E-mail: MTFinfo@isr.umich.edu
Phone: (734) 764-8365
Survey Research Center
1355 ISR Building
P.O. Box 1248
Ann Arbor, MI 48106
Runs an annual survey of high school youth that asks questions about steroid use and offers evidence on the extent of the problem among teens.

National Academy of Sports Medicine (NASM)
URL: http://www.nasm.org
E-mail: web form
Phone: (800) 460-6276

26632 Agoura Road
Calabasas, CA 91302
Provides certification and continuing education for fitness trainers, sports performance experts, and sports medicine professionals—all groups that may have to deal with use of performance-enhancing drugs by athletes.

National Strength and Conditioning Association (NSCA)
URL: http://www.nsca-lift.org
E-mail: nsca@nsca-lift.org
Phone: (719) 632-6367
1885 Bob Johnson Drive
Colorado Springs, CO 80906
Provides research-based strength and conditioning information to its members and the public.

President's Council on Physical Fitness and Sports (PCPFS)
URL: http://www.fitness.gov
E-mail: web form
Phone: (202) 690-9000
Department W
200 Independence Avenue, SW
Room 738-H
Washington, DC 20201-0004
A committee of volunteer citizens that advises the president on physical activity, fitness, and sports in America. It encourages fitness without the use of steroids and performance-enhancing drugs.

SOCIAL AND POLICY GROUPS

755 Hits
**URL: http://www.755hits.org/
about.html**
**E-mail: TeamMembers@755hits.
org**
A nonprofit organization that exists
to educate and advocate zero-tolerance policies for substances used
as a means of enhancing athletic
performance (755 Hits refers to the
career home run record of Hank
Aaron, a record reached without use
of performance-enhancing drugs).

**Association of National Anti-
Doping Organizations
(ANADO)**
**URL: http://www.anado.org/
t2.asp**
E-mail: post@antidoping.no
Phone: +47 21 02 92 00
Sognsveien 75A
0855 Oslo
Norway
An international association that
aims to promote and assist national
organizations in their goals of de-
veloping comprehensive antidoping
programs.

**Canadian Centre for Ethics in
Sport (CCES)**
URL: http://www.cces.ca
E-mail: info@cces.ca
Phone: (613) 521-3340
202-2197 Riverside Drive
Ottawa, Ontario K1H 7X3
Canada
A nonprofit organization devoted
to fair play and drug-free sport that
provides services and resources to
athletes, coaches, sports organiza-
tions, the media, and the public.

**Center for the Study of Sport in
Society (CSSS)**
**URL: http://www.northeastern.
edu/csss**
E-mail: sportinsociety@neu.edu
Phone: (617) 373-4025
360 Huntington Avenue
Suite 161 CP
Boston, MA 02115-5000
A center at Northeastern University
that aims to increase awareness of
sport and its relation to society, and
to develop programs that identify
problems, offer solutions, and promote the benefits of sport.

**Coalition for Anabolic Steroid
Precursor and Ephedra
Regulation (CASPER)**
URL: http://www.casper207.com
**E-mail: feedback@casper207.
com**
Phone: (202) 419-2521
2099 Pennsylvania Avenue, NW
Suite 850
Washington, DC 20006
A coalition of medical, public health,
and sports organizations that fo-
cuses on legislative efforts to regu-
late steroid precursors and ephedra
in dietary supplements.

**Community Anti-Drug Coalitions
of America (CADCA)**
URL: http://cadca.org
Phone: (800) 542-2322

625 Slaters Lane
Suite 300
Alexandria, VA 22314
Helps create safe, healthy, and drug-free communities by supporting its members with technical assistance and training, media strategies and marketing programs, and conferences and special events.

Healthy Competition Program
URL: http://www.
  healthycompetition.org
E-mail: healthycompetition@
  bcbsa.com
Phone: (312) 297-5824
P.O. Box 81289
Chicago, IL 60681-0289
A foundation associated with Blue Cross Blue Shield that educates parents, coaches, and teens about the dangers of performance-enhancing drugs.

National Center for Drug-Free
  Sport
URL: http://www.drugfreesport.
  com
E-mail: info@drugfreesport.com
Phone: (816) 474-8655
810 Baltimore
Kansas City, MO 64105
A company that provides testing, evaluation, and antidrug programs for sports organizations such as the National Collegiate Athletic Association.

National Coalition for the
  Advancement of Drug-Free
  Athletics (NCADFA)
URL: http://www.ncadfa.org

E-mail: info@ncadfa.org
Phone: (201) 265-868
P.O. Box 206
New Milford, NJ 07646
Supports educational, charitable, religious, and scientific organizations that teach about the dangers and prevent the use of performance-enhancing drugs. It also provides alternatives to help athletes reach their potential.

National Institute for Sports
  Reform (NISR)
URL: http://www.nisr.org
E-mail: director@nisr.org
Phone: (518) 439-7284 (fax
  only)
P.O. Box 128
Selkirk, NY 12158
An organization aiming to improve the athletic and educational experiences of young people by demanding reform of youth sports and promoting healthy competition.

Partnership for a Drug-Free
  America
URL: http://www.drugfree.org
E-mail: web form
Phone: (212) 922-1560
405 Lexington Avenue
Suite 1601
New York, NY 10174
A group working to reduce illicit use of drugs, including steroids, through research, education, and media campaigns.

Taylor Hooton Foundation
URL: http://www.taylorhooton.
  org/index.asp

E-mail: info@taylorhooton.org
Phone: (877) 503-7300
6009 West Parker Road
Suite 148
P.M.B Box 138
Plano, TX 75093
Raises awareness among the general population about the dangers of steroid abuse in order to minimize the abuse of this drug by adolescents and young adults. The foundation is named for a teen who committed suicide after experimenting with steroids.

United Nations Educational,
   Scientific and Cultural
   Organization (UNESCO)
URL: http://www.unesco.org
E-mail: bpi@unesco.org
Phone: +33 (0)1 45 68 10 00
7, place de Fontenoy
75352 Paris 07 SP
France
Among its many other activities, this organization has organized an international convention against doping in sports.

OLYMPICS

Court of Arbitration for Sport
   (CAS)
URL: http://www.tas-cas.org
E-mail: info@tas-cas.org
Phone: (41 21) 613 50 00
Château de Béthusy
Avenue de Beaumont 2
CH-1012 Lausanne
Switzerland
An international court that provides a means of resolving sports disputes, is adapted to the specific needs of the international sporting community, and avoids recourse to national courts.

Fédération Internationale de
   Natation (FINA)
URL: http://www.fina.org
Phone: (+4121) 310 47 10
Avenue de l'Avant-Poste, No. 4
1005 Lausanne
Switzerland
The international governing body of swimming, diving, water polo, synchronized swimming, and open water swimming.

International Association of
   Athletics Federations (IAAF)
URL: http://www.iaaf.org/
   antidoping
E-mail: info@iaaf.org
Phone: (+377) 93 10 8888
17 rue Princesse Florestine
BP 359
MC98007 Monaco
A governing body for international athletic competition in track and field that sets rules, promotes sports, and standardizes events across nations. It takes a strong antidoping stand.

International Olympic
   Committee (IOC)
URL: http://www.olympic.org
Phone: (41.21) 621 61 11
Château de Vidy
1007 Lausanne
Switzerland
Promotes the Olympic movement and the smooth running of the Olympic Games.

International Olympic Committee Medical Commission
URL: http://www.olympic.org/
uk/organisation/commissions/
medical/index_uk.asp
Case postale 356
Château de Vidy
1001 Lausanne
Switzerland
Created in 1967 to deal with the emerging problem of doping, it now works with the World Anti-Doping Agency to enforce doping policies and addresses medical issues in international Olympic competition.

International Ski Federation (FIS)
URL: http://www.fis-ski.com
E-mail: mail@fisski.ch
Phone: +41 (33) 244 6161
Marc Hodler House
Blochstrasse 2
CH-3653 Oberhofen,
Thunersee
Switzerland
The governing body of international skiing.

International University Sports Federation (FISU)
URL: http://www.fisu.net/site/
page_950.php
E-mail: fisu@fisu.net
Phone: 32 2 6406873
Château de la Solitude
54, avenue Charles Schaller
1160 Brussels
Belgium
Supervises the World University Championships, a competition open

to student-athletes across the world, and follows the antidoping code of the World Anti-Doping Agency.

International Weighlifting Federation (IWF)
URL: http://www.iwf.net/main.
php
Phone: (30 1) 9210790-9
43 Sigrou Avenue
GR 117 73 Athens
Greece
The international governing body of Olympic weightlifting.

Ski and Snowboard Association (USSA)
URL: http://www.ussa.org
E-mail: info@ussa.org
Phone: (435) 649-9090
Box 100
1500 Kearns Boulevard
Park City, UT 84060
The national governing body for Olympic skiing and snowboarding (including alpine, cross country, disabled, freestyle, ski jumping, and nordic combined skiing, and snowboarding).

U.S. Anti-Doping Agency (USADA)
URL: http://www.usantidoping.org
E-mail: webmaster@usantidoping.
org
Phone: (866) 601-2632
1330 Quail Lake Loop
Suite 260
Colorado Springs, CO 80906-
4651
The national antidoping organization for the Olympic movement in

the United States. It is dedicated to eliminating doping in sports; it tests athletes and sponsors research and education on doping.

USA Cycling
URL: http://www.usacycling.org
E-mail: usac@usacycling.org
Phone: (719) 866-4581
One Olympic Plaza
Colorado Springs, CO 80909
The official cycling organization of the U.S. Olympic Committee. It is responsible for identifying, training, and selecting cyclists to compete in international competitions.

USA Swimming
URL: http://www.usaswimming.org
E-mail: web form
Phone: (719) 866-4578
1 Olympic Plaza
Colorado Springs, CO 80909
The national governing body of the sport of swimming. It seeks to promote swimming, achieve competitive Olympic success, and ensure compliance with doping-control rules.

USA Track and Field (USATF)
URL: http://www.usatf.org
E-mail: web form
Phone: (317) 261-0500
One RCA Dome
Suite 140
Indianapolis, IN 46225
The national governing body for track and field that selects Olympic athletes for competition and establishes rules and regulations, including those relating to doping.

USA Weightlifting (USAW)
URL: http://www.msbn.tv/usavision
E-mail: usaw@usaweightlifting.org
Phone: (719) 866-4508
1 Olympic Plaza
Colorado Springs, CO 80909
As the national governing body of Olympic weightlifting in the United States, it sponsors and selects competitors for international events.

World Anti-Doping Agency (WADA)
URL: http://www.wada-ama.org
E-mail: info@wada-ama.org
Phone: +1 514 904 9232
Stock Exchange Tower
800 Place Victoria
Suite 1700
P.O. Box 120
Montreal, Quebec H4Z 1B7
Canada
Promotes, coordinates, and monitors the international fight against doping in sport through testing, education, research, and support for national antidoping organizations.

World Olympians Association (WOA)
URL: http://www.woaolympians.com
E-mail: miami@woaoffice.org
Phone: (305) 446 6440
The Biltmore
1200 Anastasia Avenue
Suite 140
Miami, FL 33134
An organization of Olympic athletes that promotes the Olympic movement and advocates against doping and drug use.

PROFESSIONAL SPORTS ORGANIZATIONS

American Arbitration Association
URL: http://www.adr.org/
  Welcome
E-mail: websitemail@adr.org
Phone: (212) 716-5800
335 Madison Avenue
Floor 10
New York, NY 10017-4605
A company that provides dispute-resolution services, including those involving sports and antidoping disputes.

International Federation of Bodybuilding (IFBB)
URL: http://www.ifbb.com
E-mail: info@ifbb.com
Phone: (514) 731-3783
2875 Bates Road
Montreal, Quebec H3S 1B7
Canada
The governing organization of 176 national bodybuilding federations. It has adopted an antidoping policy and program modeled after the code of the World Anti-Doping Agency, but many bodybuilders continue to use steroids and other muscle-building drugs.

Major League Baseball (MLB)
URL: http://mlb.mlb.com/
  NASApp/mlb/mlb/official_
  info/index.jsp
E-mail: web form
Phone: (866) 800-1275
75 Ninth Avenue
5th Floor
New York, NY 10011

The governing body of professional baseball in the United States. It was slow to develop drug-testing policies and has been criticized for allowing the use of steroids to spread during the 1990s and 2000s.

Major League Baseball Players Association (MLBPA)
URL: http://www.mlb.com/
  NASApp/mlb/pa/info
E-mail: feedback@mlbpa.org
Phone: (212) 826-0808
12 East 49th Street
24th Floor
New York, NY 10017
The labor union and collective bargaining unit of Major League Baseball players. It opposed drug testing of players for many years and only recently agreed to regular tests and meaningful punishment.

National Amateur Bodybuilders Association (NABBA)
URL: http://www.nabba.com
Phone: (718) 882-6413
P.O. Box 531
Bronx, NY 10469
Sponsors the Mr. Universe competition, which allows bodybuilders to compete nationally and internationally as amateurs and qualify to compete as professionals.

National Basketball Association (NBA)
URL: http://www.nba.com

E-mail: web form
Phone: (212) 407-8000
645 Fifth Avenue
New York, NY 10022
The league has had few problems with performance-enhancing drugs but agreed to a new and better drug-testing policy in 2005.

National Basketball Players Association (NBPA)
URL: http://www.nbpa.com
E-mail: info@nbpa.com
Phone: (212) 655-0880
2 Penn Plaza
Suite 2430
New York, NY 10121
The NBA labor union negotiates collective bargaining agreements and protects player's rights. It agreed with the NBA to institute a new drug-testing policy in 2005.

National Collegiate Athletics Association (NCAA)
URL: http://www.ncaa.org
E-mail: web form
Phone: (317) 917-6762
700 West Washington Street
P.O. Box 6222
Indianapolis, IN 46206-6222
An organization made up of member colleges and universities that governs collegiate athletic competition and integrates sports activities into the larger mission of higher education.

National Football League (NFL)
URL: http://www.nfl.com/help
E-mail: web form

Phone: (212) 450-2000
280 Park Avenue
New York, NY 10017
The league was one of the first in professional sports to implement a strong antidrug policy and enforcement strategy.

National Football League Players Association (NFLPA)
URL: http://www.nflplayers.com
E-mail: webadmin@nflplayers.com
Phone: (202) 463-2200
2021 L Street, NW
Washington, DC 20036
The union of NFL players agreed to testing and punishment with the league much earlier than other players' unions.

National Hockey League (NHL)
URL: http://www.nhl.com
Phone: (212) 789-2000
1251 Avenue of the Americas
New York, NY 10020
The league implemented a drug-testing program in 2006.

Union Cycliste Internationale (UCI)
URL: http://www.uci.ch
E-mail: admin@uci.ch
Phone: +41 24 468 58 11
CH 186, Aigle
Switzerland
Regulates and promotes cycling, organizes international cycling events, and collaborates with the International Olympic Committee with respect to Olympic cycling competitions.

World Wrestling Entertainment (WWE)
URL: http://www.wwe.com
E-mail: web form
Phone: (203) 352-8600
1241 East Main Street
Stamford, CT 06902
Formerly the World Wresting Federation (WWF), now a publicly traded company dealing primarily with professional wrestling. The WWE maintains an antidrug policy, but there is concern that wrestlers often use performance-enhancing drugs.

PART III

APPENDICES

APPENDIX A

THE ANABOLIC STEROID CONTROL ACTS OF 1990 AND 2004

Congress amended the Controlled Substances Act in both 1990 and 2004. In 1990, the Anabolic Steroid Control Act added anabolic steroids to the list of controlled substances, and in 2004 the Anabolic Steroid Control Act added steroid precursors to the list of controlled substances. The listing of steroids and steroid precursors in the acts will interest few besides chemists and pharmacists, but the explanation of punishments helps give a sense of the concern Congress has shown about the use of steroids and steroid precursors.

ANABOLIC STEROID CONTROL ACT OF 1990
1990 H.R. 4658; 101 H.R. 4658

A BILL

To amend the Controlled Substances Act to provide criminal penalties for illicit use of anabolic steroids and for coaches and others who endeavor to persuade or induce athletes to take anabolic steroids, and for other purposes.

Be it enacted by the Senate and House of Representatives of the United States of America in Congress assembled,

SECTION 1. SHORT TITLE.

This Act may be cited as the "Anabolic Steroids Control Act of 1990".

SEC. 2. ANABOLIC STEROID PENALTIES.

(a) COACHES AND OTHERS PERSUADING OR INDUCING USE.—Section 404 of the Controlled Substances Act (21 U.S.C. 844) is amended by inserting after subsection (a) the following:

"(b)(1) Whoever, being a physical trainer or adviser to an individual, endeavors to persuade or induce that individual to possess or use anabolic steroids in violation of subsection (a), shall be fined under title 18, United States Code, or imprisoned not more than 2 years, or both. If such individual has not attained the age of 18 years, the maximum imprisonment shall be 5 years.

"(2) As used in this subsection, the term 'physical trainer or adviser' means any professional or amateur coach, manager, trainer, instructor, or other such person, who provides any athletic or physical instruction, training, advice, assistance, or other such service to any person.".

(b) ADDITION OF ANABOLIC STEROIDS TO SCHEDULE III.—Schedule III of section 202(c) of the Controlled Substances Act (21 U.S.C. 812(c)) is amended by adding at the end the following:

"(e) Anabolic steroids."

(c) DEFINITION OF ANABOLIC STEROID.—Section 102 of the Controlled Substances Act (21 U.S.C. 802) is amended by adding at the end the following:

"(41) The term 'anabolic steroid' means any drug or hormonal substance that promotes muscle growth in a manner pharmacologically similar to testosterone, and includes-—

"(A) Boldenone.
"(B) Chlorotestosterone.
"(C) Clostebol.
"(D) Dehydrochlormethyltestosterone.
"(E) Dihydrotestosterone.
"(F) Drostanolone.
"(G) Ethylestrenol.
"(H) Fluoxymesterone.
"(I) Mesterolone.
"(J) Methandienone.
"(K) Methandranone.
"(L) Methandriol.
"(M) Methandrostenolone.
"(N) Methyltestosterone.
"(O) Mibolerone.
"(P) Nandrolone.
"(Q) Norethandrolone.
"(R) Oxandrolone.
"(S) Oxymesterone.
"(T) Oxymetholone.
"(U) Stanolone.

"(V) Stanozolol.

"(W) Testolactone.

"(X) Testosterone.

"(Y) Trenbolone; and

"(Z) any salt, ester, or isomer of a drug or substance described or listed in this paragraph, if that salt, ester, or isomer promotes muscle growth.".

SEC. 3. PENALTY FOR DISTRIBUTION OF HUMAN GROWTH HORMONE.

Subsection (e) of section 303 of the Federal Food, Drug, and Cosmetic Act (21 U.S.C. 333) is amended——

(1) by striking "anabolic steroid" each place it appears and inserting "human growth hormone"; and

(2) by adding at the end the following:

"(3) As used in this subsection, the term 'human growth hormone' means somatrem, somatropin, or an analogue of either of them.".

SEC. 4. CLERICAL CORRECTION.

Section 404 of the Controlled Substances Act (21 U.S.C. 844) is amended by inserting "(a)" before "It shall be unlawful" in the first undesignated paragraph.

ANABOLIC STEROID CONTROL ACT OF 2004
108 P.L. 358; 118 STAT. 1661; 2004
ENACTED S. 2195; 108 ENACTED S. 2195

AN ACT

To amend the Controlled Substances Act to clarify the definition of anabolic steroids and to provide for research and education activities relating to steroids and steroid precursors.

Be it enacted by the Senate and House of Representatives of the United States of America in Congress assembled,

SECTION 1. SHORT TITLE.

This Act may be cited as the "Anabolic Steroid Control Act of 2004".

Drugs and Sports

SEC. 2. AMENDMENTS TO THE CONTROLLED SUBSTANCES ACT.

(a) Definitions.—Section 102 of the Controlled Substances Act (21 U.S.C. 802) is amended—(1) in paragraph (41)—

(A) by realigning the margin so as to align with paragraph (40); and

(B) by striking subparagraph (A) and inserting the following:

"(A) The term 'anabolic steroid' means any drug or hormonal substance, chemically and pharmacologically related to testosterone (other than estrogens, progestins, corticosteroids, and dehydroepiandrosterone), and includes—

"(i) androstanediol—
    "(I) 3β, 17β-dihydroxy-5α-androstane; and
    "(II) 3α, 17β-dihydroxy-5α-androstane;
"(ii) androstanedione (5α-androstan-3, 17-dione);
"(iii) androstenediol—
    "(I) 1-androstenediol (3β, 17β-dihydroxy-5α-androst-1-ene);
    "(II) 1-androstenediol (3α, 17β-dihydroxy-5α-androst-1-ene);
    "(III) 4-androstenediol (3β, 17β-dihydroxy-androst-4-ene); and
    "(IV) 5-androstenediol (3β, 17β-dihydroxy-androst-5-ene);
"(iv) androstenedione—
    "(I) 1-androstenedione (5α-androst-1-en-3, 17-dione);
    "(II) 4-androstenedione (androst-4-en-3, 17-dione); and
    "(III) 5-androstenedione (androst-5-en-3, 17-dione);
"(v) bolasterone (7α, 17α-dimethyl-17β-hydroxyandrost-4-en-3-one);
"(vi) boldenone (17β-hydroxyandrost-1,4,-diene-3-one);
"(vii) calusterone (7β, 17α-dimethyl-17β-hydroxyandrost-4-en-3-one);
"(viii) clostebol (4-chloro-17β-hydroxyandrost-4-en-3-one);
"(ix) dehydrochloromethyltestosterone (4-chloro-17β-hydroxy-17α-methyl-androst-1,4-dien-3-one);
"(x) Δ 1-dihydrotestosterone (a.k.a. '1-testosterone') (17β-hydroxy-5α-androst-1-en-3-one);
"(xi) 4-dihydrotestosterone (17β-hydroxy-androstan-3-one);
"(xii) drostanolone (17β-hydroxy-2α-methyl-5α-androstan-3-one);
"(xiii) ethylestrenol (17α-ethyl-17β-hydroxyestr-4-ene);
"(xiv) fluoxymesterone (9-fluoro-17α-methyl-11β, 17β-dihydroxyan-drost-4-en-3-one);
"(xv) formebolone (2-formyl-17α-methyl-11α, 17β-dihydroxyan-drost-1,4-dien-3-one);
"(xvi) furazabol (17α-methyl-17β-hydroxyandrostano[2,3]-c-furazan);
"(xvii) 13β-ethyl-17α-hydroxygon-4-en-3-one;
"(xviii) 4-hydroxytestosterone (4, 17β-dihydroxy-androst-4-en-3-one);

236

Appendix A

"(xix) 4-hydroxy-19-nortestosterone (4, 17β-dihydroxy-estr-4-en-3-one);

"(xx) mestanolone (17α-methyl-17β-hydroxy-5α-androstan-3-one);

"(xxi) mesterolone (1α-methyl-17β-hydroxy-5α-androstan-3-one);

"(xxii) methandienone (17α-methyl-17β-hydroxyandrost-1,4-dien-3-one);

"(xxiii) methandriol (17α-methyl-3β, 17β-dihydroxyandrost-5-ene);

"(xxiv) methenolone (1-methyl-17β-hydroxy-5α-androst-1-en-3-one);

"(xxv) 17α-methyl-3β, 17β-dihydroxy-5α-androstane;

"(xxvi) 17α-methyl-3α, 17β-dihydroxy-5α-androstane;

"(xxvii) 17α-methyl-3β, 17β-dihydroxyandrost-4-ene.

"(xxviii) 17α-methyl-4-hydroxynandrolone (17α-methyl-4-hydroxy-17β-hydroxyestr-4-en-3-one);

"(xxix) methyldienolone (17α-methyl-17β-hydroxyestra-4,9(10)-dien-3-one);

"(xxx) methyltrienolone (17α-methyl-17β-hydroxyestra-4,9-11-trien-3-one);

"(xxxi) methyltestosterone (17α-methyl-17β-hydroxyandrost-4-en-3-one);

"(xxxii) mibolerone (7α, 17α-dimethyl-17β-hydroxyestr-4-en-3-one);

"(xxxiii) 17α-methyl-Δ1-dihydrotestosterone (17β-hydroxy-17α-methyl-5α-androst-1-en-3-one) (a.k.a. '17-α-methyl-1-testosterone');

"(xxxiv) nandrolone (17β-hydroxyestr-4-en-3-one);

"(xxxv) norandrostenediol—

"(I) 19-nor-4-androstenediol (3β, 17β-dihydroxyestr-4-ene);

"(II) 19-nor-4-androstenediol (3α, 17β-dihydroxyestr-4-ene);

"(III) 19-nor-5-androstenediol (3β, 17β-dihydroxyestr-5-ene); and

"(IV) 19-nor-5-androstenediol (3α, 17β-dihydroxyestr-5-ene);

"(xxxvi) norandrostenedione—

"(I) 19-nor-4-androstenedione (estr-4-en-3, 17-dione); and

"(II) 19-nor-5-androstenedione (estr-5-en-3, 17-dione);

"(xxxvii) norbolethone (13β, 17α-diethyl-17β-hydroxygon-4-en-3-one);

"(xxxviii) norclostebol (4-chloro-17β-hydroxyestr-4-en-3-one);

"(xxxix) norethandrolone (17α-ethyl-17β-hydroxyestr-4-en-3-one);

"(xl) normethandrolone (17α-methyl-17β-hydroxyestr-4-en-3-one);

"(xli) oxandrolone (17α-methyl-17β-hydroxy-2-oxa-[5α]-androstan-3-one);

"(xlii) oxymesterone (17α-methyl-4, 17β-dihydroxyandrost-4-en-3-one);

"(xliii) oxymetholone (17α-methyl-2-hydroxymethylene-17β-hydroxy-[5α]-androstan-3-one);

"(xliv) stanozolol (17α-methyl-17α-hydroxy-5α-androst-2-eno3,2-c-pyrazole);

"(xlv) stenbolone (17β-hydroxy-2-methyl-[5α]-androst-1-en-3-one);
"(xlvi) testolactone (13-hydroxy-3-oxo-13, 17-secoandrosta-1,4-dien-17-oic acid lactone);
"(xlvii) testosterone (17β-hydroxyandrost-4-en-3-one);
"(xlviii) tetrahydrogestrinone (13β, 17α-diethyl-17β-hydroxygon-4,9,11-trien-3-one);
"(xlix) trenbolone (17β-hydroxyestr-4,9,11-trien-3-one); and
"(xlx) any salt, ester, or ether of a drug or substance described in this paragraph.

The substances excluded under this subparagraph may at any time be scheduled by the Attorney General in accordance with the authority and requirements of subsections (a) through (c) of section 201."; and

(2) in paragraph (44), by inserting "anabolic steroids," after "marihuana,".
(b) Authority and Criteria for Classification.—Section 201(g) of the Controlled Substances Act (21 U.S.C. 811(g)) is amended—

(1) in paragraph (1), by striking "substance from a schedule if such substance" and inserting "drug which contains a controlled substance from the application of titles II and III of the Comprehensive Drug Abuse Prevention and Control Act (21 U.S.C. 802 et seq.) if such drug"; and

(2) in paragraph (3), by adding at the end the following:
"(C) Upon the recommendation of the Secretary of Health and Human Services, a compound, mixture, or preparation which contains any anabolic steroid, which is intended for administration to a human being or an animal, and which, because of its concentration, preparation, formulation or delivery system, does not present any significant potential for abuse.".
(c) Anabolic Steroids Control Act.—Section 1903 of the Anabolic Steroids Control Act of 1990 (Public Law 101-647) < 21 USC 802 note> is amended—
(1) by striking subsection (a); and
(2) by redesignating subsections (b) and (c) as subsections (a) and (b), respectively.
(d) < 21 USC 802 note> Effective Date.—The amendments made by this section shall take effect 90 days after the date of enactment of this Act.

[*3] SEC. 3. < 28 USC 994 NOTE> SENTENCING COMMISSION GUIDELINES.

The United States Sentencing Commission shall——
(1) review the Federal sentencing guidelines with respect to offenses involving anabolic steroids;

(2) consider amending the Federal sentencing guidelines to provide for increased penalties with respect to offenses involving anabolic steroids in a manner that reflects the seriousness of such offenses and the need to deter anabolic steroid trafficking and use; and

(3) take such other action that the Commission considers necessary to carry out this section.

[*4] Sec. 4. < 42 Usc 290bb-25f> PREVENTION AND EDUCATION PROGRAMS.

(a) In General.—The Secretary of Health and Human Services (referred to in this Act as the "Secretary") shall award grants to public and nonprofit private entities to enable such entities to carry out science-based education programs in elementary and secondary schools to highlight the harmful effects of anabolic steroids.

(b) Eligibility.—

(1) Application.—To be eligible for grants under subsection (a), an entity shall prepare and submit to the Secretary an application at such time, in such manner, and containing such information as the Secretary may require.

(2) Preference.—In awarding grants under subsection (a), the Secretary shall give preference to applicants that intend to use grant funds to carry out programs based on—

(A) the Athletes Training and Learning to Avoid Steroids program;

(B) The Athletes Targeting Healthy Exercise and Nutrition Alternatives program; and

(C) other programs determined to be effective by the National Institute on Drug Abuse.

(c) Use of Funds.—Amounts received under a grant under subsection (a) shall be used for education programs that will directly communicate with teachers, principals, coaches, as well as elementary and secondary school children concerning the harmful effects of anabolic steroids. (d) Authorization of Appropriations.—There is authorized to be appropriated to carry out this section, $ 15,000,000 for each of fiscal years 2005 through 2010.

[*5] Sec. 5. < 42 USC 290aa-4 note> National Survey on Drug Use and Health.

(a) In General.—The Secretary of Health and Human Services shall ensure that the National Survey on Drug Use and Health includes questions concerning the use of anabolic steroids.

(b) Authorization of Appropriations.—There is authorized to be appropriated to carry out this section, $ 1,000,000 for each of fiscal years 2005 through 2010.

APPENDIX B

———————

VERNONIA SCHOOL DISTRICT 47J, PETITIONER V. WAYNE ACTON, ET UX., ETC., 1995

No. 94-590
SUPREME COURT OF THE UNITED STATES
515 U.S. 646; 115 S. Ct. 2386; 132 L. Ed. 2d 564; 1995 U.S. LEXIS 4275;
63 U.S.L.W. 4653; 95 Cal. Daily Op. Service 4846; 9 Fla. L. Weekly Fed.
S 229

March 28, 1995, Argued
June 26, 1995, Decided

[*This decision delivered by the Supreme Court has allowed for drug testing of student athletes. Although specifically focused on mandatory tests of high school football players, the conclusion that random urinanalysis testing of athletes does not violate the Constitution applies more widely to professional athletes.*]

JUDGES: SCALIA, J., delivered the opinion of the Court, in which REHNQUIST, C. J., and KENNEDY, THOMAS, GINSBURG, and BREYER, JJ., joined. GINSBURG, J., filed a concurring opinion, post, O'CONNOR, J., filed a dissenting opinion, in which STEVENS and SOUTER, JJ., joined, post.

OPINION: JUSTICE SCALIA delivered the opinion of the Court.

The Student Athlete Drug Policy adopted by School District 47J in the town of Vernonia, Oregon, authorizes random urinalysis drug testing of students who participate in the District's school athletics programs. We granted certiorari to decide whether this violates the Fourth and Fourteenth Amendments to the United States Constitution.

Appendix B

I

A

Petitioner Vernonia School District 47J (District) operates one high school and three grade schools in the logging community of Vernonia, Oregon. As elsewhere in small-town America, school sports play a prominent role in the town's life, and student athletes are admired in their schools and in the community.

Drugs had not been a major problem in Vernonia schools. In the mid-to-late 1980's, however, teachers and administrators observed a sharp increase in drug use. Students began to speak out about their attraction to the drug culture, and to boast that there was nothing the school could do about it. Along with more drugs came more disciplinary problems. Between 1988 and 1989 the number of disciplinary referrals in Vernonia schools rose to more than twice the number reported in the early 1980's, and several students were suspended. Students became increasingly rude during class; outbursts of profane language became common.

Not only were student athletes included among the drug users but, as the District Court found, athletes were the leaders of the drug culture. 796 F. Supp. 1354, 1357 (Ore. 1992). This caused the District's administrators particular concern, since drug use increases the risk of sports-related injury. Expert testimony at the trial confirmed the deleterious effects of drugs on motivation, memory, judgment, reaction, coordination, and performance. The high school football and wrestling coach witnessed a severe sternum injury suffered by a wrestler, and various omissions of safety procedures and misexecutions by football players, all attributable in his belief to the effects of drug use.

Initially, the District responded to the drug problem by offering special classes, speakers, and presentations designed to deter drug use. It even brought in a specially trained dog to detect drugs, but the drug problem persisted. According to the District Court:

"The administration was at its wits end and ... a large segment of the student body, particularly those involved in interscholastic athletics, was in a state of rebellion. Disciplinary actions had reached 'epidemic proportions.' The coincidence of an almost three-fold increase in classroom disruptions and disciplinary reports along with the staff's direct observations of students using drugs or glamorizing drug and alcohol use led the administration to the inescapable conclusion that the rebellion was being fueled by alcohol and drug abuse as well as the student's misperceptions about the drug culture." *Ibid.*

241

Drugs and Sports

At that point, District officials began considering a drug-testing program. They held a parent "input night" to discuss the proposed Student Athlete Drug Policy (Policy), and the parents in attendance gave their unanimous approval. The school board approved the Policy for implementation in the fall of 1989. Its expressed purpose is to prevent student athletes from using drugs, to protect their health and safety, and to provide drug users with assistance programs.

B

The Policy applies to all students participating in interscholastic athletics. Students wishing to play sports must sign a form consenting to the testing and must obtain the written consent of their parents. Athletes are tested at the beginning of the season for their sport. In addition, once each week of the season the names of the athletes are placed in a "pool" from which a student, with the supervision of two adults, blindly draws the names of 10% of the athletes for random testing. Those selected are notified and tested that same day, if possible.

The student to be tested completes a specimen control form which bears an assigned number. Prescription medications that the student is taking must be identified by providing a copy of the prescription or a doctor's authorization. The student then enters an empty locker room accompanied by an adult monitor of the same sex. Each boy selected produces a sample at a urinal, remaining fully clothed with his back to the monitor, who stands approximately 12 to 15 feet behind the student. Monitors may (though do not always) watch the student while he produces the sample, and they listen for normal sounds of urination. Girls produce samples in an enclosed bathroom stall, so that they can be heard but not observed. After the sample is produced, it is given to the monitor, who checks it for temperature and tampering and then transfers it to a vial.

The samples are sent to an independent laboratory, which routinely tests them for amphetamines, cocaine, and marijuana. Other drugs, such as LSD, may be screened at the request of the District, but the identity of a particular student does not determine which drugs will be tested. The laboratory's procedures are 99.94% accurate. The District follows strict procedures regarding the chain of custody and access to test results. The laboratory does not know the identity of the students whose samples it tests. It is authorized to mail written test reports only to the superintendent and to provide test results to District personnel by telephone only after the requesting official recites a code confirming his authority. Only the superintendent, principals, vice-principals, and athletic directors have access to test results, and the results are not kept for more than one year.

Appendix B

If a sample tests positive, a second test is administered as soon as possible to confirm the result. If the second test is negative, no further action is taken. If the second test is positive, the athlete's parents are notified, and the school principal convenes a meeting with the student and his parents, at which the student is given the option of (1) participating for six weeks in an assistance program that includes weekly urinalysis, or (2) suffering suspension from athletics for the remainder of the current season and the next athletic season. The student is then retested prior to the start of the next athletic season for which he or she is eligible. The Policy states that a second offense results in automatic imposition of option (2); a third offense in suspension for the remainder of the current season and the next two athletic seasons.

C

In the fall of 1991, respondent James Acton, then a seventh grader, signed up to play football at one of the District's grade schools. He was denied participation, however, because he and his parents refused to sign the testing consent forms. The Actons filed suit, seeking declaratory and injunctive relief from enforcement of the Policy on the grounds that it violated the Fourth and Fourteenth Amendments to the United States Constitution and Article I, § 9, of the Oregon Constitution. After a bench trial, the District Court entered an order denying the claims on the merits and dismissing the action. 796 F. Supp. at 1355. The United States Court of Appeals for the Ninth Circuit reversed, holding that the Policy violated both the Fourth and Fourteenth Amendments and Article I, § 9, of the Oregon Constitution. 23 F.3d 1514 (1994). We granted certiorari. 513 U.S. 1013 (1994).

II

The Fourth Amendment to the United States Constitution provides that the Federal Government shall not violate "the right of the people to be secure in their persons, houses, papers, and effects, against unreasonable searches and seizures..." We have held that the Fourteenth Amendment extends this constitutional guarantee to searches and seizures by state officers, *Elkins* v. *United States*, 364 U.S. 206, 213, 4 L. Ed. 2d 1669, 80 S. Ct. 1437 (1960), including public school officials, *New Jersey* v. *T. L. O.*, 469 U.S. 325, 336–337, 83 L. Ed. 2d 720, 105 S. Ct. 733 (1985). In *Skinner* v. *Railway Labor Executives' Assn.*, 489 U.S. 602, 617, 103 L. Ed. 2d 639, 109 S. Ct. 1402 (1989), we held that state-compelled collection and testing of urine, such as that required by the Policy, constitutes a "search" subject to the demands of the Fourth Amendment. See also *Treasury Employees* v. *Von Raab*, 489 U.S. 656, 665, 103 L. Ed. 2d 685, 109 S. Ct. 1384 (1989).

As the text of the Fourth Amendment indicates, the ultimate measure of the constitutionality of a governmental search is "reasonableness." At least in a case such as this, where there was no clear practice, either approving or disapproving the type of search at issue, at the time the constitutional provision was enacted,[1] whether a particular search meets the reasonableness standard "'is judged by balancing its intrusion on the individual's Fourth Amendment interests against its promotion of legitimate governmental interests.'" *Skinner, supra,* at 619 (quoting *Delaware* v. *Prouse*, 440 U.S. 648, 654, 59 L. Ed. 2d 660, 99 S. Ct. 1391 (1979)). Where a search is undertaken by law enforcement officials to discover evidence of criminal wrongdoing, this Court has said that reasonableness generally requires the obtaining of a judicial warrant, *Skinner, supra,* at 619. Warrants cannot be issued, of course, without the showing of probable cause required by the Warrant Clause. But a warrant is not required to establish the reasonableness of *all* government searches; and when a warrant is not required (and the Warrant Clause therefore not applicable), probable cause is not invariably required either. A search unsupported by probable cause can be constitutional, we have said, "when special needs, beyond the normal need for law enforcement, make the warrant and probable-cause requirement impracticable." *Griffin* v. *Wisconsin*, 483 U.S. 868, 873, 97 L. Ed. 2d 709, 107 S. Ct. 3164 (1987) (internal quotation marks omitted).

We have found such "special needs" to exist in the public school context. There, the warrant requirement "would unduly interfere with the maintenance of the swift and informal disciplinary procedures [that are] needed," and "strict adherence to the requirement that searches be based on probable cause" would undercut "the substantial need of teachers and administrators for freedom to maintain order in the schools." *T. L. O.*, 469 U.S. at 340, 341. The school search we approved in *T. L. O.*, while not based on probable cause, *was* based on individualized *suspicion* of wrongdoing. As we explicitly acknowledged, however, "'the Fourth Amendment imposes no irreducible requirement of such suspicion,'" *id.*, at 342, n. 8 (quoting *United States* v. *Martinez-Fuerte*, 428 U.S. 543, 560–561, 49 L. Ed. 2d 1116, 96 S. Ct. 3074 (1976)). We have upheld suspicionless searches and seizures to conduct drug testing of railroad personnel involved in train accidents, see *Skinner, supra;* to conduct random drug testing of federal customs officers who carry arms or are involved in drug interdiction, see *Von Raab, supra;* and to maintain automobile checkpoints looking for illegal immigrants and contraband, *Martinez-Fuerte, supra*, and drunk drivers, *Michigan Dept. of State Police* v. *Sitz,* 496 U.S. 444, 110 L. Ed. 2d 412, 110 S. Ct. 2481 (1990).

Appendix B

III

The first factor to be considered is the nature of the privacy interest upon which the search here at issue intrudes. The Fourth Amendment does not protect all subjective expectations of privacy, but only those that society recognizes as "legitimate." *T. L. O.* 469 U.S. at 338. What expectations are legitimate varies, of course, with context, *id.*, at 337, depending, for example, upon whether the individual asserting the privacy interest is at home, at work, in a car, or in a public park. In addition, the legitimacy of certain privacy expectations vis-a-vis the State may depend upon the individual's legal relationship with the State. For example, in *Griffin, supra,* we held that, although a "probationer's home, like anyone else's, is protected by the Fourth Amendment," the supervisory relationship between probationer and State justifies "a degree of impingement upon [a probationer's] privacy that would not be constitutional if applied to the public at large." 483 U.S. at 873, 875. Central, in our view, to the present case is the fact that the subjects of the Policy are (1) children, who (2) have been committed to the temporary custody of the State as schoolmaster.

Traditionally at common law, and still today, unemancipated minors lack some of the most fundamental rights of self-determination—including even the right of liberty in its narrow sense, *i. e.*, the right to come and go at will. They are subject, even as to their physical freedom, to the control of their parents or guardians. See 59 Am. Jur. 2d, Parent and Child § 10 (1987). When parents place minor children in private schools for their education, the teachers and administrators of those schools stand *in loco parentis* over the children entrusted to them. In fact, the tutor or schoolmaster is the very prototype of that status. As Blackstone describes it, a parent "may ... delegate part of his parental authority, during his life, to the tutor or schoolmaster of his child; who is then *in loco parentis*, and has such a portion of the power of the parent committed to his charge, viz. that of restraint and correction, as may be necessary to answer the purposes for which he is employed." 1 W. Blackstone, Commentaries on the Laws of England 441 (1769).

In *T. L. O.* we rejected the notion that public schools, like private schools, exercise only parental power over their students, which of course is not subject to constitutional constraints. 469 U.S. at 336. Such a view of things, we said, "is not entirely 'consonant with compulsory education laws,'" *ibid.* (quoting *Ingraham* v. *Wright*, 430 U.S. 651, 662, 51 L. Ed. 2d 711, 97 S. Ct. 1401 (1977)), and is inconsistent with our prior decisions treating school officials as state actors for purposes of the Due Process and Free Speech Clauses, *T. L. O., supra,* at 336. But while denying that the State's power over schoolchildren is formally no more than the delegated power of their parents, *T. L. O.* did not deny, but indeed emphasized, that the nature of that power is custodial and tutelary, permitting a degree of supervision and control that could not be exercised over free adults. "[A] proper educational environment requires close supervision of schoolchildren, as well as the enforcement of rules against conduct that would be perfectly permissible if undertaken by an adult." 469 U.S. at 339. While we do not, of course, suggest that public schools as a general matter have such a degree of control over children as to give rise to a constitutional "duty to protect," see *De-Shaney* v. *Winnebago County Dept. of Social Servs.*, 489 U.S. 189, 200, 103 L. Ed. 2d 249, 109 S. Ct. 998 (1989), we have acknowledged that for many purposes "school authorities act *in loco parentis*," *Bethel School Dist. No. 403* v. *Fraser*, 478 U.S. 675, 684, 92 L. Ed. 2d 549, 106 S. Ct. 3159 (1986), with the power and indeed the duty to "inculcate the habits and manners of civility," *id.*, at 681 (internal quotation marks omitted). Thus, while children assuredly do not "shed their constitutional rights ... at the schoolhouse gate," *Tinker* v. *Des Moines Independent Community School Dist.*, 393 U.S. 503, 506, 21 L. Ed. 2d 731, 89 S. Ct. 733 (1969), the nature of those rights is what is appropriate for children in school. See, *e. g., Goss* v. *Lopez*, 419 U.S. 565, 581–582, 42 L. Ed. 2d 725, 95 S. Ct. 729 (1975) (due process for a student challenging disciplinary suspension requires only that the teacher "informally discuss the alleged misconduct with the student minutes after it has occurred"); *Fraser, supra*, at 683 ("It is a highly appropriate function of public school education to prohibit the use of vulgar and offensive terms in public discourse"); *Hazelwood School Dist.* v. *Kuhlmeier*, 484 U.S. 260, 273, 98 L. Ed. 2d 592, 108 S. Ct. 562 (1988) (public school authorities may censor school-sponsored publications, so long as the censorship is "reasonably related to legitimate pedagogical concerns"); *Ingraham, supra*, at 682 ("Imposing additional administrative safeguards [upon corporal punishment] ... would ... entail a significant intrusion into an area of primary educational responsibility").

Fourth Amendment rights, no less than First and Fourteenth Amendment rights, are different in public schools than elsewhere; the "reasonableness" inquiry cannot disregard the schools' custodial and tutelary responsibility for children. For their own good and that of their classmates, public school children are routinely required to submit to various physical examinations, and to be vaccinated against various diseases. According to the American Academy of Pediatrics, most public schools "provide vision and hearing screening and dental and dermatological checks ... Others also mandate scoliosis screening at appropriate grade levels." Committee on School Health, American Academy of Pediatrics, School Health: A Guide for Health Professionals 2 (1987). In the 1991–1992 school year, all 50 States required public school students to be vaccinated against diphtheria, measles, rubella, and polio. U.S. Dept. of Health & Human Services, Public Health Service, Centers for Disease Control, State Immunization Requirements 1991–1992, p. 1. Particularly with regard to medical examinations and procedures, therefore, "students within the school environment have a lesser expectation of privacy than members of the population generally." *T. L. O., supra*, at 348 (Powell, J., concurring).

Legitimate privacy expectations are even less with regard to student athletes. School sports are not for the bashful. They require "suiting up" before each practice or event, and showering and changing afterwards. Public school locker rooms, the usual sites for these activities, are not notable for the privacy they afford. The locker rooms in Vernonia are typical: No individual dressing rooms are provided; shower heads are lined up along a wall, unseparated by any sort of partition or curtain; not even all the toilet stalls have doors. As the United States Court of Appeals for the Seventh Circuit has noted, there is "an element of 'communal undress' inherent in athletic participation," *Schaill by Kross* v. *Tippecanoe County School Corp.*, 864 F.2d 1309, 1318 (1988).

There is an additional respect in which school athletes have a reduced expectation of privacy. By choosing to "go out for the team," they voluntarily subject themselves to a degree of regulation even higher than that imposed on students generally. In Vernonia's public schools, they must submit to a preseason physical exam (James testified that his included the giving of a urine sample, App. 17), they must acquire adequate insurance coverage or sign an insurance waiver, maintain a minimum grade point average, and comply with any "rules of conduct, dress, training hours and related matters as may be established for each sport by the head coach and athletic director with the principal's approval." Record, Exh. 2, p. 30, P 8. Somewhat like adults who choose to participate in a "closely regulated industry," students who voluntarily participate in school athletics have reason to expect intrusions upon normal rights and privileges, including privacy. See *Skinner*, 489 U.S. at 627; *United States* v. *Biswell*, 406 U.S. 311, 316, 32 L. Ed. 2d 87, 92 S. Ct. 1593 (1972).

IV

Having considered the scope of the legitimate expectation of privacy at issue here, we turn next to the character of the intrusion that is complained of. We recognized in *Skinner* that collecting the samples for urinalysis intrudes upon "an excretory function traditionally shielded by great privacy." 489 U.S. at 626. We noted, however, that the degree of intrusion depends upon the manner in which production of the urine sample is monitored. *Ibid.*

Under the District's Policy, male students produce samples at a urinal along a wall. They remain fully clothed and are only observed from behind, if at all. Female students produce samples in an enclosed stall, with a female monitor standing outside listening only for sounds of tampering. These conditions are nearly identical to those typically encountered in public restrooms, which men, women, and especially school children use daily. Under such conditions, the privacy interests compromised by the process of obtaining the urine sample are in our view negligible.

The other privacy-invasive aspect of urinalysis is, of course, the information it discloses concerning the state of the subject's body, and the materials he has ingested. In this regard it is significant that the tests at issue here look only for drugs, and not for whether the student is, for example, epileptic, pregnant, or diabetic. See *id.*, at 617. Moreover, the drugs for which the samples are screened are standard, and do not vary according to the identity of the student. And finally, the results of the tests are disclosed only to a limited class of school personnel who have a need to know; and they are not turned over to law enforcement authorities or used for any internal disciplinary function. 796 F. Supp. at 1364; see also 23 F.3d at 1521.[2]

Respondents argue, however, that the District's Policy is in fact more intrusive than this suggests, because it requires the students, if they are to avoid sanctions for a falsely positive test, to identify *in advance* prescription medications they are taking. We agree that this raises some cause for concern. In *Von Raab*, we flagged as one of the salutary features of the Customs Service drug-testing program the fact that employees were not required to disclose medical information unless they tested positive, and, even then, the information was supplied to a licensed physician rather than to the Government employer. See *Von Raab*, 489 U.S. at 672–673, n. 2. On the other hand, we have never indicated that requiring advance disclosure of medications is *per se* unreasonable. Indeed, in *Skinner* we held that it was not "a significant invasion of privacy." 489 U.S. at 626, n. 7. It can be argued that, in *Skinner*, the disclosure went only to the medical personnel taking the sample, and the Government personnel analyzing it, see *id.*, at 609, but see *id.*, at 610 (railroad personnel responsible for forwarding the sample, and presumably accompanying information, to the Government's testing lab); and that disclosure to teachers and coaches—to persons who personally *know* the student—is a greater invasion of privacy. Assuming for the sake of argument that both those propositions are true, we do not believe they establish a difference that respondents are entitled to rely on here.

The General Authorization Form that respondents refused to sign, which refusal was the basis for James's exclusion from the sports program, said only (in relevant part): "I ... authorize the Vernonia School District to conduct a test on a urine specimen which I provide to test for drugs and/or alcohol use. I also authorize the release of information concerning the results of such a test to the Vernonia School District and to the parents and/or guardians of the student." App. 10–11. While the practice of the District seems to have been to have a school official take medication information from the student at the time of the test, see *id.*, at 29, 42, that practice is not set forth in, or required by, the Policy, which says simply: "Student athletes who ... are or have been taking prescription medication must provide verification (either by a copy of the prescription or by doctor's authorization) prior to being tested." *Id.*, at 8. It may well be that, if and when James was selected for random testing at a time that he was taking medication, the School District would have permitted him to provide the requested information in a confidential manner—for example, in a sealed envelope delivered to the testing lab. Nothing in the Policy contradicts that, and when respondents choose, in effect, to challenge the Policy on its face, we will not assume the worst. Accordingly, we reach the same conclusion as in *Skinner*: that the invasion of privacy was not significant.

V

Finally, we turn to consider the nature and immediacy of the governmental concern at issue here, and the efficacy of this means for meeting it. In both *Skinner* and *Von Raab*, we characterized the government interest motivating the search as "compelling." *Skinner, supra,* at 628 (interest in preventing railway accidents); *Von Raab, supra,* at 670 (interest in ensuring fitness of customs officials to interdict drugs and handle firearms). Relying on these cases, the District Court held that because the District's program also called for drug testing in the absence of individualized suspicion, the District "must demonstrate a 'compelling need' for the program." 796 F. Supp. at 1363. The Court of Appeals appears to have agreed with this view. See 23 F.3d at 1526. It is a mistake, however, to think that the phrase "compelling state interest," in the Fourth Amendment context, describes a fixed, minimum quantum of governmental concern, so that one can dispose of a case by answering in isolation the question: Is there a compelling state interest here? Rather, the phrase describes an interest that appears *important enough* to justify the particular search at hand, in light of other factors that show the search to be relatively intrusive upon a genuine expectation of privacy. Whether that relatively high degree of government concern is necessary in this case or not, we think it is met.

That the nature of the concern is important—indeed, perhaps compelling—can hardly be doubted. Deterring drug use by our Nation's schoolchildren is at least as important as enhancing efficient enforcement of the

Nation's laws against the importation of drugs, which was the governmental concern in *Von Raab, supra,* at 668, or deterring drug use by engineers and trainmen, which was the governmental concern in *Skinner, supra,* at 628. School years are the time when the physical, psychological, and addictive effects of drugs are most severe. "Maturing nervous systems are more critically impaired by intoxicants than mature ones are; childhood losses in learning are lifelong and profound"; "children grow chemically dependent more quickly than adults, and their record of recovery is depressingly poor." Hawley, The Bumpy Road to Drug-Free Schools, 72 Phi Delta Kappan 310, 314 (1990). See also Estroff, Schwartz, & Hoffmann, Adolescent Cocaine Abuse: Addictive Potential, Behavioral and Psychiatric Effects, 28 Clinical Pediatrics 550 (Dec. 1989); Kandel, Davies, Karus, & Yamaguchi, The Consequences in Young Adulthood of Adolescent Drug Involvement, 43 Arch. Gen. Psychiatry 746 (Aug. 1986). And of course the effects of a drug-infested school are visited not just upon the users, but upon the entire student body and faculty, as the educational process is disrupted. In the present case, moreover, the necessity for the State to act is magnified by the fact that this evil is being visited not just upon individuals at large, but upon children for whom it has undertaken a special responsibility of care and direction. Finally, it must not be lost sight of that this program is directed more narrowly to drug use by school athletes, where the risk of immediate physical harm to the drug user or those with whom he is playing his sport is particularly high. Apart from psychological effects, which include impairment of judgment, slow reaction time, and a lessening of the perception of pain, the particular drugs screened by the District's Policy have been demonstrated to pose substantial physical risks to athletes. Amphetamines produce an "artificially induced heart rate increase, peripheral vasoconstriction, blood pressure increase, and masking of the normal fatigue response," making them a "very dangerous drug when used during exercise of any type." Hawkins, Drugs and Other Ingesta: Effects on Athletic Performance, in H. Appenzeller, Managing Sports and Risk Management Strategies 90, 90–91 (1993). Marijuana causes "irregular blood pressure responses during changes in body position," "reduction in the oxygen-carrying capacity of the blood," and "inhibition of the normal sweating responses resulting in increased body temperature." *Id.,* at 94. Cocaine produces "vasoconstriction[,] elevated blood pressure," and "possible coronary artery spasms and myocardial infarction." *Ibid.*

As for the immediacy of the District's concerns: We are not inclined to question—indeed, we could not possibly find clearly erroneous—the District Court's conclusion that "a large segment of the student body, particularly those involved in interscholastic athletics, was in a state of rebellion," that "disciplinary actions had reached 'epidemic proportions,'" and that "the rebellion was being fueled by alcohol and drug abuse as well as by the student's misperceptions about the drug culture." 796 F. Supp. at 1357. That is an immediate crisis of greater proportions than existed in *Skinner*, where we upheld the Government's drug-testing program based on findings of drug use by railroad employees nationwide, without proof that a problem existed on the particular railroads whose employees were subject to the test. See *Skinner*, 489 U.S. at 607. And of much greater proportions than existed in *Von Raab*, where there was no documented history of drug use by any customs officials. See *Von Raab*, 489 U.S. at 673; *id.*, at 683 (SCALIA, J., dissenting).

As to the efficacy of this means for addressing the problem: It seems to us self-evident that a drug problem largely fueled by the "role model" effect of athletes' drug use, and of particular danger to athletes, is effectively addressed by making sure that athletes do not use drugs. Respondents argue that a "less intrusive means to the same end" was available, namely, "drug testing on suspicion of drug use." Brief for Respondents 45–46. We have repeatedly refused to declare that only the "least intrusive" search practicable can be reasonable under the Fourth Amendment. *Skinner, supra*, at 629, n. 9 (collecting cases). Respondents' alternative entails substantial difficulties—if it is indeed practicable at all. It may be impracticable, for one thing, simply because the parents who are willing to accept random drug testing for athletes are not willing to accept accusatory drug testing for all students, which transforms the process into a badge of shame. Respondents' proposal brings the risk that teachers will impose testing arbitrarily upon troublesome but not drug-likely students. It generates the expense of defending lawsuits that charge such arbitrary imposition, or that simply demand greater process before accusatory drug testing is imposed. And not least of all, it adds to the ever-expanding diversionary duties of schoolteachers the new function of spotting and bringing to account drug abuse, a task for which they are ill prepared, and which is not readily compatible with their vocation. Cf. *Skinner, supra*, at 628 (quoting 50 Fed. Reg. 31526 (1985)) (a drug impaired individual "will seldom display any outward 'signs detectable by the lay person or, in many cases, even the physician.'" *Goss*, 419 U.S. at 594 (Powell, J., dissenting) ("There is an ongoing relationship, one in which the teacher must occupy many roles—educator, adviser, friend, and, at times, parent-substitute. It is rarely adversary in nature...") (footnote omitted). In many respects, we think, testing based on "suspicion" of drug use would not be better, but worse.[3]

Taking into account all the factors we have considered above—the decreased expectation of privacy, the relative unobtrusiveness of the search, and the severity of the need met by the search—we conclude Vernonia's Policy is reasonable and hence constitutional.

We caution against the assumption that suspicionless drug testing will readily pass constitutional muster in other contexts. The most significant element in this case is the first we discussed: that the Policy was undertaken in furtherance of the government's responsibilities, under a public school system, as guardian and tutor of children entrusted to its care.[4] Just as when the government conducts a search in its capacity as employer (a warrantless search of an absent employee's desk to obtain an urgently needed file, for example), the relevant question is whether that intrusion upon privacy is one that a reasonable employer might engage in, see *O'Connor* v. *Ortega*, 480 U.S. 709, 94 L. Ed. 2d 714, 107 S. Ct. 1492 (1987); so also when the government acts as guardian and tutor the relevant question is whether the search is one that a reasonable guardian and tutor might undertake. Given the findings of need made by the District Court, we conclude that in the present case it is.

We may note that the primary guardians of Vernonia's schoolchildren appear to agree. The record shows no objection to this districtwide program by any parents other than the couple before us here—even though, as we have described, a public meeting was held to obtain parents' views. We find insufficient basis to contradict the judgment of Vernonia's parents, its school board, and the District Court, as to what was reasonably in the interest of these children under the circumstances.

The Ninth Circuit held that Vernonia's Policy not only violated the Fourth Amendment, but also, by reason of that violation, contravened Article I, § 9, of the Oregon Constitution. Our conclusion that the former holding was in error means that the latter holding rested on a flawed premise. We therefore vacate the judgment, and remand the case to the Court of Appeals for further proceedings consistent with this opinion.

It is so ordered.

CONCUR: JUSTICE GINSBURG, concurring.

The Court constantly observes that the School District's drug-testing policy applies only to students who voluntarily participate in interscholastic athletics. *Ante*, at 650, 657 (reduced privacy expectation and closer school regulation of student athletes), 662 (drug use by athletes risks immediate physical harm to users and those with whom they play). Correspondingly, the most severe sanction allowed under the District's policy is suspension from extracurricular athletic programs. *Ante*, at 651. I comprehend the Court's opinion as reserving the question whether the District, on no more than the showing made here, constitutionally could impose routine drug testing not only on those seeking to engage with others in team sports, but on all students required to attend school. Cf. *United States* v. *Edwards*, 498 F.2d 496,

500 (CA2 1974) (Friendly, J.) (in contrast to search without notice and opportunity to avoid examination, airport search of passengers and luggage is avoidable "by choosing not to travel by air") .

Footnote 1

Not until 1852 did Massachusetts, the pioneer in the "common school" movement, enact a compulsory school-attendance law, and as late as the 1870's only 14 States had such laws. R. Butts, Public Education in the United States From Revolution to Reform 102–103 (1978); 1 Children and Youth in America 467–468 (R. Bremner ed. 1970). The drug problem, and the technology of drug testing, are of course even more recent.

Footnote 2

Despite the fact that, like routine school physicals and vaccinations—which the dissent apparently finds unobjectionable even though they "are both blanket searches of a sort," *post*, at 682—the search here is undertaken for prophylactic and distinctly nonpunitive purposes (protecting student athletes from injury, and deterring drug use in the student population), see 796 F. Supp. at 1363, the dissent would nonetheless lump this search together with "evidentiary" searches, which generally require probable cause, see *supra*, at 653, because, from the student's perspective, the test may be "regarded" or "understood" as punishment, *post*, at 683–684. In light of the District Court's findings regarding the purposes and consequences of the testing, any such perception is by definition an irrational one, which is protected nowhere else in the law. In any event, our point is not, as the dissent apparently believes, *post*, at 682–683, that *since* student vaccinations and physical exams are constitutionally reasonable, student drug testing must be so as well; but rather that, by reason of those prevalent practices, public school children in general, and student athletes in particular, have a diminished expectation of privacy. See *supra*, at 656–657.

Footnote 3

There is no basis for the dissent's insinuation that in upholding the District's Policy we are equating the Fourth Amendment status of schoolchildren and prisoners, who, the dissent asserts, may have what it calls the "categorical protection" of a "strong preference for an individualized suspicion requirement," *post*, at 681. The case on which it relies for that proposition, *Bell*, v. *Wolfish*, 441 U.S. 520, 60 L. Ed. 2d 447, 99 S. Ct. 1861 (1979), displays no stronger a preference for individualized suspicion than we do today. It reiterates the proposition on which we rely, that "'elaborate less-restrictive-alternative arguments could raise insuperable barriers to the exercise of virtually all search-and-seizure powers.'" *Id.*, at 559, n. 40 (quoting *United States* v. *Martinez-Fuerte*, 428 U.S. 543, 556–557, n. 12, 49 L. Ed. 2d 1116, 96 S. Ct. 3074

(1976)). Even *Wolfish's arguendo* "assumption that the existence of less intrusive alternatives is relevant to the determination of the reasonableness of the particular search method at issue," 441 U.S. at 559, n. 40, does not support the dissent, for the opinion ultimately rejected the hypothesized alternative (as we do) on the ground that it would impair other policies important to the institution. See *id.*, at 560, n. 40 (monitoring of visits instead of conducting body searches would destroy "the confidentiality and intimacy that these visits are intended to afford").

Footnote 4
The dissent devotes a few meager paragraphs of its 21 pages to this central aspect of the testing program, see *post*, at 680–682, in the course of which it shows none of the interest in the original meaning of the Fourth Amendment displayed elsewhere in the opinion, see *post*, at 669–671. Of course at the time of the framing, as well as at the time of the adoption of the Fourteenth Amendment, children had substantially fewer "rights" than legislatures and courts confer upon them today. See 1 D. Kramer, Legal Rights of Children § 1.02, p. 9 (2d ed. 1994); Wald, Children's Rights: A Framework for Analysis, 12 U. C. D. L. Rev. 255, 256 (1979).

APPENDIX C

RESEARCH REPORT SERIES— ANABOLIC STEROIDS, 2000

The National Institute on Drug Abuse (NIDA), the federal government's main research organization on drug use, has summarized the basic facts on steroid use for the public. This document presents clear explanations of some technical topics and includes a list of references to support its negative views on steroid use.

FROM THE DIRECTOR

Since the 1950s, some athletes have been taking anabolic steroids to build muscle and boost their athletic performance. Increasingly, other segments of the population also have been taking these compounds. The Monitoring the Future study, which is an annual survey of drug abuse among adolescents across the country, showed a significant increase from 1998 to 1999 in steroid abuse among middle school students. During the same year, the percentage of 12th-graders who believed that taking these drugs causes "great risk" to health, declined from 68 percent to 62 percent.

Studies show that, over time, anabolic steroids can indeed take a heavy toll on a person's health. The abuse of oral or injectable steroids is associated with higher risks for heart attacks and strokes, and the abuse of most oral steroids is associated with increased risk for liver problems. Steroid abusers who share needles or use nonsterile techniques when they inject steroids are at risk for contracting dangerous infections, such as HIV/AIDS, hepatitis B and C, and bacterial endocarditis.

Anabolic steroid abuse can also cause undesirable body changes. These include breast development and genital shrinking in men, masculinization of the body in women and acne and hair loss in both sexes.

These and other effects of steroid abuse are discussed in this Research Report, which is one of a series of reports on drugs of abuse. NIDA produces this series to increase understanding of drug abuse and addiction and the health effects associated with taking drugs.

We hope that this compilation of scientific information on anabolic steroids will help the public recognize the risks of steroid abuse.

Alan I. Leshner, Ph.D.
Former Director
National Institute on Drug Abuse

WHAT ARE ANABOLIC STEROIDS?

"Anabolic steroids" is the familiar name for synthetic substances related to the male sex hormones (androgens). They promote the growth of skeletal muscle (anabolic effects) and the development of male sexual characteristics (androgenic effects), and also have some other effects. The term "anabolic steroids" will be used throughout this report because of its familiarity, although the proper term for these compounds is "anabolic-androgenic" steroids.

Anabolic steroids were developed in the late 1930s primarily to treat hypogonadism, a condition in which the testes do not produce sufficient testosterone for normal growth, development, and sexual functioning. The primary medical uses of these compounds are to treat delayed puberty, some types of impotence, and wasting of the body caused by HIV infection or other diseases.

During the 1930s, scientists discovered that anabolic steroids could facilitate the growth of skeletal muscle in laboratory animals, which led to use of the compounds first by bodybuilders and weightlifters and then by athletes in other sports. Steroid abuse has become so widespread in athletics that it affects the outcome of sports contests.

More than 100 different anabolic steroids have been developed [see the list below for some examples], but they require a prescription to be used legally in the United States. Most steroids that are used illegally are smuggled in from other countries, illegally diverted from U.S. pharmacies, or synthesized in clandestine laboratories.

Commonly Abused Steroids

Oral Steroids

- Anadrol (oxymetholone)
- Oxandrin (oxandrolone)
- Dianabol (methandrostenolone)
- Winstrol (stanozolol)

256

Injectable Steroids
- Deca-Durabolin (nandrolone decanoate)
- Durabolin (nandrolone phenpropionate)
- Depo-Testosterone (testosterone cypionate)
- Equipose (boldenone undecylenate)

WHAT ARE STEROIDAL SUPPLEMENTS?

In the United States, supplements such as dehydroepian-drosterone (DHEA) and androstenedione (street name Andro) can be purchased legally without a prescription through many commercial sources including health food stores. They are often referred to as dietary supplements, although they are not food products. They are often taken because the user believes they have anabolic effects.

Steroidal supplements can be converted into testosterone (an important male sex hormone) or a similar compound in the body. Whether such conversion produces sufficient quantities of testosterone to promote muscle growth or whether the supplements themselves promote muscle growth is unknown. Little is known about the side effects of steroidal supplements, but if large quantities of these compounds substantially increase testosterone levels in the body, they also are likely to produce thesame side effects as anabolic steroids.

WHAT IS THE SCOPE OF STEROID ABUSE IN THE UNITED STATES?

Recent evidence suggests that steroid abuse among adolescents is on the rise. The 1999 Monitoring the Future study, a NIDA-funded survey of drug abuse among adolescents in middle and high schools across the United States, estimated that 2.7 percent of 8th- and 10th-graders and 2.9 percent of 12th-graders had taken anabolic steroids at least once in their lives. For 10th-graders, that is a significant increase from 1998, when 2.0 percent of 10th-graders said they had taken anabolic steroids at least once. For all three grades, the 1999 levels represent a significant increase from 1991, the first year that data on steroid abuse were collected from the younger students. In that year, 1.9 percent of 8th-graders, 1.8 percent of 10th-graders, and 2.1 percent of 12th-graders reported that they had taken anabolic steroids at least once.

Few data exist on the extent of steroid abuse by adults. It has been estimated that hundreds of thousands of people aged 18 and older abuse anabolic steroids at least once a year.

Lifetime Users of Anabolic Steroids among 10th Graders, 1998–1999

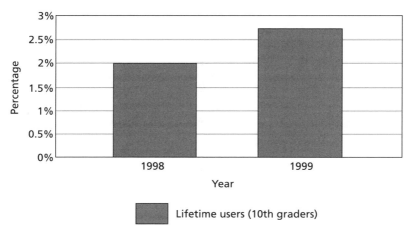

Source: Data from *Anabolic Steroid Abuse*. National Institute on Drug Abuse, April 2000. URL: http://www.drugabuse.gov/ResearchReports/Steroids/anabolicsteroids.html.

Note: "Lifetime users" indicates those who have used steroids sometime in their life.

© Infobase Publishing

Perceived Risk of Harm of Anabolic Steroid Use among High School Seniors, 1998–1999

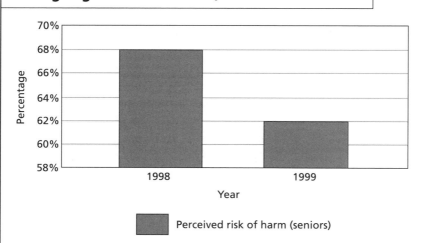

Source: Data from *Anabolic Steroid Abuse*. National Institute on Drug Abuse, April 2000. URL: http://www.drugabuse.gov/ResearchReports/Steroids/anabolicsteroids.html.

© Infobase Publishing

Among both adolescents and adults, steroid abuse is higher among males than females. However, steroid abuse is growing most rapidly among young women.

WHY DO PEOPLE ABUSE ANABOLIC STEROIDS?

One of the main reasons people give for abusing steroids is to improve their performance in sports. Among competitive bodybuilders, steroid abuse has been estimated to be very high. Among other athletes, the incidence of abuse probably varies depending on the specific sport.

Another reason people give for taking steroids is to increase their muscle size and/or reduce their body fat. This group includes some people who have a behavioral syndrome (muscle dysmorphia) in which a person has a distorted image of his or her body. Men with this condition think that they look small and weak, even if they are large and muscular. Similarly, women with the syndrome think that they look fat and flabby, even though they are actually lean and muscular.

Some people who abuse steroids to boost muscle size have experienced physical or sexual abuse. They are trying to increase their muscle size to protect themselves. In one series of interviews with male weightlifters, 25 percent who abused steroids reported memories of childhood physical or sexual abuse, compared with none who did not abuse steroids. In a study of women weightlifters, twice as many of those who had been raped reported using anabolic steroids and/or another purported muscle-building drug, compared to those who had not been raped. Moreover, almost all of those who had been raped reported that they markedly increased their bodybuilding activities after the attack. They believed that being bigger and stronger would discourage further attacks because men would find them either intimidating or unattractive.

Finally, some adolescents abuse steroids as part of a pattern of high-risk behaviors. These adolescents also take risks such as drinking and driving, carrying a gun, not wearing a helmet on a motorcycle, and abusing other illicit drugs.

While conditions such as muscle dysmorphia, a history of physical or sexual abuse, or a history of engaging in high-risk behaviors may increase the risk of initiating or continuing steroid abuse, researchers agree that most steroid abusers are psychologically normal when they start abusing the drugs.

HOW ARE ANABOLIC STEROIDS USED?

Some anabolic steroids are taken orally, others are injected intramuscularly, and still others are provided in gels or creams that are rubbed on the skin.

Doses taken by abusers can be 10 to 100 times higher than the doses used for medical conditions.

Steroid abusers typically "stack" the drugs, meaning that they take two or more different anabolic steroids, mixing oral and/or injectable types and sometimes even including compounds that are designed for veterinary use. Abusers think that the different steroids interact to produce an effect on muscle size that is greater than the effects of each drug individually, a theory that has not been tested scientifically.

Often, steroid abusers also "pyramid" their doses in cycles of 6 to 12 weeks. At the beginning of a cycle, the person starts with low doses of the drugs being stacked and then slowly increases the doses. In the second half of the cycle, the doses are slowly decreased to zero. This is sometimes followed by a second cycle in which the person continues to train but without drugs. Abusers believe that pyramiding allows the body time to adjust to the high doses and the drug-free cycle allows the body's hormonal system time to recuperate. As with stacking, the perceived benefits of pyramiding and cycling have not been substantiated scientifically.

WHAT ARE THE HEALTH CONSEQUENCES OF STEROID ABUSE?

Anabolic steroid abuse has been associated with a wide range of adverse side effects ranging from some that are physically unattractive, such as acne and breast development in men, to others that are life threatening, such as heart attacks and liver cancer. Most are reversible if the abuser stops taking the drugs, but some are permanent.

Most data on the long-term effects of anabolic steroids on humans come from case reports rather than formal epidemiological studies. From the case reports, the incidence of life-threatening effects appears to be low, but serious adverse effects may be underrecognized or underreported. Data from animal studies seem to support this possibility. One study found that exposing male mice for one-fifth of their lifespan to steroid doses comparable to those taken by human athletes caused a high percentage of premature deaths.

Possible Health Consequences of Anabolic Steroids

Hormonal System

- Men
  - infertility
  - breast development
  - shrinking of the testicles

- Women
  - enlargement of the clitoris
  - excessive growth of body hair
- Both Sexes
  - male pattern baldness

Musculoskeletal system
- short stature
- tendon rupture

Cardiovascular system
- heart attacks
- enlargement of the heart's left ventricle

Liver
- cancer
- peliosis hepatis

Skin
- acne and cysts
- oily scalp

Infection
- HIV/AIDS
- hepatitis

Psychiatric effects
- homicidal rage
- mania
- delusions

HORMONAL SYSTEM

Steroid abuse disrupts the normal production of hormones in the body, causing both reversible and irreversible changes. Changes that can be reversed include reduced sperm production and shrinking of the testicles (testicular atrophy). Irreversible changes include male-pattern baldness and breast development (gynecomastia). In one study of male bodybuilders, more than half had testicular atrophy, and more than half had gynecomastia. Gynecomastia is thought to occur due to the disruption of normal hormone balance. In the female body, anabolic steroids cause masculinization. Breast size and body fat decrease, the skin becomes coarse, the clitoris enlarges, and the voice deepens. Women may experience excessive growth of body hair but lose scalp hair. With continued administration of steroids, some of these effects are irreversible.

MUSCULOSKELETAL SYSTEM

Rising levels of testosterone and other sex hormones normally trigger the growth spurt that occurs during puberty and adolescence. Subsequently, when these hormones reach certain levels, they signal the bones to stop growing, locking a person into his or her maximum height.

When a child or adolescent takes anabolic steroids, the resulting artificially high sex hormone levels can signal the bones to stop growing sooner than they normally would have done.

CARDIOVASCULAR SYSTEM

Steroid abuse has been associated with cardiovascular diseases (CVD), including heart attacks and strokes, even in athletes younger than 30. Steroids contribute to the development of CVD, partly by changing the levels of lipoproteins that carry cholesterol in the blood. Steroids, particularly the oral types, increase the level of low-density lipoprotein (LDL) and decrease the level of high-density lipoprotein (HDL). High LDL and low HDL levels increase the risk of atherosclerosis, a condition in which fatty substances are deposited inside arteries and disrupt blood flow. If blood is prevented from reaching the heart, the result can be heart attract. If blood is prevented from reaching the brain, the result can be a stroke.

Steroids also increase the risk that blood clots will form in blood vessels, potentially disrupting blood flow and damaging the heart muscle so that it does not pump blood effectively.

LIVER

Steroid abuse has been associated with liver tumors and a rare condition called peliosis hepatis, in which blood-filled cysts form in the liver. Both the tumors and the cysts sometimes rupture, causing internal bleeding.

SKIN

Steroid abuse can cause acne, cysts, and oily hair and skin.

Appendix C

INFECTION

Many abusers who inject anabolic steroids use nonsterile injection techniques or share contaminated needles with other abusers. In addition, some steroid preparations are manufactured illegally under non-sterile conditions. These factors put abusers at risk for acquiring life-threatening viral infections, such as HIV and hepatitis B and C. Abusers also can develop infective endocarditis, a bacterial illness that causes a potentially fatal inflammation of the inner lining of the heart. Bacterial infections also can cause pain and abscess formation at injection sites.

WHAT EFFECTS DO ANABOLIC STEROIDS HAVE ON BEHAVIOR?

Case reports and small studies indicate that anabolic steroids, particularly in high doses, increase irritability and aggression. Some steroid abusers report that they have committed aggressive acts, such as physical fighting, committing armed robbery, or using force to obtain something. Some abusers also report that they have committed property crimes, such as stealing from a store, damaging or destroying others' property, or breaking into a house or a building. Abusers who have committed aggressive acts or property crimes generally report that they engage in these behaviors more often when they take steroids than when they are drug-free.

Some researchers have suggested that steroid abusers may commit aggressive acts and property crimes not because of steroids' direct effects on the brain but because the abusers have been affected by extensive media attention to the link between steroids and aggression. According to this theory, the abusers are using this possible link as an excuse to commit aggressive acts and property crimes.

One way to distinguish between these two possibilities is to administer either high steroid doses or placebo for days or weeks to human volunteers and then ask the people to report on their behavioral symptoms. To date, four such studies have been conducted. In three, high steroid doses did produce greater feelings of irritability and aggression than did placebo; but in one study, the drugs did not have that effect. One possible explanation, according to researchers, is that some but not all anabolic steroids increase irritability and aggression.

Anabolic steroids have been reported also to cause other behavioral effects, including euphoria, increased energy, sexual arousal, mood swings, distractibility, forgetfulness, and confusion. In the studies in which researchers administered high steroid doses to volunteers, a minority of the volunteers developed behavioral symptoms that were so extreme as to disrupt their ability to function in their jobs or in society. In a few cases, the volunteers' behavior presented a threat to themselves and others.

In summary, the extent to which steroid abuse contributes to violence and behavioral disorders is unknown. As with the health complications of steroid abuse, the prevalence of extreme cases of violence and behavioral disorders seems to be low, but it may be underreported or underrecognized.

ARE ANABOLIC STEROIDS ADDICTIVE?

An undetermined percentage of steroid abusers become addicted to the drugs, as evidenced by their continuing to take steroids in spite of physical problems, negative effects on social relations, or nervousness and irritability. Also, they spend large amounts of time and money obtaining the drugs and experience withdrawal symptoms such as mood swings, fatigue, restlessness, loss of appetite, insomnia, reduced sex drive, and the desire to take more steroids. The most dangerous of the withdrawal symptoms is depression, because it sometimes leads to suicide attempts. Untreated, some depressive symptoms associated with anabolic steroid withdrawal have been known to persist for a year or more after the abuser stops taking the drugs.

WHAT CAN BE DONE TO PREVENT STEROID ABUSE?

Early attempts to prevent steroid abuse concentrated on drug testing and on educating students about the drugs' adverse effects. A few school districts test for abuse of illicit drugs, including steroids, and studies are currently under way to determine whether such testing reduces drug abuse.

Research on steroid educational programs has shown that simply teaching students about steroids' adverse effects does not convince adolescents that they personally can be adversely affected. Nor does such instruction discourage young people from taking steroids in the future. Presenting both the risks and benefits of anabolic steroid use is more effective in convincing adolescents about steroids' negative effects, apparently because the students find a balanced approach more credible and less biased, according to the researchers. However, the balanced approach still does not discourage adolescents from abusing steroids.

A more sophisticated approach has shown promise for preventing steroid abuse among players on high school sports teams. In the ATLAS program, developed for male football players, coaches and team leaders discuss the potential effects of anabolic steroids and other illicit drugs on immediate sports performance, and they teach how to refuse offers of drugs. They also discuss how strength training and proper nutrition can help adolescents build their bodies without the use of steroids. Later, special trainers teach the players proper weightlifting techniques. An ongoing series of studies has shown that this multicomponent, team-centered approach reduces new steroid abuse by 50 percent. A program designed for adolescent girls on sports teams, patterned after the program designed for boys, is currently being tested.

WHAT TREATMENTS ARE EFFECTIVE FOR STEROID ABUSE?

Few studies of treatments for anabolic steroid abuse have been conducted. Current knowledge is based largely on the experiences of a small number of physicians who have worked with patients undergoing steroid withdrawal. The physicians have found that supportive therapy is sufficient in some cases. Patients are educated about what they may experience during withdrawal and are evaluated for suicidal thoughts.

If symptoms are severe or prolonged, medications or hospitalization may be needed.

Some medications that have been used for treating steroid withdrawal restore the hormonal system after its disruption by steroid abuse. Other medications target specific withdrawal symptom, for example, antidepressants to treat depression, and analgesics for headaches and muscle and joint pains.

Some patients require assistance beyond simple treatment of withdrawal symptoms and are treated with behavioral therapies.

WHERE CAN I GET FURTHER SCIENTIFIC INFORMATION ABOUT STEROID ABUSE?

Fact sheets on anabolic steroids, other illicit drugs, and related topics can be ordered free, in English and Spanish, by calling NIDA Infofax at 1-888-NIH-NIDA (1-888-644-6432) or, for those with hearing impairment, 1-888-TTY-NIDA (1-888-889-6432).

Information on steroid abuse also can be accessed through the NIDA Steroid Abuse Web Site (http://www.steroidabuse.org/). Information on illicit drugs in general can be accessed through NIDA's home page (http://www.drugabuse.gov/) or by contacting the National Clearinghouse for Alcohol and Drug Information (NCADI) Web Site (http://www.health.org/).

GLOSSARY

Addiction: A chronic, relapsing disease, characterized by compulsive drug-seeking and use and by neurochemical and molecular changes in the brain.

Anabolic effects: Drug-induced growth or thickening of the body's nonreproductive tract tissues—including skeletal muscle, bones, the larynx, and vocal cords—and decrease in body fat.

Analgesics: A group of medications that reduce pain.

Androgenic effects: A drug's effects upon the growth of the male reproductive tract and the development of male secondary sexual characteristics.

Antidepressants: A group of drugs used in treating depressive disorders.

Cardiovascular system: The heart and blood vessels.

Hormone: A chemical substance formed in glands in the body and carried in the blood to organs and tissues, where it influences function, structure, and behavior.

Musculoskeletal system: The muscles, bones, tendons, and ligaments.

Placebo: An inactive substance, used in experiments to distinguish between actual drug effects and effects that are expected by the volunteers in the experiments.

Sex hormones: Hormones that are found in higher quantities in one sex than in the other. Male sex hormones are the androgens, which include testosterone; and the female sex hormones are the estrogens and progesterone.

Withdrawal: Symptoms that occur after chronic use of a drug is reduced or stopped.

REFERENCES

Bahrke, M.S., Yesalis, C.E., and Wright, J.E. Psychological and behavioral effects of endogenous testosterone and anabolic-androgenic steroids: an update. *Sports Medicine* 22(6): 367–390, 1996.

Blue, J.G., and Lombardo, J.A. Steroids and steroid-like compounds. *Clinics in Sports Medicine* 18(3): 667–689, 1999.

Bronson, F.H., and Matherne, C.M. Exposure to anabolic-androgenic steroids shortens life span of male mice. *Medicine and Science in Sports and Exercise* 29(5): 615–619, 1997.

Brower, K.J. Withdrawal from anabolic steroids. *Current Therapy in Endocrinology and Metabolism* 6: 338–343, 1997.

Elliot, D., and Goldberg, L. Intervention and prevention of steroid use in adolescents. *The American Journal of Sports Medicine* 24(6): S46–S47, 1996.

Goldberg, L., et al. Anabolic steroid education and adolescents: Do scare tactics work? *Pediatrics* 87(3): 283–286, 1991.

Goldberg, L., et al. Effects of a multidimensional anabolic steroid prevention intervention: The Adolescents Training and Learning to Avoid Steroids (ATLAS) Program. *Journal of the American Medical Association* 276(19): 1555–1562, 1996.

Goldberg, L., et al. The ATLAS program: Preventing drug use and promoting health behaviours. *Archives of Pediatrics and Adolescent Medicine* 154: 332–338, 2000.

Gruber, A.J., and Pope, H.G., Jr. Compulsive weight lifting and anabolic drug abuse among women rape victims. *Comprehensive Psychiatry* 40(4): 273–277, 1999.

Gruber, A.J., and Pope, H.G., Jr. Psychiatric and medical effects of anabolic-androgenic steroid use in women. *Psychotherapy and Psychosomatics* 69: 19–26, 2000.

Hoberman, J.M., and Yesalis, C.E. The history of synthetic testosterone. *Scientific American* 272(2): 76–81, 1995.

Leder, B.Z., et al. Oral androstenedione administration and serum testosterone concentrations in young men. *Journal of the American Medical Association* 283(6): 779–782, 2000.

The Medical Letter on Drugs and Therapeutics. Creatine and androstenedione-two "dietary supplements." 40(1039): 105–106, 1998.

Middleman, A.B, et al. High-risk behaviors among high school students in Massachusetts who use anabolic steroids. *Pediatrics* 96(2): 268–272, 1995.

Pope, H.G., Jr., Kouri, E.M., and Hudson, M.D. Effects of supraphysiologic doses of testosterone on mood and aggression in normal men. *Archives of General Psychiatry* 57(2): 133–140, 2000.

Porcerelli, J.H., and Sandler, B.A. Anabolic-androgenic steroid abuse and psychopathology. *Psychiatric Clinics of North America* 21(4): 829–833, 1998.

Porcerelli, J.H., and Sandler, B.A. Narcissism and empathy in steroid users. *American Journal of Psychiatry* 152(11): 1672–1674, 1995.

Rich, J.D., Dickinson, B.P., Flanigan, T.P., and Valone, S.E. Abscess related to anabolic-androgenic steroid injection. *Medicine and Science in Sports and Exercise* 31(2): 207–209, 1999.

Su, T.-P., et al. Neuropsychiatric effects of anabolic steroids in male normal volunteers. *Journal of the American Medical Association* 269(21): 2760–2764, 1993.

Sullivan, M.L., Martinez, C.M., Gennis, P., and Gallagher, E.J. The cardiac toxicity of anabolic steroids. *Progress in Cardiovascular Diseases* 41(1): 1–15, 1998.

Yesalis, C.E. *Anabolic Steroids in Sports and Exercise*, 2nd edition. Champaign, IL: Human Kinetics. In press.

Yesalis, C.E. *Androstenedione*. Sport Dietary Supplements Update, 2000, E-SportMed.com.

Yesalis, C.E. Trends in anabolic-androgenic steroid use among adolescents. *Archives of Pediatrics and Adolescent Medicine* 151: 1197–1206, 1997.

Yesalis, C.E., Kennedy, N.J., Kopstein, A.N., and Bahrke, M.S. Anabolic-androgenic steroid use in the United States. *Journal of the American Medical Association* 270(10): 1217–1221, 1993.

Zorpette, G. Andro angst. *Scientific American* 279(6): 22–26, 1998.

Source: NIDA National Institute on Drug Abuse, Abuse, April 2000 (URL: http://www.drugabuse.gov/ResearchReports/Steroids/anabolicsteroids.html)

INDEX

Page numbers in **boldface** indicate biographical entries. Page numbers followed by *g* indicate glossary entries.

269

Index

Index

Index

Index

Index

279

Index

281

Index